JUSTIFIED SINNERS

BY

TIMOTHY MUSGRAVE

A WHOLLY OWNED SUBSIDIARY OF **TBN**

PROFESSIONAL PUBLISHING MEETS POWERFUL PROMOTION

Trilogy Christian Publishers

A Wholly Owned Subsidiary of Trinity Broadcasting Network

2442 Michelle Drive

Tustin, CA 92780

10 9 8 7 6 5 4 3 2 1

Library of Congress Cataloging-in-Publication Data is available.

ISBN 979-8-89041-989-7

ISBN 979-8-89041-990-3 (ebook)

Reviews

"As a former elementary teacher, I appreciate the gift that Tim has to take a complex concept, break it apart into smaller pieces, and put it back together in a way that helps the reader to understand how the pieces all fit together. As a visual learner, I love the many charts and diagrams he uses to show these concepts. Best of all are the many Scripture references that he uses to justify his statements. This is a book truly grounded in God's Word."

–Chris Bolin, retired teacher
and social worker

"Mr. Musgrave, an incisive student of the Bible, has condensed the Bible into lessons, I believe, it was intended to teach. Yet, he uses the entirety of the Bible to reference and source every statement making up each lesson. The lessons follow a logical progression and are explained in such a way as to make it easy to understand the Bible. This book is indispensable for the layperson who wishes to do Bible study on his own. The Ordained would also

find this book useful in developing sermons using the individual lessons and resourcing the references and sources to fill out the lessons as time allows. I highly recommend the reading of this book to all who are seeking the lessons contained within the Bible but find the distillation process a daunting task."

–Terry Rasmussen MSG (ret.) NEARNG
thirty-two years of combined service

"It is a thorough investigation of the themes covered. It presents orthodox evangelical positions on those themes. It was a blessing to go so deeply into the subjects covered."

–Keith Swarzbaugh, Registrar,
Rio Grande Bible Ministries

TABLE OF CONTENTS

Reviews iii

Foreword ix

Acknowledgments xv

Introduction and Purpose xvii

Redeeming God's Image-Bearers (Online Outline) xxi

The Redemption Story Overview 1

Redemptive Cycle: Baptism and Communion 7

  1. Trinity 11

  2. God-man 20

  3. Image of God 33

  4. The Fall Resulted in Death 39

  5. Sin Nature 46

  6. Imputation of Sin 46

  7. Atonement 50

  8. Imputation of Righteousness 54

  9. As Righteous Judge and Justifier of Sinful Man 59

  10. Gift, Not Works 62

  11. Jesus Is the Only Way to Heaven 65

  12. Eternal Security 69

13. Church: *What's Its Make-Up?* 74

14. Baptism 79

15. Communion 83

Redemptive Cycle: Baptism and Communion 93

16. Church: *What Are Its Functions?* 96

17. Spiritual Gifts 99

18. Sanctification: The Process of Becoming
    Conformed to the Image of Christ 104

19. Battle of Two Natures: Flesh vs. Spirit 108

20. Eternal Rewards 111

Redemption Cycle (Short) 119

Redemptive Cycle: Baptism and Communion 137

Study A: Tabernacle 140

Study B: Old Testament Sacrifices 154

Study C: Seven Biblical Feasts 172

Redemption Cycle (Long) 189

Be Sanctified 214

End Times Framework 217

Study D: Daniel's Seventy Weeks 222

21. 1st Coming 233

22. 2nd Coming 240

23. Two General Resurrections 246

24. Millennium 251

Study E: The New Covenant 264

25. Tribulation 277

26. Rapture 285

Study F: Church Age: 294

27. Eternal State 310

Redeeming God's Image-Bearers Throughout History 315

About the Author 343

Foreword

"The grass withers, the flower fades, But the word of God stands forever" (Isaiah 40:8; NASB20).

Isaiah 40:8 is a familiar passage. Many of us have either formally or informally memorized it. The Apostle Peter quotes this verse to provide proof of our everlasting salvation (1 Peter 1:24–25). I suspect if you are reading this book, you affirm this yourself. I commend you for taking God's Word seriously and for your willingness to consider investing time into further understanding His revealed message.

Before engaging with God's Word, it is worth asking: what is God's Word? God, the creator of the world, has chosen to communicate with His creation. There are several ways in which God has communicated, including the natural revelation of creation itself. From the tiny details of a simple leaf to incomprehensible stars throughout the universe, it is difficult to look at this creation and not be awestruck by its beauty and complexity. This revelation should help us "see" God. It does, but we are corrupted by sin and cannot see clearly. God also sent His only Son, Jesus, to share our experiences, live a perfect life, fulfill the Law, and die in our place in order that our sins may be forgiven and a proper relationship with God, the Father, be restored. It is interesting that the Apostle John uses the term "Word" (Logos) to introduce Jesus in his Gospel (John 1:1). Jesus was involved in creation itself (John 1:3) and entered into His creation (John 1:14). Everything that Jesus did was revelation from God.

Simply put, "revelation" is God who is not part of this world acting within it. It is mind-boggling that God Himself would send His only Son (also God) not only to live with us but also to die in our place. This is a life-saving revelation that provides salvation for a world without hope.

Now, returning to my initial inquiry: what is God's Word? God's Word, as contained in the Bible, is God's special revelation to us. It contains a message that came from outside of this creation. It is through Scripture that we learn what Jesus accomplished for us. It is through Scripture that we discover the intricacies of salvation. It is through Scripture that we can understand the world.

Let this sink in for a moment: God, the Creator of the universe and Savior of His people, chose to communicate with us. Because the Bible is direct revelation in which God communicates to His people, it is worth every effort to understand. I ask myself consistently, do I really believe the Bible is direct communication from God to humanity? Yes, I know that it is true, but do I really believe it? What in my life suggests that I believe that Scripture is really God's Word?

Scripture needs to orient the way in which we see the world. We need to allow the Bible to speak to us. We must submit ourselves to God's message and allow it to shape our beliefs and practices. Given the many potential distractions we face daily, we must consciously allow the Bible to mold us into the children of God. To use a common figure of speech, we must view everything through the lens of Scripture.

This is not easy, but it should not be stressful. The Holy Spirit can guide us in this process. In fact, guidance is part of His role here. Read Scripture. Listen to others who read Scripture. Walk by faith. Trust the Holy Spirit to guide you in this process and make changes as you go. We will not be perfect. We cannot be perfect. Perfection cannot be our goal. Rather, we can be faithful. It is faithfulness that God desires from us.

In the pages that follow, the author, Timothy Musgrave, has provided a map organizing many aspects of the Bible into understandable units. Timothy is not your ordinary travel guide. I have known Timothy since his days as a ThM student at Dallas Theological Seminary. He has always had a desire to dig deep into the text of Scripture. Since seminary, he has devoted hundreds of more hours to this task. On the one hand, much of the Bible is easy to understand. However, it is quite long and covers much theological ground. It is easy to get lost. Timothy's purpose for writing this book it to provide that necessary map to navigate through this difficult theological terrain. He believes that a comprehensive understanding of the whole will help the Bible reader to understand the parts and relationships among those parts. Further, Timothy's goal is to help believers to be able to defend their precious faith. Here, one will find solid doctrine. Equipped with a thorough understanding of what is right, one will be able to recognize what is incorrect and misleading. Finally, Timothy's purpose is not limited to the present; he desires this book to be a resource for many in the future, including those who are left behind after the Rapture. Timothy Musgrave has created a map. Follow this map with an open Bible. Pray for understanding, humility, and wisdom. Remember, it is God's Word that makes an impact.

It is likely wrong to state the obvious at the end of the foreword. However, it nevertheless goes without saying that people following God will produce the fruits of the Spirit in their lives: "love, joy, peace, patience, kindness, goodness, faithfulness, gentleness, self-control" (Galatians 5:22–23, NASB20). Timothy's purpose for this book is not simply to know doctrine. He also intends for readers to be able to live faithfully. Again, we will not live perfectly. Only Jesus did. Nevertheless, Scripture study should be producing such fruit in all our lives.

In these complex times, clarity is often elusive. Daily, we are faced with countless decisions. Many of these decisions impact not only our own lives but the lives of those we love. How is one supposed to respond to all that confronts us? First, know that God is always with us. Second, read Scripture to know more about God and how to live. Finally, allow the Holy Spirit to produce His fruit in you as you read God's Word. Be faithful. This process will result in Christian growth and produce a means by which you can approach life. Returning to the earlier figure of speech, this process will produce a biblical lens through which you can live your life and make proper decisions. This book can be part of this process. Study Scripture to know God better.

Study Scripture to live a life pleasing to God.

—Dr. Joseph D. Fantin

Professor, New Testament (twenty years)

Dallas Theological Seminary

Acknowledgments

This work is the product of nine years of effort, mainly made possible by the sacrifice of my wife, Juany Musgrave. She poured her life into supporting me as I studied at Dallas Theological Seminary for eight years while simultaneously raising our three children. Her efforts enabled me to compile my study to create this book. She encouraged me to take the necessary steps to finance and publish it, without which I would have never finished. Without her, this work would have never been possible.

I'm appreciative to Chris Bolin. I started with a simple request to have her look over a couple of sections, and she ended up spending a lot of time helping with the editing process, including the charts that accompany each section. When needed, she simplified the terminology and helped clarify key terms. Keith Baumfalk was a support for me emotionally and spiritually and simultaneously advised Chris. As a couple, they have been a tremendous support and encouragement in our times of suffering.

This book brought physical, emotional, and spiritual trials, and we faced much opposition during the writing process. We experienced tremendous spiritual warfare and attacks from unexpected people and places, and each time,

God enabled us to persevere and rebound. Ephesians 6:12 (NASB95) says, "For our struggle is not against flesh and blood, but against the rulers, against the powers, against the world forces of this darkness, against the spiritual forces of wickedness in the heavenly places."

Introduction and Purpose

How well do we understand our Christian beliefs? How capable are we of explaining and defending them? What key biblical concepts should we grasp? How should an understanding of our faith play out in our daily living? If we genuinely believe the Word of God, it will govern our thought processes and behavior.

This material is designed for someone who goes to church and has no formal Bible school training. It is for the reader to understand his faith, know how to articulate it, scripturally defend it, and apply it to his daily decision-making. Theology is not about puffed-up knowledge. It is about regulating our decision-making.

This study does not pull from various authors, but it lets the Word of God speak for itself. Everything revolves around the theme that the Triune God, from the beginning to the end of human history, is redeeming fallen, sinful mankind, His image-bearers back into full relationship with Himself. And it is a call for Christians, who are justified sinners, to be continually cleansed in order to be in a right relationship with Holy God. The purpose of this study is *not* to accumulate *information* but to call for action: the cleansing of individual believers and the cleansing of the Church of God as a whole.

The layout is divided into two parts: the first part is the *redemptive cycle*, and the second part is the *end times* framework, which defines one's position on end times events and how they relate to the redemptive cycle. Baptism and Communion together are a snapshot of the whole redemptive cycle. As such, they are repeated throughout various parts of this study to help the reader understand what the bigger picture is: Redeeming God's image-bearers.

This work incorporates key biblical concepts across seven essential theological areas: the Trinity, the Study of Man, Sin, Salvation, the Church, Sanctification, and the End Times. It also incorporates six individual studies (the Tabernacle, Old Testament Sacrifices, Seven Biblical Feasts, Daniel's seventy weeks, the New Covenant, and the Church Age) to help us better understand these biblical concepts and tie them together as part of a unified whole. Each section is accompanied by charts to help the reader visualize and better grasp the material; go to https://rbeteach71.wixsite.com/justified-sinners/charts.

The common theme throughout this study is how Holy God is working to redeem sinful mankind to Himself. This is also seen in how God works throughout history and that He calls His chosen people, Israel, to national repentance. While the Trinity remains a mystery, it is foundational to this study on *Justified Sinners* and is underlined wherever it appears throughout this work. To visually grasp each concept and chapter in this book, reference the outline on the following page. Following the online charts (https://rbe-teach71.wixsite.com/justified-sinners/charts) will enable the reader to better comprehend each concept as a whole with its interrelated parts.

Keep in mind that an understanding of biblical knowledge is not useful unless applied. James 1:22–23 (NASB95) states, "For if anyone is a hearer of the word and not a doer, he is like a man who looks at his natural face in a mirror; for once he has looked at himself and gone away, he has immediately forgotten what kind of person he was." But the Word of God does have power to transform lives, change one's thought processes, and govern one's behavioral choices.

Scripture quotations are taken from the New American Standard Bible®, Copyright © 1995 by the Lockman Foundation.

Redeeming God's Image-Bearers

Part 1: Redemption Cycle

Overview

1. Redemption Story Overview *1–6*

2. Redemptive Cycle: Baptism and Communion *7–10*

Trinity

3. *(1)* Trinity *11–19*

4. *(2)* God-man *20–32*

Study of Man

5. *(3)* Image of God *33–38*

Sin

6. *(4)* The Fall *39–45*

7. *(5–6)* Sin Nature and Imputation of Sin *46–49*

Salvation

8. *(7)* Atonement *50–53*

9. *(8)* Imputation of Righteousness *54–58*

10. *(9)* Judge and Justifier *59–61*

11. *(10)* Gift, Not Works *62–64*

12. *(11)* Jesus Is the Only Way *65–68*

13. *(12)* Eternal Security *69–73*

The Church

14. *(13)* Church: What Is Its Make-Up? *74–78*

15. *(14)* Baptism *79–82*

16. *(15)* Communion *83–92*

17. Redemptive Cycle: Baptism and Communion *93–95*

18. *(16)* Church: What Are Its Functions? *96–98*

19. *(17)* Spiritual Gifts *99–103*

Sanctification

20. *(18)* Sanctification *104–107*

21. *(19)* Battle of Two Natures *108–110*

22. *(20)* Eternal Rewards *111–118*

Overview

23. Redemption Cycle (short) *119–136*

24. Redemptive Cycle: Baptism and Communion *137–139*

25. Study A: Tabernacle *140–153*

26. Study B: Old Testament Sacrifices *154–171*

27. Study C: Seven Biblical Feasts *172–188*

28. Redemption Cycle (long) *189–213*

Application

29. Be Sanctified *214–216*

Part 2: Redemption Cycle Throughout History
Study of the End Times

30. End Times Framework *217–221*

31. Study D: Daniel's Seventy Weeks *222–232*

32. *(21)* 1st Coming *233–239*

33. *(22)* 2nd Coming *240–245*

34. *(23)* Two General Resurrections *246–250*

35. *(24)* Millennium *251–264*

36. Study E: New Covenant *264–276*

37. *(25)* Tribulation *277–284*

38. *(26)* Rapture *285–293*

39. Study F: Church Age (long) *294–309*

40. *(27)* Eternal State *310–316*

Overview

41. Redemption Throughout History *317–340*

THE REDEMPTION STORY OVERVIEW

Introduction: In this opening lesson, we are going to get a bird's eye view of the redemption story. This brief overview reveals how the Triune God is redeeming mankind. The redemptive process is made up of four phases: Sin, the Cross, the Cleansing of Justified Sinners, and the Resurrection. It covers the biblical doctrines of the Trinity, the study of Man, Sin, Salvation, the Church, Sanctification, and the End Times.

Redeeming God's image bearers. It is the restoration of lost fellowship between the Triune God and mankind as His image bearers[1] due to sin. In the redemptive process, at the beginning, mankind was in full fellowship with the Triune God.

1. The first phase is **Sin, which is broken fellowship** between mankind and his Creator. First, we will look at the Fall, where man sinned, resulting in physical and spiritual death.[2] Adam and Eve disobeyed God's command not to eat of the tree of the "Knowledge of Good and Evil."[3] So sin

---

[1]   Genesis 1:26–27; 2:7; 9:6
[2]   Genesis 2:17; Romans 5:18–19
[3]   Genesis 3:6

entered the world,[4] breaking that fellowship. Man was eternally separated from God, utterly unable to come back to his Maker on his own terms. God is a Holy God and cannot tolerate sin. So He cannot have sinful mankind in His presence. When Adam sinned, not only did he become a sinner, but he passed down that sin nature to every one of his descendants, every single man, woman, and child in the human race from the beginning to the end of human history.[5] As Romans 3:23 says, "All have sinned and fallen short of the glory of God." No one can meet God's holy standards. Everybody falls short of God, and no one can come to Him on their terms.[6] Because of this, we need a Savior.

2. Cross (price of redemption): The second phase is the cross, the price of redemption. Because God loved mankind,[7] He came up with a plan that included all three members of the Triune God.[8] God the Father sent the Son to be the Savior of the world.[9] The Holy Spirit impregnated Mary,[10] giving Jesus the Father's nature.[11] He had God's nature, the divine nature

---

4   Romans 5:12
5   Romans 5:18–19
6   Ephesians 2:8–9
7   John 3:16
8   1 Peter 1:18–20
9   1 John 4:14
10   Matthew 1:18–23
11   Hebrews 1:3 with John 10:30

free from sin,[12] and He also had the human nature,[13] frail that it is in one, the God-man. He was the only one who was born without sin and who did not have a sin nature throughout the entire human race.[14] He lived a perfect life and completed the requirements of God's law on behalf of the human race.[15] Because of that, He could die as a man in mankind's place[16] to satisfy God's wrath against sin.[17] And because He was God simultaneously,[18] the sacrifice of Himself[19] could take the punishment of the sin of every man, woman, and child throughout human history from Adam until the end of the world. The cross was the price of redemption for the human race.[20] As the God-man, He was the only one who could meet God's requirements and, as man, save mankind. For everyone who accepts Jesus' gift of righteousness, God the Father takes their sin nature and their sins and places it on Jesus at the cross. He takes Jesus' nature and places it on them.[21] They receive Jesus' righteousness,[22] and the

---

[12] Jesus knew no sin (2 Corinthians 5:21), did no sin (1 Peter 2:22), and in Him is no sin (1 John 3:5).

[13] Hebrews 2:17–18; John 1:14

[14] Hebrews 4:15

[15] Galatians 4:4–5; Matthew 5:17

[16] Philippians 2:7–8; Hebrews 2:17

[17] Romans 1:18; 3:25; 1 John 2:2

[18] John 1:14; Philippians 2:6–7

[19] Hebrews 7:26–27; 9:11–12

[20] Acts 20:28

[21] 2 Corinthians 5:21

[22] Romans 5:17

Father sees Jesus' righteousness instead of the image-bearers' sin.[23]

3. Cleansing (Justified Sinners): After the cross, we will look at the third phase, the cleansing of justified sinners. Those who receive Jesus' righteousness are baptized by the Holy Spirit into Jesus' body, the Church.[24] Now, those who have accepted Jesus Christ as their Lord and Savior, believing that He died on the cross to take away their sins and rose from the grave and that He is God, are justified sinners.[25] They belong to God as children of God,[26] the Triune God, but they are still sinners. They still have the sin nature,[27] but they have the divine nature,[28] the Triune nature in them, and there is a battle throughout their entire life of submitting to the Holy Spirit or their own sinful nature.[29] In this cleansing process, where justified sinners are living in fellowship with Holy God, there are two aspects: the Church and the individual believers. First, they have their identity as the Church, and God cleanses the Church who lives in fellowship with

---

[23]   Philippians 3:9
[24]   1 Corinthians 12:13
[25]   Romans 3:22–24
[26]   John 1:12
[27]   Galatians 5:16–17; Romans 7:25b; 8:4
[28]   2 Peter 1:4
[29]   Galatians 5:16–23

Him.[30] Secondly, He also cleanses individual believers.[31] It is a life-long struggle of learning to submit oneself to God individually and as a local church body and be continually cleansed from sin to be in fellowship with God as His children. This struggle will continue from the time one accepts Jesus as his Savior until death.

4. Resurrection: The fourth and final stage of the redemptive process is the Resurrection of the Saints. In the resurrection, they are perfected; they are glorified. They have no sin nature.[32]

End: They are restored in fellowship with the Triune God.[33] This is the Eternal state, when sinful mankind has been redeemed, perfected, and is living without sin with the Triune God, the Father, the Son, and the Holy Spirit for all eternity in heaven.

Overview: This is the redemptive process. This study is redeeming God's image bearers. It is the story of the restoration of lost fellowship between the Triune God and mankind as His image bearers due to sin. To view the

---

[30]   Ephesians 5:25–27

[31]   Hebrews 12:7–10 with 1 Corinthians 11:27–30 (The Lord's Supper acts as a heart preparation/cleansing to be in fellowship with God individually and with the Church body.)

[32]   Philippians 3:20–21; 1 John 3:2

[33]   Revelation 21:3

chart for this section, go to https://rbeteach71.wixsite.com/ justified-sinners/charts.

REDEMPTIVE CYCLE: BAPTISM AND COMMUNION

As a snapshot, the two Church ordinances, Baptism and Communion, cover the entire *redemptive cycle:* sin, the cross, the cleansing of justified sinners, and the resurrection. They have to do with restoring lost fellowship between the Triune God and sinful mankind.

Baptism is a symbol of entrance into the family of God. It focuses on the *beginning and the end of the Christian walk* and deals with the redemptive stages of sin, the cross, and the resurrection. Baptism is a very concise illustration of a believer being united to Jesus in His death to sin on the cross and resurrection from the dead. Jesus' death to sin becomes our death to sin. Jesus' resurrection becomes our resurrection. This is our position in Christ and our future reality when we are transformed according to His image. Romans 6:3–5 proclaims, "Or do you not know that all of us who have been baptized into Christ Jesus have been baptized into His death? Therefore we have been buried with Him through baptism into death, so that as Christ was raised from the dead through the glory of the Father, so we too might walk in newness of life. For if we have become united with Him in the likeness of His death, certainly we shall also be in the likeness of His resurrection." Philippians 3:20–21 speaks of this resurrection. "For our citizenship is in heaven, from which also we eagerly wait for a Savior, the Lord Jesus Christ; who will transform the body of our humble state into conformity with the body of His glory, by the exertion of the power that He has even to subject all things to Himself."

Communion acts as a heart cleansing or preparation for justified sinners to be in fellowship with Holy God. It focuses on the *ongoing Christian walk* and deals with sin, the cross, and the cleansing of justified sinners. It is about actively remembering Jesus' sacrifice on the cross for our sins. It also addresses how we as believers can fellowship with Holy God. We are to examine ourselves before taking part in the bread and the cup, for if we take it in an unworthy manner, we become guilty of the body and blood of Jesus, bringing judgment upon ourselves. Being conscious of this pushes us to settle accounts with God and people before taking Communion. This requires us to be continually cleansed to freely fellowship with Him. This goes on throughout our entire Christian walk from beginning to end.

The two ordinances that all Christians are to practice are concise, visual, and participatory illustrations covering the entire redemptive cycle: sin, the cross, the cleansing of justified sinners, and the resurrection. They have to do with restoring lost fellowship between the Triune God and sinful mankind.

Baptism and Communion combined provide a snapshot of the entire redemptive cycle. The first biblical doctrine provides a foundation for understanding the redemption story, the Trinity.

To view the chart for this section, go to https://rbeteach71. wixsite.com/justified-sinners/charts.

Introduction

Redeeming God's image bearers is the restoration of lost fellowship between the Triune God and mankind as His image bearers due to sin. The foundation for understanding the Redemption story is the Trinity. In the beginning, innocent mankind, made in the image of the Triune God, is in fellowship with Him. The Trinity is involved throughout the entire redemptive process, and while many times it is not clearly stated, it is the backbone underlying everything. In fact, the New Testament has 117 Trinitarian passages, which is in every book except for Philemon, James, and 2, 3 John. Today, we will take a good look at what the Trinity is, as this concept is weaved throughout the entire study.

1. TRINITY

The Trinity is one God in three persons. The Father is God,[34] the Son, Jesus Christ is God,[35] and the Holy

---

[34]   John 6:27; Ephesians 4:6
[35]   John 1:1; Hebrews 1:8

Spirit is God,[36] yet the Father is not the Son,[37] and the Father is not the Holy Spirit.[38] The Son is not the Father, and the Son is not the Holy Spirit.[39] The Holy Spirit is not the Father, and the Holy Spirit is not the Son. We are going to keep this chart in mind as we look at both aspects of the Trinity, one God and three persons.

God is one, yet there is a plurality of persons[40] in that oneness. Just as a simple rooftop has two opposite sides, whose unified form is only seen when joined together, so God is one,[41] yet three persons,[42] and is best understood as a plurality of oneness.

The Father,[43] Son,[44] and Holy Spirit[45] as distinct persons are each the one same God. Each one has His own distinct

---

[36]   Acts 5:3–4

[37]   Luke 23:4–6; John 20:17

[38]   Luke 11:13; John 14:26

[39]   John 14:26; Acts 2:33

[40]   Horrell, Scott. ST102 Class Notes. Dallas: Dallas Theological Seminary, ch 6 pg 23, 2008.

[41]   Deuteronomy 6:4

[42]   Isaiah 48:16; Mark 1:8–12

[43]   John 6:27

[44]   John 1:1–3, 18

[45]   Acts 5:3–4, 9

will,[46] mind,[47] and emotions.[48] The Father,[49] who has His own will, mind, and emotions, has certain functions that belong only to Him. He is the Source of all things.[50] He is the great initiator.[51] The **Father** is the Sovereign Ruler over all things,[52] and in the end, all things return to Him so that He might be all in all.[53]

The **Son** has His own will, mind, and emotions and is begotten of the Father.[54] He has certain roles that belong specifically to Him. He is our Creator.[55] He holds the universe together.[56] As God, Jesus also became man,[57] thus fully sharing in man's humanity[58] (except without a sin nature[59]) and remains God at the same time,[60] in one personality. His

---

46   Father's will (John 6:38); Son's will (Luke 22:41–44); Holy Spirit's will (Acts 16:6)

47   Father's mind (1 Corinthians 2:11); Son's mind (1 Corinthians 2:16); Holy Spirit's mind (Romans 8:27)

48   Father's emotions (Luke 3:21–22); Son's emotions (Hebrews 5:7); Holy Spirit's emotions (Ephesians 4:30)

49   1 Corinthians 8:6

50   Acts 17:24–31

51   Matthew 28:18 (implied passively by coming from the Father; see John 17:1–2); Ephesians 1:17–23

52   1 Timothy 6:15–16

53   1 Corinthians 15:24–28

54   John 1:14, 18

55   John 1:3; Colossians 1:16

56   Hebrews 1:3; Colossians 1:17

57   Philippians 2:6–7

58   Hebrews 2:17–18; John 1:14

59   Hebrews 4:15

60   John 10:30

divine nature sustained His human nature,[61] and the two natures exist without confusion, change, division, or separation.[62] His dual nature happened when the Father sent the Son to the world,[63] by which the Holy Spirit impregnated the Virgin Mary,[64] who then gave birth to the Son of God.[65] His dual nature of humanity and divinity was necessary for various reasons. In regard to His human nature, as sinless man,[66] He was able to redeem mankind by completing the requirements of God's law for the human race.[67] His humanity was necessary because, as man, He died in mankind's place.[68] And because He shared in man's humanity, He is able to act as our sympathetic high priest.[69] His divine nature was necessary because, as God simultaneously,[70] the sacrifice of Himself at the cross paid for the sins of the whole world.[71] And as God, He acts as our advocate before God the Father

---

[61]   John 10:17–18; Luke 23:46 (A crucified man almost dead can't cry out in a loud voice. He gave up His life.)

[62]   Sellers, R. V. Council of Chalcedon: A Historical and Doctrinal Survey. London: SPCK, 1954 (210–211).

[63]   John 3:16–17

[64]   Matthew 1:18–23

[65]   Luke 1:35

[66]   Jesus knew no sin (2 Corinthians 5:21), did no sin (1 Peter 2:22), and in Him is no sin (1 John 3:5).

[67]   Galatians 4:4–5; Matthew 5:17

[68]   Philippians 2:7–8; Hebrews 2:17

[69]   Hebrews 2:14–18

[70]   Philippians 2:6–7

[71]   Hebrews 9:26; 1 John 2:2

when we sin.[72] Jesus is not only our Savior and the Savior of the world[73] but is also our judge and the judge of the world because the judgment was passed from the Father to the Son.[74] He will carry out the judgment of all humanity at the resurrections of the righteous and the wicked.[75]

The **Holy Spirit** is the Spirit of the Father and of the Son,[76] yet is distinct from them, having His own will, mind, and emotions, and proceeds from the Father.[77] He has certain roles that belong to Him. He convicts the world of sin.[78] He seals the believers for the Day of Redemption.[79] The Holy Spirit gives them assurance that they are children of God.[80] He intercedes for them to the Father.[81] He uses the Bible to confront and speak to their innermost being, including the hidden thoughts and intentions of their hearts.[82] He com-

---

[72]   1 John 2:1–2

[73]   Matthew 1:21; John 3:17

[74]   John 5:22, 27

[75]   John 5:25–29

[76]   Romans 8:9

[77]   John 15:26

[78]   He convicts believers and non-believers alike (John 16:8)

[79]   Ephesians 1:13–14 (Upon believing in Jesus, the Holy Spirit is given to indwell the believer, waiting for the day when he is resurrected and conformed to the image of the Triune God. Being sealed by the Holy Spirit acts like a man giving his fiancé an engagement ring, with the future promise of marriage.)

[80]   Romans 8:15–16

[81]   Romans 8:26–27

[82]   Hebrews 4:12

forts the believers.[83] He is their Counselor.[84] He teaches them the Bible and all truth. He reminds them of what they were previously taught.[85] And He gives them spiritual gifts and ministries to build them up to spiritual maturity as He sees fit and to prepare them for ministry.[86]

The Father, Son, and Holy Spirit as distinct persons are each the one same God. We see this in that they possess the same attributes. They are eternal.[87] They are all-knowing.[88] They are everywhere at once.[89] They are all-powerful.[90] They are holy.[91] They personify truth.[92] Each person of the Trinity is a giver and sustainer of life,[93] and they are worthy of the same glory.[94] In the Old Testament, God said He would not share His glory with anyone,[95] yet we see them sharing in the same glory. As distinct persons, the Father, Son, and Holy Spirit are in relationship with one another. They per-

---

[83]   Acts 9:31

[84]   John 14:26

[85]   John 14:26

[86]   1 Corinthians 12:4–11; Ephesians 4:7–16

[87]   Father (Revelation 1:8); Son (Isaiah 9:6); Holy Spirit (Hebrews 9:14)

[88]   Father (1 John 3:20); Son (John 21:17); Holy Spirit (1 Corinthians 2:10)

[89]   Son (Matthew 18:20, 28:20); Father and the Holy Spirit (Psalm 139:1, 7–10)

[90]   Son (Matthew 28:18); Father and Spirit (Isaiah 40:13–18)

[91]   Plurality in one (Isaiah 6:3, 8); Father (Revelation 4:8); Son (Mark 1:24); Holy Spirit (Ephesians 4:30)

[92]   Son and Father (John 1:14); Son (John 14:6); Holy Spirit and Father (John 15:26)

[93]   Father and Son (John 5:21); Son (Hebrews 1:3); Holy Spirit (Romans 8:11)

[94]   Father and Son (John 17:1, 5); Holy Spirit (1 Peter 4:14)

[95]   Isaiah 42:8

sonally relate to one another in community.[96] They know and testify of one another.[97] They demonstrate self-giving love.[98] They mutually indwell one another (while remaining distinct).[99] And the Father is the head of the three persons, yet equal, not superior to the other two.[100]

Jesus testified to the plurality of oneness quoting from the Old Testament while proclaiming that the Lord our God is One Lord.[101] This God distinct from God is seen in Old Testament books[102] and Revelation.[103] God talks to Himself using plural pronouns, first five times in Genesis 1–11,[104] then again in Isaiah 6:8. His names of Elohim and Adonai also allow for plurality of oneness as in "mi señores."[105] Jesus most clearly stated the plurality of oneness in the Great Commission,

---

[96] Father, Son, and Holy Spirit (John 16:13–15) Son with Father (John 1:1–2); Holy Spirit and Father (1 Corinthians 2:11–12)

[97] Father and Son (John 10:15); Father and Spirit (1 Corinthians 2:11–12); Son and Spirit (John 15:26)

[98] Fathers' love for Son (John 3:35); Son's love for the Father (John 14:31)

[99] Father and Son (John 17:21–23); Son and Holy Spirit: Holy Spirit came from within Jesus to the disciples (John 20:22)

[100] Father's authority over Son (1 Corinthians 15:24, 28); Father's authority over Holy Spirit (John 15:26); Holy Spirit's authority over Son (Matthew 4:1); Son's authority over Holy Spirit (John 16:7); Father's authority over all (Ephesians 4:4–6)

[101] Mark 12:29, 35–37

[102] Psalm 2:7–12; 110:1; Isaiah 44:6; 48:16

[103] God the Father calls Himself the Alpha and Omega, the beginning and the end (Revelation 1:8) as does Jesus (Revelation 22:13).

[104] Genesis 1:26 (3x); 3:22; 11:6–7

[105] Horrell, Scott. ST102 Class Notes. Dallas: Dallas Theological Seminary, 2008.

where He told the disciples to baptize them in the **name** of the Father and of the Son and of the Holy Spirit. [106]

As stated before, the Trinity is the foundation for the entire redemptive process. But what does it have to do with people's everyday lives? Let us look at three specific areas in which the Trinity effects the Christian walk.

Application

1. First, the Trinity is actively working throughout human history to redeem sinful mankind to Himself by restoring the corrupted image of God in mankind. And the Trinity is actively working to redeem individual believers from a sinful lifestyle.

2. Secondly, the Holy Spirit assures believers they belong to God. Paul talks about this in Romans and in Galatians. Romans 8:15–16 says, "For you have not received a spirit of slavery leading to fear again, but you have received a spirit of adoption as sons by which we cry out, Abba! Father!" Paul again talks about the Holy Spirit giving assurance to His children that they are sons of God. It says in Galatians 4:6, "Because you are

---

[106] Matthew 28:19 (one name = one essence, yet this one essence consists of three distinct persons)

sons, God has sent forth the Spirit of His on into our hearts, crying, Abba! Father!"

3. And lastly, the disciples of Jesus walk in fellowship with the Triune God. At the beginning of the discipleship, they are to be baptized, which is a demonstration that they are starting their Christian walk. The baptism talks about being in fellowship with the Triune God because it states in Matthew 28:19–20, "Go therefore and make disciples of all the nations, baptizing them in the name of the Father and the Son and the Holy Spirit, teaching them to observe all that I commanded you; and lo, I am with you always, even to the end of the age."

In this lesson, we have seen the three persons of the Trinity. In the following lesson, we will focus on the second person of the Trinity, the God-man. To view the chart for this section, go to https://rbeteach71.wixsite.com/justified-sinners/charts.

2. GOD-MAN

In the last session, we looked at how the Trinity is the foundation for understanding the redemptive process, which is the restoration of lost fellowship between the Triune God and mankind as His image-bearers due to sin. As previously mentioned, the three persons of the Trinity are described in 117 distinct places throughout the New Testament. Today, we will take a closer look at the Trinity by focusing on its 2nd person, the God-man.

Concept:

The second person of the Trinity, the Son, is Jesus. Jesus, as the God-man, is the most visible part of the Trinity. Who is Jesus? What is His identity? We will not just look at His time on earth but other time periods as well. We will look at His time before Creation, during Creation, in the Old Testament, His time on earth as the God-man, and in the future as judge.

Before the creation of the world, He was in relationship with the Father.[107] He was loved by the Father.[108] He even shared in His Father's glory.[109]

---

[107]   John 1:1–2
[108]   John 17:24
[109]   John 17:5

During Creation, Jesus created the world,[110] speaking it into existence.[111] While it was the work of the Trinity,[112] Jesus was the one referred to in Genesis 1:1 when it said, "In the beginning God created the heavens and the earth." As the Creator, He holds the universe together.[113]

He appears in the Old Testament several times as someone who is equal to God yet distinct from God. This is revealed in various ways. He is the Commander of the Lord's army.[114] He is the coming Messiah.[115] He is the future ruler in Israel.[116] Sometimes, the angel of the Lord refers to Him.[117]

During His time on earth, He was the God-man. As God, Jesus also became man,[118] thus fully sharing in man's humanity[119] (except without a sin nature[120]) and remains God at the same time,[121] in one personality. His dual nature happened when the Father sent the Son to the world,[122] by which the

---

[110]   John 1:3; Colossians 1:16

[111]   Genesis 1:1, 3, 6, 9, 11, 14, 20, 24, 26

[112]   Hebrews 1:2; Genesis 1:2, 26

[113]   Hebrews 1:3; Colossians 1:17

[114]   Joshua 5:13–15

[115]   Isaiah 9:6

[116]   Micah 5:2

[117]   God distinct from God is revealed where the angel of the Lord is mentioned and given equal standing as God (Genesis 22:11–18; Exodus 3:1–6 [with Mark 12:26–27]; Judges 2:1–3).

[118]   Philippians 2:6–7

[119]   Hebrews 2:17–18

[120]   Hebrews 4:15

[121]   John 10:30

[122]   John 3:16–17

Holy Spirit impregnated the Virgin Mary,[123] who then gave birth to the Son of God.[124] His divine nature sustained His human nature,[125] and the two natures exist without confusion, change, division, or separation.[126] His dual nature of humanity and divinity was necessary for various reasons. In regard to His human nature, He was able to redeem mankind by completing the requirements of God's law for the human race.[127] His humanity was necessary because, as sinless man,[128] He died in mankind's place.[129] Because He shared in man's humanity, He is able to act as our sympathetic high priest.[130] His divine nature was necessary because, as God simultaneously,[131] the sacrifice of Himself at the cross paid for the sins of the whole world.[132] And as God, He acts as our Advocate before God the Father when we sin.[133]

In regards to His human nature, Jesus was fully human. From birth, Jesus developed like other people, matur-

---

[123]   Matthew 1:18–23

[124]   Luke 1:35

[125]   John 10:17–18; Luke 23:46 (A crucified man almost dead can't cry out in a loud voice. He gave up His life)

[126]   Sellers, R. V. Council of Chalcedon: A Historical and Doctrinal Survey. London: SPCK, 1954 (210–211)

[127]   Galatians 4:4–5; Matthew 5:17

[128]   Jesus knew no sin (2 Corinthians 5:21), did no sin (1 Peter 2:22), and in Him is no sin (1 John 3:5).

[129]   Philippians 2:7–8; Hebrews 2:17

[130]   Hebrews 2:14–18

[131]   Philippians 2:6–7

[132]   Hebrews 9:26; 1 John 2:2

[133]   I John 2:1–2

ing physically, maturing mentally, maturing socially, and even maturing spiritually.[134] He became hungry,[135] He was thirsty,[136] He grew tired,[137] He longed for fellowship with close friends,[138] He felt genuine sorrow,[139] at times, He struggled bitterly to obey His Father's will instead of His own,[140] and He even struggled with sin's temptations in every way as we have.[141] Being God, He was simultaneously completely human, except He did not have a sin nature.

Jesus is not only the Savior of the world[142] but also its judge,[143] which He will carry out at the resurrection of the righteous and the wicked.[144] At the Great White Throne judgment, Jesus will judge all of the unsaved from the beginning of the world until its end according to their works and because their name is not found in the Book of Life. They will be thrown into the lake of fire.[145]

The tendency is to focus on Jesus as just His time on earth as Savior, but gaining a grasp of who He is from before Cre-

---

[134] Luke 2:40, 52
[135] Matthew 4:2
[136] John 4:7
[137] John 4:6
[138] Luke 22:15
[139] John 11:35
[140] Hebrews 5:7–8
[141] Hebrews 4:14–15
[142] Matthew 1:21; John 3:17
[143] John 5:22, 27–29
[144] John 5:25–29
[145] Revelation 20:11–15

ation to the end of time brings a deeper reverence and awe of Him. But how does learning who Jesus is help Christians in their daily walk? We are going to look at eleven things.

Application: Who Is Jesus?

1. **He thoroughly understands who we are because He is our Creator.** He is intimately acquainted with our personality, our temperament, and how we think. Genesis 2:7 says, "Then the Lord God formed man of dust from the ground, and breathed into his nostrils the breath of life; and man became a living being." He made us to be who we are, and He intimately knows us. Psalm 139:1–4 says, "Oh Lord, you have searched me and known me. You know when I sit down and when I rise up. You understand my thought from afar. You scrutinize my path and my lying down, and are intimately acquainted with all my ways. Even before there is a word on my tongue, behold O Lord, you know it all." Psalm 139 also tells us that He knows us because He made us. He fashioned us to be who we are. Verse 13–16 says, "For you formed my inward parts. You wove me in my mother's womb. I will give thanks to you, for I am fearfully and wonderfully made. Wonderful are your works, and my soul knows

it very well. My frame was not hidden from you, when I was made in secret, and skillfully rot in the depths of the earth. Your eyes have seen my unformed substance: and in your book were all written the days that were ordained for me, when as yet there was not one of them." And lastly, He knows how we think. He says in verse 23, "Search me, O God, and know my heart; Try me and know my anxious thoughts." So why is it important that we know who Jesus is? It is so that we recognize that He thoroughly understands who we are because He is the one who made us. And He made us with the personality, He made us with the skills, and with the genes just as He wanted us to be. He does not make mistakes. He is intimately acquainted with our personality, temperament, and the way we think.

2. **It matters that we know who Jesus is because He identifies with our need for relationships.** Luke 22:15 says, "And he said to them, I have earnestly desired to eat this Passover with you before I suffer." He longed for fellowship with them.

3. **Jesus understands our limitations and weaknesses. He knows what it feels like personally.** Hebrews 2:14, 17 says, "Therefore, since the

children share in flesh and blood, He Himself likewise also partook of the same, that through death He might render powerless him who had the power of death, that is, the devil. Therefore he had to be made like his brethren in all things, so that He might become a merciful and faithful high priest in things pertaining to God, to make propitiation for the sins of the people." So, He understands our limitations and weaknesses.

4. **Jesus intimately understands our struggle against temptation.** Hebrews 4:14–15 says, "Therefore, since we have a great high priest who has passed through the heavens, Jesus the Son of God, let us hold fast our confession. For we do not have a high priest who cannot sympathize with our weaknesses, but One who has been tempted in all things as we are, yet without sin."

5. **Jesus can help us overcome temptation.** Hebrews 2:17–18 says, "Therefore he had to be made like his brethren in all things, so that He might become a merciful and faithful high priest in things pertaining to God, to make propitiation for the sins of the people. For since He Himself was tempted in that which He has suffered,

He is able to come to the aid of those who are tempted."

6. **It matters that we understand who Jesus is so we understand the price of our forgiveness.** God poured out His wrath toward sin on Jesus at the cross instead of on us so we could be forgiven. Second Corinthians 5:21 says, "He made Him who knew no sin to be sin on our behalf, so that we might become the righteousness of God in Him." And it also says in Isaiah 53:5–6, "But He was pierced through for our transgressions, He was crushed for our iniquities; The chastening for our well-being fell upon Him, and by His scourging we are healed. All of us like sheep have gone astray, each one of us has turned to his own way; but the Lord has caused the iniquity of us all to fall on Him." So God poured out His wrath toward sin on Jesus at the cross instead of us. That was the price of forgiveness.

7. **It matters that we know who Jesus is because He knows firsthand how hard it can be to choose to obey God instead of His own will.** And He knows how hard it can be for you to choose to obey God instead of your own will. Hebrews 5:7–8 says, "In the days of his flesh, He offered up both prayers and supplications with loud

crying and tears to the One able to save him from death, and He was heard because of His piety. Although He was a Son, He learned obedience from the things which he suffered." In Luke 22:41–44, it describes the struggle where Jesus is in the Garden of Gethsemane. "And He withdrew from them about a stone's throw, and He knelt down and began to pray, saying, Father, if you are willing, remove this cup from Me; yet not My will, but Yours be done. Now an angel from heaven appeared to Him strengthening Him. And being in agony He was praying very fervently. And his sweat became like drops of blood falling down upon on the ground." It was not easy for Jesus to obey His Father while in the flesh, so He understands why we have a hard time being obedient as well. And He can help us with that.

8. **It matters that we know who Jesus is because He is our lawyer who defends us before the Father when Satan accuses us.** Romans 8:34 says, "Who is the one who condemns? Christ Jesus is He who died, yes, rather who was raised, who is at the right hand of God, who also intercedes for us." First John 2:1–2 also tells us that Jesus is our lawyer or our Advocate. "My little children, I am writing these things to you so that

you may not sin. And if anyone sins, we have an Advocate with the Father, Jesus Christ the righteous; And He Himself is the propitiation for our sins; and not for ours only, but also for those of the whole world." Jesus is the best lawyer, period, who never loses.

9. **It matters that we know who Jesus is because He can cleanse our guilty conscience.** Hebrews 9:14 says, "How much more will the blood of Christ, who through the eternal spirit offered Himself without blemish to God, cleanse your conscience from dead works to serve the living God?" Hebrews 10:22 says, "Let us draw near with a sincere heart in full assurance of faith, having our hearts sprinkled clean from an evil conscience and our bodies washed with pure water." As believers, we can have a conscience that continues to afflict us. He can cleanse our guilty conscience.

10. **It is important to know who Jesus is because He is the gatekeeper to heaven.** John 14:6 says, "Jesus said to him, I am the way, and the truth, and the life; no one comes to the Father but through Me." It matters that we know who Jesus is because He is the only one God provided to come to Him.

11. **And lastly, we are accountable to Him for how we live our lives, as He is our ultimate Judge.** He is not only our Savior but our judge. "If we confess our sins," as it says in 1 John 1:9, "He is faithful and just to forgive us our sins and to cleanse us from all unrighteousness." But if we have unconfessed sin, if the Spirit of God is pressing us to settle accounts and we ignore Him, we will have to give an account for that later. Second Corinthians 5:10 states, "For we must all appear before the judgment seat of Christ, so that each one may be recompensed for his deeds in the body, according to what he has done, whether good or bad." While God cleanses us, if we have unconfessed sin, if we have hidden sin, after we pass away, our sin will be exposed at the judgment seat of Christ. Jesus was given the right to be judge, for it says in John 5:22, "For not even the Father judges anyone, but He has given all judgment to the Son." And verses 27–29 say, "And He gave Him authority to execute judgment, because He is the Son of Man. Do not marvel at this; for an hour is coming, in which all who are in the tombs will hear His voice, and will come forth; those who did the good deeds to a resurrection of life, those who committed the evil

deeds to a resurrection of judgment." Jesus is not only our Savior. He is our judge.

In the previous session, we looked at the Trinity. Let's compare an aspect of the Trinity and Jesus as the God-man. This chart shows that the Triune God has one nature, or essence, yet has three persons. The God-man has one person yet two natures: the divine nature and the human nature.

Trinity and Christology Compared

TRINITY	ONE NATURE	THREE PERSONS
CHRIST	ONE PERSON	TWO NATURES

In the next session, we will see how understanding the Trinity and Jesus' role as the God-man in the redemptive process sheds light on mankind's identity as being made in the image of God. To view the charts for this section, go to https://rbeteach71.wixsite.com/justified-sinners/charts.

3. IMAGE OF GOD

Concept: This study is about God's image-bearers, which means that mankind was created in the image of God. The first session examined the Trinity, which is the foundation for mankind's creation. Because people are not only made in the image of God, they are made in the image of the Triune God.[146] The New Testament says they are made in the image of the Son.[147] They are made in the image of the Father.[148] They are made in the image of the Father and the Son.[149] They are made in the image of the Son and the Holy Spirit.[150] And in the Old Testament, it says people are made in the image of God, in which God uses plural pronouns to refer to Himself. Genesis 1:26–27 says, "Then God said, 'let Us make man in Our image, according to Our likeness; and let them rule over the fish of the sea and over the birds of the sky and over the cattle and over all the earth, and over every creeping thing that creeps on the earth.' God created man in His own image, in the image of God He created him; male

---

[146] Genesis 1:26–27; 2:7; 9:6
[147] Romans 8:29; Philippians 3:20–21
[148] James 3:9
[149] James 3:9 with Hebrews 1:3
[150] 2 Corinthians 3:18

and female He created them." People are made in the image of the Triune God.

Think through the social effects of a biblical view of mankind being fashioned in the image of God. The value of human life affects all social interaction. Our belief about it dictates how we relate to our spouses, children, and parents. It controls our decision-making in abortion, suicide, and euthanasia. It even governs how we treat our own bodies. First Corinthians 3:16 states, "Do you not know that you are the temple of God and that the Spirit of God dwells in you?" Because we are made in the image of God, we do not have the right to do whatever we want with our bodies, for it belongs to God. Public education, orphans and the welfare system, homeless people, employer-employee relationships, colleagues, families, etc.... are directly influenced by one's (and society's) belief in what is the value of human life. Understanding the social effects of a biblical view of mankind can radically change how people (and society) interact socially towards one another and support the rights of others they have any influence over or say in. Jesus went as far as to say that how people treat His own, they treat Him.[151]

Application

So, what does that have to do with us in our decision-making? How would we treat others around us if we

---

[151]   Matthew 10:40–42; 25:31–45

truly believed they were made in the image of the Triune God? I am going to give you nine different scenarios, and I would like you to take the time to think through each one separately.

1. If we believed that our spouse was made in the image of God and our treatment of him or her was how we were treating His image, how would that change the way we fight, boss him or her around, or care for his or her needs? If we saw our spouse as God's son or daughter, what would change? How would our approach change?

2. If we believed that our children were made in the image of God and our treatment of them was how we were treating His image, how would that change the way we instruct them or discipline them?

3. If we believed that our parents were made in the image of God and our treatment of them was how we were treating His image, how would that change the way we obey them (if still under their care) or respect and honor them?

4. If we believed that our boss was made in the image of God and our treatment of him or her was how we were treating His image, how would that change the way we relate to him or her,

respect him or her, or do what he or she tells us to do?

5. If we believed that our employees were made in the image of God and our treatment of them was how we were treating His image, how would that change the way we relate to them or manage them?

6. If we believed that our colleagues were made in the image of God and our treatment of them was how we were treating His image, how would that change the way we relate to them or work out difficulties between us and them when they come?

7. If we believed that our neighbors were made in the image of God and our treatment of them was how we were treating God, how would that change the way we interact with them or relate to them when tensions arise between us?

8. Pay attention to this one. If we believed that our bodies were made in the image of God and our treatment of ourselves is how we take care of His image, how would that change the way we treat ourselves or behave when no one else is looking? For we do not belong to our own. We

are a temple of God, and the Holy Spirit dwells within us.

9. And lastly, if we wholeheartedly believed that everyone (no matter how they act or how much money they have) was made in the image of God, how would we interact socially towards them and support the rights of others we have any influence over or say in?

The reason we look at these different scenarios is that what people believe about the value of human life (whether they are made in the image of God or have the same or similar value to animals) controls how they perceive people and interact with those they come in contact with.

Our society's belief about the value of human life decides government and people's decision-making on social issues like abortion, suicide, euthanasia, public education, orphans and the welfare system, homeless people, the care of the elderly, etc.

<u>How would the way you treat others around you look like if you truly believed they were made in the image of the Triune God?</u> Would it change? If so, how? Or would it stay the same? Why? If you believe human life doesn't have this value and is worth the same or not much more than animals, how would you act differently? Would it change from the way you act now? How? Or would it stay the same? Why?

Understanding that mankind is made in the image of the Triune God helps people view others with value, regardless of their social position or personal choices. But God made mankind perfect. What happened? How did people become twisted? In session four, we will look at the beginning of the redemptive cycle, sin, and how the Fall resulted in physical and spiritual death.

To view the chart for this section, go to https://rbeteach71.wixsite.com/justified-sinners/charts.

4. THE FALL RESULTED IN DEATH

Concept: In the last session, we learned that mankind was made in the image of the Triune God. So, how did people become twisted and messed up like we see in the world today? In this session, we will look at the beginning of the redemptive cycle, Sin, and how the Fall resulted in mankind's physical and spiritual death. When God made people, they were perfect, and the world was perfect.[152] God placed Adam and Eve in the Garden of Eden to be its caretakers.[153] They were to rule over creation as God's image bearers.[154] Everything they wanted was theirs. They could eat and drink what they wanted, they were in complete harmony with the animal kingdom and nature as their overseers,[155] and God visited them every evening.[156] They were naked and completely unashamed of their condition.[157] They did not possess

---

[152]   Genesis 1:31
[153]   Genesis 2:8, 15
[154]   Genesis 1:26–27
[155]   Genesis 1:28–30
[156]   Genesis 3:8
[157]   Genesis 2:25

a sin nature, nor did they age.[158] Adam and Eve loved each other and were completely united.[159]

God only gave them one negative command. "Do not eat from the 'Tree of the Knowledge of Good and Evil,' for in the day that you eat from it, you will surely die."[160] Satan possessed the serpent, the most beautiful creature in the Garden, using it to deceive Eve. Listening to the serpent's deceptive argument, Eve disobeyed God and ate of the forbidden fruit.[161] Adam, who was not deceived, was beside her and did not try to stop her. He knowingly took of the fruit Eve gave him, outright disobeying God.[162] ***Everything changed!*** Everything in the world changed.

At that moment, our first parents[163] *took on a sin nature, and death entered the world.*[164] As a result of sin entering the world and as a result of God's image-bearers (the human race) becoming corrupted through sin, God subjected nature to meaninglessness (which is a lack of purpose), enslaved to corruption. In that state, God's whole creation continually suffers and groans together in agony.[165]

---

158   Romans 5:12, 14; Genesis 2:17
159   Genesis 2:22–24
160   Genesis 2:17
161   Genesis 3:1–6
162   Genesis 3:6; 1 Timothy 2:14
163   Genesis 3:20
164   Romans 5:12, 14
165   Romans 8:19–22

Adam and Eve became ashamed of their nakedness and afraid because they disobeyed God, so they hid from Him.[166] When confronted, Adam blamed his wife, and she blamed the serpent.[167] They were no longer completely united. Sin brought consequences. God cursed the ground so it wouldn't grow crops like before[168] and increased women's pain in childbirth.[169] He put woman into subjection under man while at the same time giving her a desire to control him.[170] Adam and Eve were removed from the Garden of Eden, lest they live forever in their sin by eating from the Tree of Life.[171] They could not freely fellowship with God because of their sin. They were separated spiritually from Him, and apart from His direct intervention, they and every one of their descendants would go to hell after death.

In their sinful state, God showed them how to approach Him by killing a lamb as a sacrifice for their sins.[172] As seen in the story of Cain and Abel, God required that man come to Him on God's terms, not man's way.[173] From this point

---

[166] Genesis 3:7–10

[167] Genesis 3:11–13

[168] Genesis 3:17–19; 5:29

[169] Genesis 3:16a

[170] Genesis 3:16b. In the word desire, see also Genesis 4:7

[171] Genesis 3:22–24

[172] Genesis 3:21 with 4:4 (Abel learned that God wanted a lamb sacrifice for sin because his parents taught him. They learned from God, starting in Genesis 3:21).

[173] Genesis 4:3–5

on, mankind, with his sin nature, would naturally turn away from God.[174]

Let's take a look at the chart to see what specifically changed in the entire human race because of Adam and Eve's disobedience. *Mankind's relationship to God changed.* He went from no sin[175] to having a sin nature.[176] He went from a state of innocence[177] to depravity.[178] He changed his position towards God from fellowship and free access to God[179] to separation from God.[180] He used to be naturally inclined to obey God,[181] but due to his sin nature, he naturally rebels and strays from God.[182]

Human relationships changed because of Adam and Eve's disobedience. They went from openness and transparency among one another[183] to shame.[184] They went from confidence and security[185] to fear.[186] Instead of mutual

---

[174]   Isaiah 53:6; Romans 3:10–12
[175]   Romans 5:12
[176]   Psalm 51:5; Ephesians 2:3
[177]   Genesis 2:25
[178]   Jeremiah 17:9; Romans 3:10–12
[179]   Genesis 3:8
[180]   Genesis 2:17; Romans 5:18–19
[181]   Romans 5:12
[182]   Isaiah 53:6; Romans 3:10–12
[183]   Genesis 2:24–25
[184]   Genesis 3:7–10
[185]   Genesis 2:24–25
[186]   Genesis 3:8–10

acceptance,[187] people entered the blame game and started inter-fighting.[188] They went from equality[189] to dominance,[190] even in the marriage relationship.

Adam and Eve's disobedience changed the natural order. In the beginning, people did not age or die,[191] yet growing old and dying is now a part of life.[192] The ground was not cursed, but now it is cursed.[193] It is hard work to get food. Work used to be easy, but it became tiresome.[194] In the beginning, there was little pain in childbirth, but now it is extremely painful.[195]

Adam and Eve's disobedience towards God changed the relationship between the human race and nature. Before, mankind lived in paradise,[196] but he was banished from it.[197] In the beginning, there was harmony with nature and the animal kingdom,[198] but now there is conflict with it, and people abuse it. In the beginning, nature and the animal kingdom was in harmony with itself, and mankind was its

---

187   Genesis 2:23–25
188   Genesis 3:11–13
189   Genesis 2:20–24
190   Genesis 3:16b
191   Genesis 2:17; Romans 5:12
192   Romans 5:12, 14
193   Genesis 3:17–19
194   Genesis 5:29
195   Genesis 3:16a
196   Genesis 2:8
197   Genesis 3:23–24
198   Genesis 1:28–30

caretaker.[199] But because sin entered the world, God subjected nature to meaninglessness, which is a lack of purpose, enslaved to corruption. In that state, God's whole creation suffers and groans together in agony.[200] Adam and Eve's disobedience brought sin into the world, changing literally everything. Let's look at life application.

What Effects Does the Fall Have on People Today?

1. First, mankind is separated from God because of his sin. It is his fault, and there is nothing he can do to return to God by his own efforts. Apart from God's direct intervention, man has no hope.

2. Second, we can't blame God for our sin. It is our fault. Until we recognize and take responsibility for our wrongdoings, He can't save us.

3. Third, our fallen world is a direct result of man's sin nature.

The Fall resulted in corrupting God's image in mankind. Sin brought physical and spiritual death. In the next session, we will look at the sin nature and how it was passed on to every one of Adam and Eve's offspring. To view the chart

---

[199]   Genesis 1:28–30; Romans 8:20a
[200]   Romans 8:20–22

for this section, go to https://rbeteach71.wixsite.com/justified-sinners/charts.

5. SIN NATURE

Concept: In the last session, we learned about the Fall, when sin entered the world, resulting in broken fellowship between mankind and his Creator. Adam and Eve's disobedience brought a series of horrific consequences, climaxing in physical and spiritual death. As a result, everyone throughout history is born with a sin nature[201] and is sinful by nature.[202] Everyone who is born has the natural tendency to sin. When I was born, I inherited the name Musgrave. I did not choose my parents, last name, or genetic make-up. In the same way, when I was born, I had already inherited a sin nature. Even little children and babies sin because it comes naturally. No one has to teach a little child how to do wrong. It comes instinctively. Everyone is born with a sin nature. This is because of the imputation of sin.

6. IMPUTATION OF SIN

Concept: There are two main categories of imputation. Actual imputation is crediting something to someone that he earned (like a paycheck). Judicial imputation is to credit

---

201   Psalm 51:5

202   Ephesians 2:3

to one's account something that he did not earn (is not inherently his). I inherited the last name "Musgrave." Imputation of sin is being credited with a sin nature before ever doing anything wrong. Adam's sin of direct disobedience in the Garden of Eden is judicially imputed to everyone's account in the entire world, passed down through ancestry.[203] His sin nature was judicially imputed to all of his descendants, bringing judgment to every person, resulting in their condemnation.[204] Because people are born in sin, whether or not they commit sins, they are already condemned before God because of their sin nature. This is proven by the concept of death. Just as Adam's sin nature is judicially imputed to everyone, so death is judicially imputed to everyone.[205] Death did not exist before Adam's sin. There was no death in the Garden of Eden before then. Death was a direct consequence of sin entering the world. So, how does our sin nature and sin imputed to our account affect us personally?

Application

1. We are not basically good. Psalm 51:5 says, "Behold, I was brought forth iniquity, and in sin my mother conceived me." Romans 3:10 states, "As it is written, there is none righteous, not

---

[203] Romans 5:12–21; 1 Corinthians 15:22, 45–59
[204] Romans 5:18–19
[205] Romans 5:12, 14; Genesis 2:17; 1 Corinthians 15:22

even one." We are prone to sin. Ephesians 2:3 announces, "Among them we too all formally left in the lusts of our flesh, indulging the desires of the flesh and of the mind, and were by nature children of wrath, even as the rest."

2. We are prone to stray from our Creator. Isaiah 53:6 affirms this. "All of us like sheep have gone astray, each of us has turned to his own way; but the Lord has caused the iniquity of us all to fall on Him."

3. Our hearts are by nature deceptive, not only toward others but also towards our own selves. Jeremiah 17:9 declares, "The heart is more deceitful than all else and desperately sick; who can understand it?"

4. As sinners, there is nothing we can do to win God's approval by our own efforts. Romans 3:10–12 and 23 points out, "As it is written, there is none righteous, not even one; there is none who understands, there is none who seeks for God; all have turned aside, together they have become useless; there is none who does good, there is not even one." "For all have sinned and fall short of the glory of God." Galatians 3:11 adds, "Now that no one is justified by the Law before

God is evident; for, 'The righteous man shall live by faith.'"

Conclusion

As we can see, our sin nature and sin imputed to our account affects us profoundly. This places mankind in a hopeless condition. It is in understanding and accepting this fate that opens people's eyes to the need for a Savior. In the last two sessions, we have been addressing the devastating consequences of sin. <u>Throughout the next six sessions, we will come to understand the Triune God's sovereign plan of redemption through the cross.</u> In the following lesson, we will look at the Atonement, which reveals how sinful mankind is allowed to approach Holy God. To view the chart for this section, go to https://rbeteach71.wixsite.com/justified-sinners/charts.

7. ATONEMENT

Introduction

S in separates mankind from his Creator. Understanding one's hopeless state before God reveals why people need a Savior. In the last session, we learned how our sin nature and sin imputed to our account places us in a desperate situation. In this lesson, we will look at the Atonement, which reveals how sinful mankind is allowed to approach Holy God.

Concept: The Atonement is the innocent shedding their blood to pay for the sins of the guilty. As innocent, perfect sacrifices, animal blood was shed, killed to pay for people's wrong doings.[206] Leviticus 17:11 proclaims, "For the life of the flesh is in the blood, and I have given it to you upon the altar to make atonement for your souls; for it is the blood that makes atonement for the soul."

Once a year in Israel, on the Day of the Atonement, the high priest shed the blood of sin offerings for himself and God's people. He entered the Holy of Holies and sprinkled the blood on the Mercy Seat in God's presence to cover their

---

[206]   Leviticus 6:7

sins.[207] A scapegoat was also chosen, and the high priest would lay his hands on it, confessing the sins of Israel over it and transferring their sins to it. The goat would carry all their sins. Then, the goat would be cast out into the wilderness. By bearing the sins of the people, the goat would make atonement for their sins.[208] In the same way the high priest placed the sins of Israel on the scapegoat, God the Father placed the sins of the world on Jesus at the cross. Second Corinthians 5:21 writes, "He (God) made Him (Jesus) who knew no sin to be sin on our behalf..." God made Jesus guilty by transferring the world's sins to Him. Isaiah chapter 53 explicitly declares this. God took man's sin and put it on His Servant (Jesus).[209] It also says, "Each of us has turned to his own way; but the Lord has caused the iniquity of us all to fall on Him."[210] And again, "...My Servant will justify the many, as He will bear their iniquities."[211] The Old Testament sacrificial system of shedding innocent blood to pay for the sins of the guilty was a foreshadowing of what Jesus did. He was the perfect, sinless sacrificial lamb who shed his blood to pay for the sins of the world.[212] It was one sacrifice that paid for everyone's sins forever, never to be repeated.[213] The Atone-

---

207   Leviticus 16:2, 14–15 (Hebrews 9:7), 33–34

208   Leviticus 16:10, 20–22

209   Isaiah 53:4–6, 10, 11

210   Isaiah 53:6

211   Isaiah 53:11

212   John 1:29; Hebrews 9:26

213   Hebrews 10:10, 12, 14

ment results in mankind's forgiveness,[214] appeasing God's wrath toward sin[215] and removal of sin.[216] What effect does the Atonement have on people's daily lives?

Application

1. Recognize that because we are guilty, there is nothing we can do to make ourselves presentable before God.

2. Accept the fact that all our sins have been paid for. Hebrews 10:10, 12, 14 professes, "By this will we have been sanctified through the offering of the body of Jesus Christ, once for all. but He, having offered one sacrifice for sins for all time, sat down at the right hand of God... For by one offering He perfected for all time those who are sanctified."

3. Know that we cannot earn God's forgiveness but can only choose to receive it. Matthew 26:28 reveals, "for this is My blood of the covenant, which is poured out for many for the forgiveness of sins." Ephesians 1:7 points out, "In Him we have redemption through His blood, the forgive-

---

[214] Matthew 26:27–28; Ephesians 1:7
[215] Romans 1:18; 3:25; 1 John 2:2
[216] Isaiah 53:10–11

ness of our trespasses, according to the riches of His grace..."

The Atonement reveals how sinful mankind is allowed to approach Holy God. In the following session, we will further examine this by taking a careful look at the imputation of righteousness. To view the chart for this section, go to https://rbeteach71.wixsite.com/justified-sinners/charts.

8. IMPUTATION OF RIGHTEOUSNESS

Concept: In the last session, we looked at the Atonement, which reveals how sinful mankind is allowed to approach Holy God. This lesson will further examine this by taking a careful look at the imputation of righteousness. There are two main categories of imputation. First, actual imputation is crediting something to someone that he earned (like a paycheck). Second, judicial imputation is to credit to someone's account something that he did not earn (is not inherently his). I inherited the last name, Musgrave.

To clearly understand the imputation of righteousness, it is necessary to see it in context with the imputation of sin. The imputation of sin means being credited with a sin nature before ever doing anything wrong. Adam's sin of direct disobedience in the Garden of Eden is judicially imputed to everyone's account in the entire world, passed down through ancestry. His sin nature was judicially imputed to all of his descendants, bringing judgment to every person, resulting in their condemnation. Because people are born in sin, whether or not they commit sins, they are already condemned before God because of their sin nature. The imputation of righteousness is Jesus's righteousness being credited to one's account so that His righteousness becomes one's own. Both the imputation of sin and the imputation of righteousness are inherited, the first received by birth and the second as a gift by faith in Jesus.

How do people receive the imputation of righteousness? Jesus came to earth to give His life as the full payment for sin.[217] His act of obedience[218] was very costly.[219] At the cross, God imputed the sins of the world to Jesus. Second Corinthians 5:21 affirms, "He (God) made Him (Jesus) who knew no sin to be sin on our behalf..." God made Jesus guilty by transferring mankind's sins and sin nature to Him. The prophet Isaiah explicitly declares that God took man's iniquity and put it on His Servant (Jesus).[220] Isaiah 53:6 declares, "Each of us has turned to his own way; but the Lord has caused the iniquity of us all to fall on Him." And verse 11 adds, "...My Servant will justify the many, as He will bear their iniquities." Jesus' one act of obedience (death on the cross) brought righteousness to everyone who trusts in Him by faith.[221]

God the Father imputed mankind's sin nature and sins to Jesus on the cross and imputed Jesus' righteousness to those who accept Jesus as their Lord and Savior.[222] Jesus'

---

217   Mark 10:45; 8:31
218   Romans 5:19; Philippians 2:8
219   Luke 22:41–44; Hebrews 5:7–8
220   Isaiah 53:4–6, 10–11
221   Romans 5:19
222   2 Corinthians 5:21 (See also Romans 4:6–8; 5:18; 10:3, 6–10; Isaiah 53:11)

righteousness is credited to people's account.[223] One can't earn this righteousness. It can only be judicially credited to the account of those who place their faith in Jesus,[224] just as the sin nature is judicially credited to everyone's account by birth.[225] The results of receiving Jesus's righteousness are one, justification, which is being declared righteous before God;[226] two, becoming reconciled to God,[227] which means being brought into a relationship with Him; and three, reigning eternally with Him.[228] How does the imputation of righteousness apply to our lives personally?

Application

1. First, just as I inherited a sin nature, I inherited Jesus' righteousness. Psalm 51:5 proclaims, "Behold, I was brought forth in iniquity, and in sin my mother conceived me. Romans 5:18–19 counters with, "So then as through the one man's disobedience the many were made sinners, even so through one act of righteousness there resulted justification of life to all men. For as through the one man's obedience of the One

---

223   Romans 5:17
224   Philippians 3:9
225   Psalm 51:5
226   Romans 5:16, 18
227   Romans 5:10
228   Romans 5:17; Revelation 22:5

the many will be made righteous." The truth is, no efforts on my own earn either a sin nature or Jesus' righteousness.

2. Second, even though I am a sinner, I can have a relationship with a holy, perfect God because of Jesus. Romans 5:10 asserts, "For if while we were enemies we were reconciled to God through the death of His Son, much more, having been reconciled, we shall be saved by His life." Second Corinthians 5:18–19 states, "Now all things are from God, who reconciled us to Himself through Christ and gave us the ministry of reconciliation, namely that God was in Christ reconciling the world to Himself, not counting their trespasses against them, and He has committed to us the word of reconciliation."

3. Third, as ambassadors of Christ, God makes His appeal of reconciling people to Himself through us. Second Corinthians 5:20 points out, "Therefore, we are ambassadors for Christ, as though God were making an appeal through us; we beg you on behalf of Christ, be reconciled to God." So, each of these are direct ways of how the imputation of righteousness affects our lives personally.

We are familiar with John 3:16. "For God so loved the world." God the Father loves the people He created so much that He sent His only Son Jesus to save them. The imputation of sin received at birth condemns mankind, but the imputation of righteousness received by faith in Jesus reconciles mankind to God the Father. This is how sinful mankind is allowed to approach Holy God. In the next session, we will further discover how God the Father can be just and justify sinners simultaneously. To view the chart for this section, go to https://rbeteach71.wixsite.com/justified-sinners/charts.

9. AS RIGHTEOUS JUDGE AND JUSTIFIER OF SINFUL MAN

Concept: Through the cross, a way was created for sinful mankind to be restored in fellowship with his Creator. In the last two sessions, we looked at the Atonement and the imputation of righteousness, both of which reveal how sinful man is allowed to approach Holy God. In this lesson, we will further examine this by looking at the Judge and Justifier. How can holy, perfect God maintain His standard and declare sinful people righteous? Or how can a judge be just and let a murderer go free? When people are saved, God the Father changes their legal status. He looks at the shed blood of Jesus and counts His death as the perfect sacrifice that covers all of people's sins—past, present, and future. Even while believers are sinners, even while they are continually falling short of God's glory, they are declared righteous before God their judge because Jesus has paid the price for their sin.[229] The Old Testament sacrifices could not really pay for sins;[230] all they could do was to point to one who could. But they illustrated a very important point: the

---

[229]   Romans 3:23–24

[230]   Hebrews 10:4, 11

death of an innocent, perfect life is required to satisfy a Holy God's wrath against sinners. This is what we learned in the Atonement.

Every year, the Israelites celebrated the Passover. In preparation for the first Passover, God told Israel to kill a lamb and smear blood on the door frame, then have all household inhabitants inside so He would pass over the house and not kill the firstborn.[231] When God brought the final plague on the Egyptians so Pharaoh would let His people go, the death angel came to every household in Egypt to kill the firstborn. When the death angel saw the blood of the acceptable sacrifice over the door frame, he passed over it.[232] In the same way, Old Testament sins were overlooked when people offered acceptable sacrifices to God by faith. It is only in the cross where God fully satisfies His own righteousness against sin and thus demonstrates His righteousness.[233] This is how God could "pass over the sins previously committed;" only by looking forward to the actual payment for sins by His own Son, Jesus. Through the work of the cross, God the Father transfers people's sins to Jesus and credits Jesus' righteousness to their account.[234] This is the imputation of righteousness.

---

[231]   Exodus 12:3, 5–7, 21–23

[232]   Exodus 12:11–13, 26–27, 29–32

[233]   Romans 3:21–26

[234]   2 Corinthians 5:21

He demonstrates His righteousness by demanding full payment for sin through His sinless and perfect Son, Jesus, offering His body and shed blood as payment for it. This payment is sufficient one time, forever, for all who take hold of it through faith in Jesus.[235] Jesus' substitutionary death allows God the Father to maintain His holy standard of righteousness before sinners and, at the same time, declare them righteous.

God is our judge and justifies us as sinners simultaneously. This is deeply personal, for it allows us to approach a Holy God directly. God the Father replaces my sin with Jesus' righteousness, so while I'm sinful, He sees Jesus' righteousness, not my sin. Second Corinthians 5:21 reveals this. "He (God the Father) made Him (Jesus) who knew no sin to be sin on our behalf, so that we might become the righteousness of God in Him."

The lessons on the Atonement, the imputation of righteousness, and Judge and Justifier each reveal how sinful man is allowed to approach Holy God. In the next session, we will understand how entrance to heaven is received as a gift and cannot be earned. To view the chart for this section, go to https://rbeteach71.wixsite.com/justified-sinners/charts.

---

[235]   Hebrews 9:26; 10:10, 12, 14

10. GIFT, NOT WORKS

Concept: In the redemptive process, we have been discovering how God uses the cross to restore people to Himself. The last session on Judge and Justifier revealed how sinful man is allowed to approach Holy God. In this lesson, we will understand that getting into heaven is not based on good works. Salvation can't be earned. There is nothing anyone can do to be declared righteous in God's sight and earn his way to heaven. David was credited with righteousness apart from his good deeds after he had committed adultery and murder. Romans 4:5 declares, "But to him who does not work (these are good deeds), but believes on Him who justifies the ungodly, his faith is accounted for righteousness..." God promised Abraham he would have a son through Sarah and that he would be the father of many nations. Twenty-five years later, he was a hundred years old, and his wife Sarah was ninety and still barren. Even so, Abraham continued to believe in God's promise. Romans 4:3 reveals, "Abraham believed God, and it was counted to him for righteousness." His righteousness did not come from his good works but through faith in what God promised. Jesus' gift of righteousness is credited toward one's account without one doing anything to earn it.[236] There is nothing one can do to earn enough good deeds before God and enter heaven. It is solely God's gift by grace given to those who place their faith in Jesus. Ephesians 2:8–9 says, "For by grace you have been saved through faith (in Jesus); and that not of yourselves. It is the gift of God, not as a result of works, so that no one may boast."

This affects how we, as believers, live before God. Our good works cannot secure a place in heaven, but it does change our experience in heaven, which we will look at later in the lesson on eternal rewards.

Application

1. As Christians, we don't live righteously before God by our good works in our own efforts. We live righteously before God by faith, which is demonstrated through our works. Jesus, the author and perfecter of our faith, helps us in our struggle, just as He has helped the multitude of people of faith before us who were also sinful.

In this lesson, we clearly see how salvation is obtained as a gift and can't be earned. In the next lesson, we will put everything together. The Atonement, Imputation of Righteousness, Judge and Justifier, and Gift, not works, all

---

[236] Romans 5:15–18

point to the truth that Jesus is the only way. To view the chart for this section, go to https://rbeteach71.wixsite.com/justified-sinners/charts.

11.   JESUS IS THE ONLY WAY TO HEAVEN

Concept: In the redemptive cycle, we have been examining different aspects of the cross, ways in which Holy God paid a costly price to restore sinful mankind to Himself. The lesson on Jesus is the only way to encompasse every one of the different concepts of the cross: the Atonement, Imputation of Righteousness, Judge and Justifier, Gift, not works, and the following lesson on Eternal security. Jesus is the only way to heaven. He is the only answer to the dilemma: how can holy, perfect God maintain His standard and declare sinful people righteous? It would be like, "How can a judge be just and let murderers go free?" God is perfect and can't allow sin in heaven. The punishment for everyone's sin is eternal separation from Him in hell. [237] It is impossible to remove one's sin. It is impossible to earn one's way to heaven.[238] Payment for sin can't come from an animal or any other creature. It needs to come from mankind. Man must be offered as the sacrifice for man. But if the sin nature is passed to all of Adam's descendants, how would there be anyone free from sin? So, this is the answer. God the

---

[237]   Romans 6:23a

[238]   Ephesians 2:8–9

Father sent His Son to the world,[239] by which the Holy Spirit impregnated the Virgin Mary,[240] who then gave birth to the Son of God.[241] This is how Jesus had God's nature and man's nature at the same time, yet without sin.[242] His dual nature of humanity and divinity was necessary, for as fully man, He redeemed mankind by completing the requirements of God's law for the human race,[243] and as sinless man, He died in man's place.[244] As fully God simultaneously, the sacrifice of Himself[245] at the cross paid for the sins of the world.[246]

Atonement is the innocent shedding their blood to pay for the sins of the guilty. The sacrifice of innocent animals without defect covered the sins of the guilty. But it is only in the cross where God fully satisfies His own righteousness against sin, and thus demonstrates His righteousness.[247] Through the work of the cross, God the Father transfers people's sins to Jesus and credits Jesus' righteousness to their account.[248] He demonstrates His righteousness by demanding full payment for sin by sinless, perfect Jesus offering His

---

[239]   John 3:16–17

[240]   Matthew 1:18–23

[241]   Luke 1:35

[242]   Jesus knew no sin (2 Corinthians 5:21), did no sin (1 Peter 2:22), and in Him is no sin (1 John 3:5).

[243]   Galatians 4:4–5; Matthew 5:17

[244]   Philippians 2:7–8; Hebrews 2:17

[245]   Hebrews 7:26–27; 9:11–12

[246]   Hebrews 9:26; 1 John 2:2

[247]   Romans 3:21–26

[248]   2 Corinthians 5:21

body and shed blood as payment for it. This payment is sufficient one time, forever, for all who take hold of it through faith in Jesus.[249] Jesus' substitutionary death allows God to maintain His holy standard of righteousness before sinners, and simultaneously declare them righteous. There is no one else who is sinless who can pay for the human race's punishment for sin and give them God's righteousness in its place. That is why He is the only mediator between God and man.[250] People must believe in Him or be condemned.[251] First John 5:12 declares, "He who has the Son has life. He who doesn't have the Son doesn't have eternal life." Jesus is the light of the world[252] and the only way to heaven,[253] the only one who can give people direct access to God.[254]

Jesus, as the only way, radically separates Christianity from any other religion. Entrance to heaven cannot be obtained by trying hard and doing good. It can only be obtained by accepting Jesus' gift of righteousness. I invite you to reflect on this question. How would you behave differently in your everyday life, living, knowing you needed to work your way to heaven vs. accepting eternal life as a priceless gift from Jesus?

---

[249]   Hebrews 9:26; 10:10, 12, 14
[250]   1 Timothy 2:5
[251]   John 3:36
[252]   John 8:12
[253]   John 14:6
[254]   John 14:6

Jesus is the only way to heaven. In the next lesson, we will see that the Triune God, not us as individual believers, is responsible for safeguarding our salvation. To view the chart for this section, go to https://rbeteach71.wixsite.com/justified-sinners/charts.

12. ETERNAL SECURITY

Concept: We have been examining different aspects of the cross and how Jesus is the only way God the Father provided to go to heaven. But is it possible to lose one's salvation? That's what we are going to talk about in the biblical concept of eternal security. The key question concerning eternal security is who is responsible for safeguarding one's salvation: individual believers or the Triune God? Is each individual believer responsible for securing his salvation and making sure it isn't lost, or is the Triune God responsible for preserving his salvation regardless of what choices he may make?

Scripture clearly states that once a person is a believer, he can't lose his salvation, for his position and future destiny is held fast by the Triune God, not himself. The three persons of the Trinity work together to ensure the believer's eternal security.

Let's look at the Father: He chose them for salvation from before the world was made. [255] He predestined them to be adopted as sons by Jesus.[256] He keeps them secure in sal-

---

[255] Ephesians 1:4
[256] Ephesians 1:5

vation. Those He foreknew, He predestined, called, justified, and will bring to glorification. None are lost in the process.[257]

Let's look at the Son's role in securing salvation: He redeemed the believer.[258] He removed the wrath of God the Father from him.[259] He justified him.[260] He provided forgiveness.[261] The Son sanctified him.[262] He prays to the Father for them to be with Him for eternity.[263] He is their Advocate before God the Father when their sin condemns them,[264] and He continually intercedes for them as their High Priest.[265]

The Holy Spirit also takes an active role in safeguarding one's salvation: He baptizes the believer into the body of Christ.[266] He regenerates the believer, giving him life.[267] He indwells the believer forever,[268] and He seals the believer until the Day of Redemption.[269]

The following passages in the chart clearly state the position of eternal security. John 3:16; John 5:24; John 6:37, 39;

---

[257]   Romans 8:29–30

[258]   Ephesians 1:7

[259]   Romans 3:25; 5:9

[260]   Romans 5:1, 9

[261]   Ephesians 1:7; Colossians 2:13

[262]   1 Corinthians 1:2

[263]   John 17:24 (20–24)

[264]   Romans 8:34; 1 John 2:1

[265]   Hebrews 7:25

[266]   1 Corinthians 12:13

[267]   Titus 3:5

[268]   John 14:16–17

[269]   Ephesians 1:13–14; 4:30

John 10:27–29; Romans 8:29–30; Hebrews 7:25 and Jude 21–14. John 3:16 confirms eternal security. "For God so loved the world, that He gave His only begotten Son, that whoever believes in Him shall not perish, but have eternal life." John 5:24 adds to this, "Truly, truly I say to you, he who hears My word, and believes Him who sent Me, has eternal life, and does not come into judgment, but has passed out of death into life."

One aspect of eternal security is true believers and false believers. Only the Triune God knows without a doubt who belongs to Him. Matthew 7:21–23 talks about this, as well as Matthew 13:24–30 and 36–43, and 1 John 2:18–19. Matthew 7:21–23 claims, "Not everyone who says to me, 'Lord, Lord,' will enter the kingdom of heaven, but he who does the will of My Father who is in heaven will enter. May will say to Me on that day, 'Lord, Lord, did we not prophesy in Your name, and in Your name cast out demons, and in Your name preform many miracles?' And then I will declare to them, 'I never knew you; depart from Me, you who practice lawlessness.'

True and false believers should be known by what fruit they produce. We see this in Matthew 7:15–20 and Luke 6:43–45. Matthew 7:15–20 says, "Beware of the false prophets, who come to you in sheep's clothing, but inwardly are ravenous wolves. You will know them by their fruits. Grapes are not gathered from thorn bushes nor figs from thistles, are they? So, every good tree bears good fruit, but the bad tree bears bad fruit. A good tree cannot produce bad fruit, nor can a bad tree produce good fruit. Every tree that does not bear good fruit is cut down and thrown into the fire. So then, you will know them by their fruits."

Even though only some become believers, the Triune God died for the sins of the world and desires repentance for everyone. There are people who are going to heaven, and there are people who are going to hell, but God died for everyone in the world and wishes that everyone repent. This is addressed in Ezekiel 18:23, 32, John 3:16–17, 1 Timothy 2:4, Titus 2:11, 2 Peter 3:9, and 1 John 2:1–2. John 3:16–17 proclaims, "For God so loved the world, that He gave His only begotten Son, that whoever believes in Him shall not perish, but have eternal life. For God did not send the Son into the world to judge the world, but that the world might be saved through Him." Second Peter 3:9 stresses this too. "The Lord is not slow about His promise, as some count slowness, but is patient toward you, not wishing for any to perish but for all to come to repentance."

Eternal security governs how believers live their lives before God. Here are three ways how eternal security affects us as believers.

Application

1. Our salvation is sure because it doesn't depend on us but on the Triune God.

2. We can live without fear of the future after this life.

3. Believers can be deceived by those who profess to be Christians yet are false, but God always knows who belongs to Him.

Once an individual accepts Jesus as their Savior, Eternal Security does not depend on the individual believer. The Triune God is responsible for safeguarding one's salvation. Good works do not secure one's place in heaven, but good works done with the right motive do have eternal consequences. We will look at this in a later lesson on eternal rewards.

We have studied different biblical concepts about the cross. In the next lesson, we will transition to the following stage in the redemptive cycle, the Cleansing of Justified Sinners. We will start with what makes up the Church, the body of Jesus. To view the chart for this section, go to https://rbeteach71.wixsite.com/justified-sinners/charts.

13. CHURCH: *WHAT'S ITS MAKE-UP?*

Concept: In the previous stage of the redemptive cycle, we studied different biblical concepts about the cross. In this lesson, we are transitioning to the next stage, the Cleansing of Justified Sinners. The cleansing of justified sinners is made up of two parts: the Church and the individual believers. We will start with the Church and what makes it up: the body of Jesus.

The Church is the people of God on earth in the era between the Day of Pentecost and the Rapture, called the Church Age. It is the time period when God chooses to primarily work with the Gentiles as the people of God, instead of the nation of Israel, and is placed in the prophetic calendar of Daniel's seventy weeks between the **69**th and **70**th week.[270] Paul wrote that the nation of Israel as a whole (except for a Jewish remnant[271]) is excluded from the people of God for a time,[272] and Gentile believers are grafted into it in their place.[273] The majority of God's saving work would

---

[270]   Daniel 9:26

[271]   God has not rejected the people of Israel but has kept a remnant of believing Jews during this time period (Romans 11:1–6).

[272]   Romans 11:15, 17, 19–20, 24–27

[273]   Romans 11:11–24

be with the Gentiles, not the Jews, until the fullness of the Gentile believers has come in.[274] During the Church Age, the people of Israel are spiritually hardened,[275] and there is just a remnant of Jews. The Church began on the Day of Pentecost[276] and ends at the Rapture, before the Tribulation, Daniel's 70th week.[277] It was a mystery not previously revealed in the Old Testament.[278]

The New Testament gives the Church various names. It is called the flock.[279] Another name is God's field or cultivated land.[280] The Church is referred to as the household of God.[281] It is God's building.[282] Another reference is a dwelling place of God in the Spirit.[283] The Church is known as the Body of Christ[284] and the Bride of Christ.[285] It is spoken of as a new man.[286] It is also described as the pillar and support of truth.[287]

---

[274]   Romans 11:25

[275]   Romans 11:7–10, 25

[276]   The day of Pentecost is the birth of the Church (Acts 2:1 with Acts 2).

[277]   See the concept, "Rapture."

[278]   Colossians 1:24–27 **(25–26)**

[279]   John 10:16

[280]   1 Corinthians 3:9

[281]   1 Timothy 3:15

[282]   1 Corinthians 3:9

[283]   Ephesians 2:22

[284]   1 Corinthians 12:12, 27

[285]   2 Corinthians 11:2

[286]   Ephesians 2:15

[287]   1 Timothy 3:15

Everyone who has put their faith in Jesus as their Lord and Savior is a member of the Church, which is the body and bride of Christ. Everyone who believes is, at that instant, baptized by the Holy Spirit into Jesus' body[288] and indwelt by the Holy Spirit.[289] God the Father instituted Jesus as its head,[290] who purchased the Church with His own blood,[291] and Jesus is completely in charge of the churches.[292] The Spirit unifies the body.[293] The end goal of the Church is unity among all of its members and between the Church as a whole and the Triune God.[294] As one body, the Church is made up of many diverse members.[295] These members should have the same care for one another. "And if one member suffers, all the members suffer with it; or if one member is honored, all the members rejoice with it."[296] When one hurts his toe, the whole body reacts. When one member is hurting, a healthy church body reacts, too. The Church is one body, one Spirit, one Lord, one faith, and one baptism.[297] These items should

---

288   1 Corinthians 12:13; Romans 6:3

289   1 Corinthians 6:19; Ephesians 1:13–14

290   Ephesians 1:17, 20–23

291   Acts 20:28

292   Revelation 1–3 (1:20)

293   Ephesians 2:19–22

294   John 17:21–23

295   1 Corinthians 12:12–27

296   1 Corinthians 12:26

297   Ephesians 4:4–5

cross individual church boundaries, for they are all part of the same Church.

How does the institution of the Church affect people's everyday lives and how they make decisions?

Application

1. First, in a healthy church, its members truly care for one another. According to 1 Corinthians 12:25–26, when one suffers, the body suffers with it. When one member is honored, others should not become jealous but should rejoice with that person.

2. Secondly, in a healthy church, while its members have their differences, they are unified, not divided.

3. Third, Jesus said the people of God are more important than one's earthly family. Listen to that again. Jesus said that the people of God are more important than one's earthly family. Mark 3:31–35 reads, "Then His mother and His brothers arrived, and standing outside they sent word to Him and called Him. A crowd was sitting around Him, and they said to Him, Behold, Your mother and Your brothers are outside looking for You. Answering them, He said, 'Who are My

mother and My brothers?' Looking about at those who were sitting around Him, He said, 'Behold, My mother and My brothers! For whoever does the will of God, he is My brother and sister and mother.'" Jesus said that one's church family is more important than one's earthly family.

In this lesson, we have seen what the Church is made up of and the time period in which it exists on earth. In the next two lessons, we will learn about two of its ordinances or practices: Baptism and Communion. To view the chart for this section, go to https://rbeteach71.wixsite.com/justified-sinners/charts.

14. BAPTISM

Concept: In the last session, we examined the make-up of the Church. In this lesson, we will look at one of the two Church ordinances or practices: Baptism. Baptism is a symbol of entrance into the family of God. *It looks at the beginning of the Christian life and the end.* It is a very concise visual illustration of a believer being united to Jesus in His death to sin on the cross and resurrection from the dead.[298] Everyone who believes in Jesus is, at that instant, baptized by the Holy Spirit into His body, which is a believer's identification and participation in the death and resurrection of Jesus. His death was our death to sin. Jesus' resurrection is our resurrection. This is our position in Him and our future reality when we are transformed to His image. Baptism looks back to Jesus' 1st Coming through the cross and forward to His 2nd Coming with the believers' resurrection. Distinct yet closely tied to the baptism of the Holy Spirit and salvation, water baptism[299] is directly related to calling on the name of Jesus,[300] believing and receiving the Gospel,[301] repenting,[302]

---

[298] Romans 6:3–5
[299] Acts 8:12, 14–17 with 10:44–48
[300] Acts 22:16
[301] Acts 8:5, 12, 14–15; 8:35–37
[302] Acts 2:38

being forgiven,[303] brought into the Body of Christ,[304] saved from a life of sin,[305] making a public profession of faith,[306] [307] and starting a life of discipleship.[308] There is only one baptism,[309] which is through the Holy Spirit, but demonstrated by water baptism. Baptism and Communion, also called the Lord's Supper, are the only sacraments and ordinances of the Church. We practice baptism by immersion because it is a visual demonstration of being united with Jesus in His death, burial, and resurrection. It is done in the name of the Father, the Son, and the Holy Spirit, the Triune God.[310] How does baptism personally affect believers?

Application

1. Every Christian should be baptized, as commanded by the Lord in Matthew 28:19. "Go therefore and make disciples of all the nations, baptizing them in the name of the Father and the Son and the Holy Spirit..." *It is a public symbol of entrance into the family of God.*

---

303   Colossians 2:11–**13**

304   1 Corinthians 12:13

305   Romans 6:3–**6**

306   1 Peter 3:21

307   Ceslas Spicq and James D. Ernest, *Theological Lexicon of the New Testament* (Peabody, MA: Hendrickson Publishers, 1994), 32.

308   Matthew 28:19

309   Ephesians 4:4–5

310   Matthew 28:19

2. Biblically, once one is baptized as a believer, he should not have to be baptized again if he later joins another church. Ephesians 4:4–5 reveals, "There is one body and one Spirit, just as also you were called in one hope of your calling; one Lord, one faith, one baptism…"

3. *It is important to know what Baptism means. When we were baptized by the Holy Spirit into Jesus' body, the Church, the same instant we believed in Jesus, His death became our death to sin. Jesus' resurrection is our resurrection. This is our position in Him, and our future reality when we are transformed to His image.* Listen to what Romans 6:3–5 says, "Or do you not know that all of us who have been baptized into Christ Jesus have been baptized into His death? Therefore we have been buried with Him through baptism into death, so that as Christ was raised from the dead through the glory of the Father, so we too might walk in newness of life. For if we have become united with Him in the likeness of His death, certainly we shall also be in the likeness of His resurrection." Philippians 3:20–21 speaks of this resurrection. "For our citizenship is in heaven, from which also we eagerly wait for a Savior, the Lord Jesus Christ; who will transform the body

of our humble state into conformity with the body of His glory, by the exertion of the power that He has even to subject all things to Himself."

So, Baptism is a concise visual illustration of a believer's position in Jesus and the Triune God. It is a public demonstration that one already belongs to the family of God and symbolizes the beginning and end of the Christian walk. The following lesson is on Communion, the second Church ordinance or practice. While Baptism focuses on the beginning and end of the Christian walk, Communion looks at the ongoing Christian walk. To view the chart for this section, go to https://rbeteach71.wixsite.com/justified-sinners/charts.

15. COMMUNION

Concept: In the redemptive cycle, we are looking at the Cleansing of Justified Sinners and the Church. Last session was the first of the two Church ordinances or practices, Baptism, which has to do with the beginning and end of the Christian walk. This lesson is the second Church ordinance, Communion, which has to do with the ongoing Christian walk, the Cleansing of Justified Sinners. Believers are saints and sinners simultaneously, and Communion acts as a heart cleansing or preparation to be in fellowship with Holy God.

Communion, or *the Lord's Supper,*[311] *is a symbol of Christian fellowship* in which only believers should be allowed to participate. It looks back to Jesus' death on the cross and looks forward to His return at the Second Coming. *The bread that believers break and eat in fellowship is participating in the body of Jesus, and drinking the cup together is taking part in the blood of Jesus.*[312] When believers eat the bread and drink the cup, they state publicly, or announce, Jesus' death until He returns.[313]

---

[311] 1 Corinthians 11:20–30
[312] 1 Corinthians 10:16; Luke 22:17
[313] 1 Corinthians 11:26

The bread represents Jesus' body that was offered up as a substitutionary sacrifice for our sins.[314] The breaking of the same bread together is a symbol of fellowship among those who participate together. The early believers used one loaf of bread in communion, signifying they are taking part together in the same body of Jesus.[315] Even though they are many different believers, they make up the same body.[316]

The cup,[317] the fruit of the vine,[318] represents three things. *First, it symbolizes Jesus' blood poured out, proclaiming His sacrificial death and what it does for the believers.* The blood represents the substitutionary death of the innocent (Jesus) paying for the sins of the guilty (everyone in the world).[319] He was the only one who could do this because He is fully God and fully man. Because He was sinless,[320] Jesus as man could redeem mankind by completing the requirements of God's law on the human race's behalf.[321] As sinless man, He died in mankind's place.[322] As God simultaneously,[323] the sacrifice of

---

314   Hebrews 9:26, 28
315   1 Corinthians 10:16–17
316   1 Corinthians 12:12–27
317   Matthew 26:27
318   Matthew 26:29
319   Hebrews 9:11–12, 28
320   Jesus knew no sin (2 Corinthians 5:21), did no sin (1 Peter 2:22), and in Him is no sin (1 John 3:5).
321   Galatians 4:4–5; Matthew 5:17
322   Philippians 2:7–8; Hebrews 2:17
323   John 1:14; Philippians 2:6–7

Himself[324] at the cross paid for the sins of the whole world.[325] Let's see what His death does for the believer. It obtained eternal redemption[326] and satisfied God's wrath towards sin.[327] This brings believers the forgiveness of their sins,[328] justification before God,[329] and reconciliation to God[330] and between Jews and Gentiles (warring factions among mankind), who are now one in Jesus.[331] As believers drink the cup together, they participate in and announce Jesus' sacrificial death and what it does for them.

Secondly, the cup represents Jesus' blood, which was shed, starting the beginning of the New Covenant.[332] "The New Covenant was announced by Jeremiah,[333] but it was not confirmed until the sacrifice was made as payment. Jesus announced the cutting of the covenant, which would take place when He shed His blood on the cross.[334] The covenant began at Jesus' death, and the Church,[335] by her union with

---

324   Hebrews 7:26–27; 9:11–12
325   Hebrews 9:26; 1 John 2:2
326   Ephesians 1:7; Hebrews 9:12
327   Romans 1:18; 3:25; 1 John 2:2
328   Matthew 26:27–28
329   Romans 5:16, 18
330   Romans 5:10
331   Ephesians 2:11–16
332   Matthew 26:27–29
333   Jeremiah 31:31–34
334   Hebrews 9:14–15; 13:20
335   Ephesians 1:22–23

Him,[336] shares in many of the spiritual blessings promised to Israel[337] through a partial completion of the New Covenant.[338] But although the Church's participation in the New Covenant is real, it is not the ultimate fulfillment of God's promise. Believers today enjoy many of the spiritual blessings of the New Covenant: the forgiveness of sins,[339] eternal redemption,[340] being perfected for all time those who are being sanctified,[341] direct access to God without a priest as a go-between,[342] having an advocate to God through Jesus as our lawyer who defends us before God the Father, [343] a clean conscience,[344] and the indwelling of the Holy Spirit.[345] However, the national and physical blessings will be realized by the nation of Israel in the future[346] in the Millennium.

---

[336] **Galatians 3:16** (Christ fulfills the promise that the families and nations of the earth will be blessed through Abraham's offspring); Galatians 3:27–29 (in being united to Christ, there is no distinction between Jews and Gentiles).

[337] Romans 11:11–24; Ephesians 2:11–22; 2 Corinthians 3:6 with New Covenant in Hebrews (The New Covenant is a superior ministry [Hebrews 8:1–6] and has a superior mediator [Jesus] than the Palestinian Covenant [Hebrews 8:6–13], providing spiritual blessings).

[338] See the concept, "New Covenant," 'New Covenant.'

[339] Hebrews 9:15, 26; 10:17–18

[340] Hebrews 9:12

[341] Hebrews 10:10, 14

[342] Hebrews 10:19–20

[343] Hebrews 9:24

[344] Hebrews 9:8–9 with 9:14; 10:22

[345] Romans 8:9, 1 Corinthians 6:19

[346] The houses of Israel and Judah, will become one nation (Ezekiel 37:15–22), will return to the land (Ezekiel 37:21), and live there forever in peace and safety with David as their king, God dwelling in their midst as their God, a rebuilt temple, *and distinct from the other nations of the earth* (Ezekiel 37:25–28);

That still awaits the day when Israel will acknowledge her sin, turn to the Messiah they rejected and killed,[347] and be forgiven and cleansed at His 2nd Coming.[348]

And third, the cup in the Lord's Supper looks towards the restoration of Israel's kingdom at the Second Coming when Jesus establishes His kingdom on earth, then feasts in fellowship with the people of God in the Millennial kingdom. At the Last Supper, Jesus said, "from now on I shall not drink of the fruit of the vine until the kingdom of God comes."[349] This refers to the future restoration of Israel's kingdom, which takes places during the Millennium[350] when Jesus reigns as Israel's king[351] and king over the earth.[352] The climax and finale of salvation in the kingdom of God is pictured as a

---

Zechariah 9:9–**11** (The New Covenant will occur when Israel's awaited king is ruler over the earth); Romans 11:25–**27** (This passage clarifies that the New Covenant will occur after the "Time of the Gentiles." This does not happen until after Daniel's 70th week [Daniel 9:27 – Tribulation] when God's earthly kingdom is set up [Daniel 2:35, 44 with 7:13–14, 27]).

[347] The day of Jesus' triumphal entry when he came riding into Jerusalem on a donkey (Matthew 21:1–11), He prophesied over Jerusalem saying that because the nation of Israel rejected Him as king and Messiah, He would not return until they embraced Him as their king and Messiah (Matthew 23:37–**39**). When they see Him at His return (Revelation 1:7), they will nationally repent (Isaiah 59:20; Ezekiel 36:31–33a) and individually mourn over their king and Messiah whom they had previously rejected and killed (Zechariah 12:10–14).

[348] Zechariah 13:1; Romans 11:26–27

[349] Luke 22:18. See also Luke 22:16 on the kingdom of God

[350] It was expected the kingdom would be restored to Israel (Ezekiel 37:15–28). The Old Testament predicted this coming kingdom (Zechariah 9:9–10; 14:9) and New Testament passages confirm they were waiting for it (Matthew 19:28; Luke 19:11; **Acts 1:6**).

[351] Micah 5:2

[352] Zechariah 9:9–10; 14:9, 16–17

banquet or feast.[353] The parables of the marriage feast[354] and the great banquet[355] look forward to the time of feasting with Jesus and the people of God. As illustrated in the parables, Jews and Gentiles alike are invited to the celebration in His kingdom. *So the cup, the fruit of the vine, represents the sacrificial death of Jesus and what it does for the believer, the inauguration of the New Covenant, and the anticipation of the restoration of Israel's kingdom when Jesus feasts in fellowship with the people of God in the Millennium.*

In the early church, Christians believed Jesus is bodily present in the Lord's Supper, but they have no explanation as to how this takes place.[356] Some church groups believe that the bread becomes His body, and the fruit of the vine becomes His blood, which is called transubstantiation. Some say there is some mystical union when people partake of the bread and cup. What the Scripture clearly does state is that the bread and cup are a memorial of the body and blood of Jesus, as believers were to take part together in the bread and cup to proclaim the Lord's death on the cross until His return at the Second Coming. Jesus said, "do this in remembrance of Me."[357]

---

[353]   Matthew 8:11; Luke 13:29

[354]   Matthew 22:1–14

[355]   Luke 14:15–24

[356]   Svigel, Michael. "Class notes," *ST105 Sanctification and Ecclesiology,* Dallas: Dallas Theological Seminary, Fall 2009.

[357]   Luke 22:19; 1 Corinthians 11:24–25

Believers must take Communion seriously. They are to first examine themselves, for if they take part in the Lord's Supper in an unworthy manner, they become guilty of the body and blood of Jesus, bringing judgment upon themselves.[358] Understanding this heightens the need for believers to make a heart preparation or cleansing, as they are justified sinners preparing themselves to be in fellowship with Holy God. Communion has a profound effect on believers' lives and decisions. How does this affect our daily living?

Application

4. According to 1 Corinthians 11:27–30, we should not participate in Communion when we are consciously practicing sin. If we do, we are guilty of the body and blood of Jesus, bringing judgment upon ourselves. So, being conscious of this pushes us to settle accounts with God and people before taking Communion. If we are acting wrongly towards others, we need to correct our behavior before taking part in the bread and cup so we don't bring judgment upon ourselves.

---

[358]   1 Corinthians 11:27–30

5. *Taking part in the Lord's Supper is a participatory act in our identification with Jesus, which means, as believers, we share in His sufferings and death and eternal glory.* I Peter 2:21 reveals, "For you have been called for this purpose, since Christ also suffered for you, leaving you an example for you to follow in His steps..." *If we share in His sufferings on earth **(suffer for our allegiance to Him and service for Him)**, we will share in His glory in heaven.* Romans 8:17–18 affirms this, "...and if children, heirs also, heirs of God and fellow heirs with Christ, if indeed we suffer with Him so that we may also be glorified with Him. For I consider that the sufferings of this present time are not worthy to be compared with the glory that is to be revealed to us." In reality, *our momentary affliction is preparing for us an eternal weight of glory.* Second Corinthians 4:17–18 announces, "For momentary, light affliction is producing for us an eternal weight of glory far beyond all comparison, while we look not at the things which are seen, but at the things which are not seen; for the things which are seen are temporal, but the things which are not seen are eternal."

6. We are to continually remember Jesus' death together and how it causes us to see our lives

differently than before. It causes us to live in a fundamentally different way than before we were Christians. Matthew 26:27–28 says that we are not under condemnation, but our sins are forgiven. Romans 5:16 and 18 point out, we are not sinners but have been made righteous before God. Romans 5:10 reveals that we used to be God's enemies but have been brought back in relationship with Him. We used to be separated from God, but Hebrews 10:19 declares that we now have direct access to Him. Hebrews 9:24 testifies that when we sin, Jesus is our advocate or lawyer before God the Father. And Hebrews 10:22 announces that instead of living with a guilty conscience, we can have a clean conscience through the blood of Jesus. So, Jesus' death radically changed how we live our lives.

7. *Finally, Communion reminds us that we are to live our lives waiting expectantly for Jesus' return at any time.* First Corinthians 11:26 points out, "For as often as you eat this bread and drink the cup, you proclaim the Lord's death until He comes." *Those who wait for His return will receive the crown of righteousness.* Second Timothy 4:7–8 asserts, "I have fought the good fight, I have finished the course, I have kept the faith; in the

future there is laid up for me the crown of righteousness, which the Lord, the righteous Judge, will award to me on that day; and not only to me, but also to all who have loved His appearing." *In other words, we are to live our lives preparing for our eternal home, not just accumulating our treasures here on earth.*

Communion is about actively remembering Jesus' sacrifice on the cross for our sins. It also addresses how we as believers can fellowship with Holy God. We are part of the family of God, but we are also justified sinners in the presence of Holy God. This requires us to be continually cleansed to freely fellowship with Him. This happens throughout our entire Christian walk, from beginning to end. That is how Communion focuses on the ongoing Christian walk, while Baptism focuses on its beginning and end.

In these two lessons, we have examined the two Church ordinances or practices. Now, we are going to review the Redemptive cycle, Baptism and Communion, to understand how they work together to provide a snapshot of the entire Redemptive cycle. To view the chart for this section, go to https://rbeteach71.wixsite.com/justified-sinners/charts.

REDEMPTIVE CYCLE: BAPTISM AND COMMUNION

As a snapshot, the two Church ordinances, Baptism and Communion, work together to cover the entire redemptive cycle: sin, the cross, the cleansing of justified sinners, and the resurrection. They have to do with restoring lost fellowship between the Triune God and sinful mankind.

Baptism is a symbol of entrance into the family of God. It focuses on the *beginning and the end of the Christian walk* and deals with the redemptive stages of sin, the cross, and the resurrection. Baptism is a very concise illustration of a believer being united to Jesus in His death to sin on the cross and resurrection from the dead. Jesus' death to sin becomes our death to sin. Jesus' resurrection becomes our resurrection. This is our position in Christ and our future reality when we are transformed according to His image. Romans 6:3–5 proclaims, "Or do you not know that all of us who have been baptized into Christ Jesus have been baptized into His death? Therefore we have been buried with Him through baptism into death, so that as Christ was raised from the dead through the glory of the Father, so we too might walk in newness of life. For if we have become united with Him in the likeness of His death, certainly we shall also be in the likeness of His resurrection." Philippians 3:20–21 speaks of this resurrection. "For our citizenship is in heaven, from which also we eagerly wait for a Savior, the Lord Jesus Christ; who will transform the body of our humble state into conformity with the body of His glory, by the exertion of the power that He has even to subject all things to Himself."

Communion acts as a heart cleansing or preparation for justified sinners to be in fellowship with Holy God. It focuses on the *ongoing Christian walk* and deals with sin, the cross, and the cleansing of justified sinners. It is about actively remembering Jesus' sacrifice on the cross for our sins. It also addresses how we as believers can fellowship with Holy God. We are to examine ourselves before taking part in the bread and the cup, for if we take it in an unworthy manner, we become guilty of the body and blood of Jesus, bringing judgment upon ourselves. Being conscious of this pushes us to settle accounts with God and people before taking Communion. This requires us to be continually cleansed to freely fellowship with Him. This goes on throughout our entire Christian walk from beginning to end.

The two ordinances that all Christians are to practice are concise, visual, and participatory illustrations covering the entire redemptive cycle: sin, the cross, the cleansing of justified sinners, and the resurrection. They have to do with restoring lost fellowship between the Triune God and sinful mankind.

Baptism and Communion combined provide a snapshot of the entire redemptive cycle. In the following lesson, we will take a look at the functions of the Church. To view the chart for this section, go to https://rbeteach71.wixsite.com/justified-sinners/charts.

16.   CHURCH: *WHAT ARE ITS FUNCTIONS?*

Concept: The redemptive cycle stage, the cleansing of justified sinners, has two parts: the Church and individual believers. In the last two sessions, we examined the two Church ordinances or practices, Baptism and Communion. This lesson will briefly focus on the functions of the Church. We looked at the make-up of the Church and will now turn our attention to how it is supposed to operate. The functions of the Church, as one body with many diverse members, are not only the responsibility of its spiritual leaders but the body as a whole. The Church body is to display God's mercy,[359] grace,[360] and wisdom[361] to the world. It is to proclaim the Gospel and make disciples worldwide.[362] Its members should care for one another as part of the same body of Jesus.[363] The Church is to build up its members to spiritual maturity and prepare them for ministry through gifts and ministries given to each one by the Spirit as He

---

[359]   Romans 9:23–24

[360]   Ephesians 2:7

[361]   Ephesians 3:10

[362]   Matthew 28:19–20

[363]   1 Corinthians 12:25–26

sees fit.[364] It is to be holy and blameless before God[365] and walk in good works.[366] Its purpose is to glorify God.[367] The Church should be known for its love for one another[368] and the world around it,[369] including its enemies.[370]

The Trinity is seen in the functions of the Church. The Church is to glorify God the Father and build up the Church, Jesus' body, to spiritual maturity, empowered by the Holy Spirit who lives within each believer. How do the functions of the Church apply to decisions we make every day?

Application

1. First, as part of the church body, everybody in the Church is called to actively serve, not just the church leadership.

2. Secondly, service to God should not just be in the Church but should extend to those we interact with in our day-to-day living.

3. Third, as Jesus' ambassadors, we are called to share Him through our daily living.

---

[364] Ephesians 4:7–16
[365] Colossians 1:22
[366] Ephesians 2:10
[367] Ephesians 1:5–6, 12, 14; 3:21
[368] John 13:34–35
[369] Matthew 22:37–40 (**39**)
[370] Matthew 5:43–47

4. Fourth, according to Ephesians 2:8–10, we are to do good works, not to earn our way to heaven, but in response to what Jesus did to save us.

In this study, we have looked at the functions of the Church and how they are not only the responsibility of its spiritual leaders but the body as a whole. The next lesson builds on this with spiritual gifts. To view the chart for this section, go to https://rbeteach71.wixsite.com/justified-sinners/charts.

17. SPIRITUAL GIFTS

Concept: We are looking at the Cleansing of Justified Sinners and the Church. In the last session, we looked at the functions of the Church. This lesson builds on it with spiritual gifts.

Spiritual gifts are not the same as natural abilities. Why do they matter? They are gifts given by the Holy Spirit for building up the body of Jesus to spiritual maturity and equipping the saints for the work of the ministry God has designated to them.[371] Who has them? Each believer has at least one spiritual gift given by the Holy Spirit.[372] As Romans 12:1–2 precedes Romans 12:3–8, one's relationship to God needs to go before one's service to Him. First Peter 4:10 says, "As each one has received a gift, use it to serve one another..." Romans 12:4 and 6 states, "For as we have many members in one body, but all the members do not have the same function... having then gifts differing according to the grace that is given to us, let us use them." Which are more important? The differing members of the same body of Jesus are given different gifts and ministries assigned by the Holy Spirit as He sees are needed.[373] No one has the right to brag or feel

---

[371] Ephesians 4:12; 1 Corinthians 14:12

[372] 1 Peter 4:10

[373] 1 Corinthians 12:4–7, 11. See also Hebrews 2:4

more important about their gift than another, for each was given according to what God assigned.[374]

The list of spiritual gifts can be found in four biblical passages: First Corinthians 12:1–11, 27–31; Romans 12:3–8; Ephesians 4:7–16; and 1 Peter 4:10–11. Here is the following chart on spiritual gifts. We have the *Word, Service, Others,* and *Sign* gifts. In the Word, the gifts are apostleship, prophecy, teaching, wisdom, exhorting, evangelism, and pastoring. Pastoring can also go under Service. In Service, the gifts are administration or leadership, service or helping, showing mercy, and giving. We can also include pastoring. Under Others, we have faith and discernment of spirits. And the Sign gifts are miracles, healings, tongues, and interpretation of tongues.

In 1 Corinthians 12:9, gifts and healings are both in the plural form in Greek. Physical healing may also include emotional, mental, and spiritual healing. There is debate as to how sign gifts are used. The three main views are:

a. First, they are gifts given by the Spirit today, like any of the other spiritual gifts.

b. Second, the sign gifts are used today in places where there are no established churches or where the presence of the gospel and God's Word is new in an area and needs to be vali-

---

[374] Romans 12:3, 6

dated. Where there is an established presence, they are not needed.

c. Or third, while God is not limited to working this way and does when He chooses to, these are spiritual gifts that were for the time of the early church to build it up and validate its message but are no longer given today.

Concerning the sign gifts of tongues, Paul wrote that the gift of speaking in tongues needs to be accompanied by an interpretation of it. Otherwise, he should keep silent in church and speak only to himself and God.[375] It is to be done by up to two, at most three, each one taking turns.[376] One who speaks in tongues should pray that another interprets.[377] The one who speaks in tongues only builds up himself in the church,[378] for tongues are a sign for unbelievers, not believers.[379] Tongues are known languages people in the world speak,[380] but unintelligible speech to the speaker.[381] First Corinthians 14:14–15 reads, "For if I pray in a tongue, my spirit prays but my mind is unfruitful. What am I to do? I will

---

[375] 1 Corinthians 14:27–28

[376] 1 Corinthians 14:27

[377] 1 Corinthians 14:13

[378] 1 Corinthians 14:2–4

[379] 1 Corinthians 14:22

[380] 1 Corinthians 14:9–11

[381] 1 Corinthians 14:9

pray with my spirit, but I will pray with my mind also; I will sing praise with my spirit, but I will sing with my mind also." Those who speak in tongues are not building anyone else up in the church by it[382] unless they have someone to interpret what they said.

Prophecy is a more important spiritual gift than tongues.[383] While tongues only edify the speaker (unless one interprets), prophesy builds up the church.[384] Tongues are a sign for unbelievers, but prophesy is a sign for believers.[385] And just like tongues, prophesy is to be done by up to two or three, each taking their turn.[386]

How do spiritual gifts affect the way we live and our service in the Church?

Application

1. First, our service to God needs to come from our relationship with God.

2. Second, as believers, we are to serve God with our spiritual gifts to build up the body of Christ to spiritual maturity and equip the saints for the

---

[382]   1 Corinthians 14:17

[383]   1 Corinthians 14:5

[384]   1 Corinthians 14:4

[385]   1 Corinthians 14:22

[386]   1 Corinthians 14:29–31

work of the ministry. This is every believer's responsibility, not just the church leadership.

3. Third, we need to know what our spiritual gift(s) is and use it.

4. Fourth, people with more prominent spiritual gifts aren't superior to those with less noticeable spiritual gifts.

5. Fifth, differing spiritual gifts means interdependence. We need each other.

While examining spiritual gifts, we looked at how they build up believers to spiritual maturity and equip them for the work of the ministry. They highlight the need for dependence on one another in the body of Jesus. In the cleansing of justified sinners, we have focused on the Church. Starting next lesson, we will draw our attention to individual believers. To view the chart for this section, go to https://rbeteach71.wixsite.com/justified-sinners/charts.

18. SANCTIFICATION: THE PROCESS OF BECOMING CON-FORMED TO THE IMAGE OF CHRIST

Concept: We are looking at the redemptive stage, the Cleansing of Justified Sinners. Until now, the focus has been on the Church. Starting with this lesson, we will focus on individual believers. In the last lesson, we looked at spiritual gifts. In this lesson, we will look at sanctification, which is being conformed to the image of Jesus. Being conformed to His image is having the image of God, which was distorted by sin, be progressively restored in the believer's life until, in heaven, it will be sinless again. The process of becoming conformed to His image[387] is the ever-increasing need to rely on the Holy Spirit to be conformed to the life of Jesus. We must become more dependent on God for that transformation, just as a handicapped person with a debilitating disease progressively grows in dependence on another person to care for him. Some people try to be more good by their own efforts, but this results in failure. This battle of trying to obey

---

[387]   2 Corinthians 3:18

and serve God in one's own efforts is described in Romans chapter 7. Sanctification is not the process of becoming more good by oneself. It is the process of a person with all his sin choosing to increasingly depend on the Holy Spirit in place of his own desires, attitudes, and actions. That is why Jesus said in Luke 9:23, "If anyone wishes to come after Me, let him deny himself, and take up his cross *daily*, and follow me."[388] This increasing dependence on the Holy Spirit instead of one's efforts or flesh is a daily effort.

God helps us in this process. Two things that He uses in our lives to accomplish this are discipline and suffering. First, just as earthly parents discipline their children according to how they think best, God disciplines His children throughout their life for their spiritual maturity so that they will take part in His holiness.[389] During this time, believers are taking part in Jesus' nature.[390] Second, as believers, we share in His sufferings.[391] If we share in His sufferings on earth (which means *suffer for our allegiance to Him and service for Him*), we will share in His glory in heaven.[392] Our momentary affliction is preparing for us an eternal weight of glory.[393]

---

[388] See also Matthew 10:38; Luke 14:27

[389] Hebrews 12:7–10

[390] 2 Peter 1:4

[391] 1 Peter 2:21; 4:12–16 (**13**)

[392] Romans 8:17–18; 1 Peter 5:1, 10

[393] 2 Corinthians 4:17–18

The process goes on until the believer dies. It is only after one's physical death that Jesus will make him perfect without sin and give him a glorified or perfect body, thus finishing the work of conforming the believer to His own image.[394]

Application

1. First, God will continue to work to conform us to His image until death. He will not give up on working on us. Philippians 1:6 asserts, "For I am confident of this very thing, that He who began a good work in you will perfect it until the day of Christ Jesus."

2. Second, we should not focus on trying to be good. We should focus on being aware of our sinful state and continually submit our desires, attitudes, and actions to the Holy Spirit to become more Christ-like.

3. Third, be glad when God disciplines you because of your sin or for spiritual maturity. His discipline is for your good, so you will share in His holiness. His discipline is a sign you belong to Him, for He disciplines His children, but not those who don't belong to Him. Hebrews 12:7–10 states, "It is for

---

[394] Philippians 3:20–21; 1 John 3:2

discipline that you endure; God deals with you as with sons; for what son is there who his father does not discipline? But if you are without discipline, of which all have become partakers, then you are illegitimate children and not sons. Furthermore, we had earthly fathers to discipline us, and we respected them; shall we not much rather be subject to the Father of spirits and live? For they disciplined us for a short time as seemed best to them, but He disciplines us for our good, so that we may share in His holiness."

Sanctification is a significant part of the Christian walk as it deals with how justified sinners can have fellowship with Holy God. In the next lesson, we will see how this is an ongoing battle in the battle of the flesh and the Spirit. To view the chart for this section, go to https://rbeteach71.wixsite.com/justified-sinners/charts.

19.   BATTLE OF TWO NATURES: FLESH VS. SPIRIT

Concept: In the cleansing of justified sinners, we are focusing on the individual believers. In the last lesson, we looked at sanctification, as it deals with how justified sinners can have fellowship with Holy God. This lesson builds on this with the ongoing battle of two natures: the flesh and the Spirit.

When one becomes a believer, he now has two natures: the sin nature[395] and the divine nature.[396] He remains a slave. He used to be a slave of sin but has become a slave of righteousness. Slavery means he is not in control but has to obey his master. He must choose which to submit to. He can either present his body as an instrument of unrighteousness to sin or present his body as an instrument of righteousness to God.[397] That is why it says in Galatians 5:16–23 that the flesh, the sin nature, and the Spirit are at war with each other. Either one submits to the Holy Spirit, which enables him to fulfill the fruit of the Spirit, or he lets the sin nature

---

[395]   Galatians 5:16–17; Romans 7:25b; 8:4

[396]   2 Peter 1:4

[397]   Romans 6:12–13, 16–20, 22

take control and carry out its works through him. The fruit of the Spirit is love, joy, peace, patience, kindness, goodness, faithfulness, gentleness, and self-control. The deeds of the flesh are immorality, impurity, sensuality, idolatry, sorcery, enmities, strife, jealously, outbursts of anger, disputes, dissensions, factions, envying, drunkenness, and carousing. This tug of war between the flesh and the Spirit is also played out in Romans 8:3–8. People must act according to nature. There are two natures at war within the believer, and the battle is won not through fighting but through submitting. This is why Paul says in Romans 12:1–2, "I beseech you brothers, by the mercies of God, that you present your bodies a living sacrifice, holy, acceptable to God, which is your reasonable service." This concept is fundamental to our Christian thinking and how we act. Let's see how it directly applies to us.

Application

1. First, you are a slave. Depending on which master you submit to will dictate what you do.

2. Second, you can't live a righteous life by trying to be good. You can only live a righteous life by submitting to the Holy Spirit. It is He who will enable you to live out the fruit of the Spirit: love, joy, peace, patience, kindness, goodness, faithfulness, gentleness, and self-control.

3. Third, it is impossible to try to be genuinely good in your efforts, for you attempt through your sin nature. Instead, strive to live by the Holy Spirit by submitting your desires, actions, and attitudes to Him.

The battle of two natures, the flesh and the Spirit, reveals that believers are not in control. They give control to one of their masters. This is an ongoing battle from the beginning until the end of the Christian walk. Motivation helps us with this continuous struggle. This is what the next lesson is about: eternal rewards. To view the chart for this section, go to https://rbeteach71.wixsite.com/justified-sinners/charts.

20. ETERNAL REWARDS

I n the redemptive stage, the Cleansing of Justified Sinners, we first examined the Church, then individual believers. In the last lesson, we looked at the battle of two natures, the flesh and the Spirit. This lesson on eternal rewards is the final lesson, not only of individual believers but also of the redemptive stage: the Cleansing of Justified Sinners.

Concept: In this lesson, we will cover the following topics. First, eternal rewards are motivation to live godly lives. Second, how a Christian lives his life on earth determines his position and rewards in heaven. Third, prioritize investing one's time and efforts in eternal rewards over earthly rewards because they will last forever instead of wearing out. Fourth, doing works for Jesus will be rewarded. And fifth, Paul challenges believers to strive for rewards and to not lose them.

First, eternal rewards are important to motivate Jesus' followers to live godly lives out of their love for God. The most powerful motivation to obey someone is out of love for that person. Jesus said, "If you love me you will obey my commandments."[398] Rewards are also a compelling motivation to follow and obey Him. Believe it or not, the New Testament

---

[398]   John 14:15

is filled with at least 124 passages and separate verses on this topic.

Second, how a Christian lives his life on earth determines his position and rewards in heaven. In order to obtain the rewards, it is necessary to have faith God will keep His promises.[399] It is not sufficient to know God's Word. Knowledge has no real value unless one acts upon it.[400] Just as the believer's eternal destiny hinges on his relationship to Jesus,[401] his eternal rewards depend on his faithfulness and obedience to Him.[402] Jesus Himself often explicitly stated that one's position in heaven is a result of how one lives for Him on earth.[403] While one's salvation is secure, heaven is not the same for everybody. There is a hierarchy determined by how one lives the Christian life while on earth. First Corinthians 3:10–15 says that one's life on earth is for building a foundation of eternal rewards. "According to the grace of God which was given to me, like a wise master builder I laid a foundation, and another is building on it. But each man must be careful how he builds on it. For no man can lay a foundation other than the one which is laid, which is Jesus Christ. Now if any man builds on the foundation with gold, silver, precious stones, wood, hay, straw, each man's

---

[399]   Hebrews 11:1, 6

[400]   #2 Luke 11:28; Romans 2:13b

[401]   Matthew 25:31–46

[402]   Parable of talents (Luke 19:11–27) and #6 Overseer held accountable (Matthew 24:45–51)

[403]   Matthew 20:25–27; Mark 10:42–44

work will become evident; for the day will show it because it is to be revealed with fire, and the fire itself will test the quality of each man's work. If any man's work which he has built on it remains, he will receive a reward. If any man's work is burned up, he will suffer loss; but he himself will be saved, yet so as through fire." At the judgment seat of Christ, everyone will give an account for how he lived.[404] One's good deeds and bad deeds will be publicly brought to light.[405] I personally believe the bad deeds are only the unconfessed sin the believer didn't deal with because of what 1 John 1:9 says. And then one will receive the eternal rewards he has earned.[406] *How a Christian lives his life on earth determines his position and rewards in heaven.*

Third, Jesus counseled His followers to make a priority of investing one's time and efforts in eternal rewards over earthly rewards because they would last forever, instead of wearing out.[407] He instructed them to serve Him while waiting for His return, for He could arrive at any time, like a thief in the night.[408] Choosing to follow Him would create problems, for Jesus said that the worldly system hates Him and also hates those who follow Him.[409] Those who would

---

404   Romans 14:10, 12
405   1 Corinthians 4:5; 2 Corinthians 5:10
406   1 Corinthians 3:10–15; Revelation 22:12
407   Matthew 6:19–21
408   Luke 12:35–40; Revelation 16:15
409   Matthew 10:22

live for Him would be persecuted.[410] When that happens, He challenged them to confess His name before people, for then He would confess them before God the Father and the angels.[411] Following Him may require having to choose loyalty to Him over family, even a loss of possessions. If this were to happen, they would receive a reward of a hundred-fold of what they gave up for following and serving Him.[412] In serving Him, Jesus advised them to do good deeds to those who could not repay the favor, for they would be richly repaid at the judgment seat of Christ.[413] The writer of Hebrews described this earthly loss for eternal gain very well when he wrote, "By faith Moses, when he had grown up, refused to be called the son of Pharaoh's daughter, choosing rather to endure ill-treatment with the people of God than to enjoy the passing pleasures of sin, considering the reproach of Christ greater riches than the treasures of Egypt; for he was looking to the reward." This is found in Hebrews 11:24–26.

Fourth, doing good works for Jesus (not man's praise) *will be rewarded,* even for things as small as giving a cold cup of water to someone.[414] The good works one does for Jesus'

---

410   Matthew 5:10, 11–12
411   Matthew 10:32–33
412   Mark 10:28–30
413   Luke 14:12–14
414   Matthew 10:42

people is counted as doing it to Him.[415] When doing good works, Jesus warned people to not do it publicly for man's praise, for that would be their reward. Instead, do it without drawing attention to themselves, so what is done secretly would be rewarded by the Father publicly in heaven.[416] There are five different crowns that can be won as rewards. An imperishable crown is rewarded for running the spiritual race, disciplining oneself to serve Jesus for the duration of the race.[417] A crown of righteousness is for those who long for Jesus' return.[418] A crown of life is for those who endure trials because of their love for God,[419] and for those who endure to the point of dying as a martyr.[420] A crown of glory is given to those who faithfully shepherd the flock of God.[421] A crown of rejoicing is given to those who win souls for Jesus.[422] Daniel 12:3 also says that those who turn people to God will be very richly rewarded. In evangelism, not only those who lead others to Jesus receive a reward, but all who are involved in the process. First Corinthians 3:8 says, "Now he who plants and he who waters are one; but each will receive his own reward according to his own labor."

---

[415]   Matthew 10:40 and John 13:20
[416]   Matthew 6:2–4, 5–6, 16–18
[417]   1 Corinthians 9:24–27
[418]   2 Timothy 4:7–8
[419]   James 1:12
[420]   Revelation 2:10
[421]   1 Peter 5:2–4
[422]   1 Thessalonians 2:19–20

And fifth, Paul challenges Christians to strive for rewards and to not lose them. He describes the process in Philippians 3:12–**14.** "Not that I have already obtained it or have already become perfect, but I press on so that I may lay hold of that for which also I was laid hold of by Christ Jesus. Brethren, I do not regard myself as having laid hold of it yet; but one thing I do: forgetting what lies behind and reaching forward to what lies ahead, I press on toward the goal for the prize of the upward call of God in Christ Jesus." Earning eternal rewards is a continuous effort. Jesus tells people to persist and to not lose heart in doing good works so they will receive their reward and not lose it.[423] He likens the way we live our lives for eternal rewards versus earthly rewards in the following story in Matthew 7:24–27.[424] "Therefore everyone who hears these words of Mine and acts on them, may be compared to a wise man who built his house on the rock. And the rain fell, and the floods came, and the winds blew and slammed against that house; and yet it did not fall, for it had been founded on the rock. Everyone who hears these words of Mine and does not act on them, will be like a foolish man who built his house on the sand. The rain fell, and the floods came, and the winds blew and slammed against that house; and it fell–and great was its fall."

---

[423] Galatians 6:7b-9; 2 John 1:8

[424] See also Luke 6:47–49

The Trinity is seen assisting believers in earning their eternal rewards. In a Christian's striving to follow God the Father, the Holy Spirit empowers him to do what is right, and Jesus promises eternal rewards when He judges the righteous for their deeds. We live radically differently when we choose to live for eternal rewards instead of earthly rewards. Let's see how this is.

Application

1. First, what or who do you primarily worship and serve on a regular basis? Jesus, money, fame, an actor or famous person, sex, drugs, hobby, or some other passion?

2. Second, you treasure whatever you consistently invest your time, effort, and money towards. If it is for earthly things, the payoff will be temporary. If it is for eternal things, the investments will last forever. Matthew 6:19–21 warns us, "Do not store up for yourselves treasures on earth, where moth and rust destroy, and where thieves break in and steal. But store up for yourselves treasures in heaven, where neither moth nor rust destroys, and where thieves do not break in or steal; for where your treasure is, there your heart will be also."

Many churches do not place much emphasis on eternal rewards, but they are a significant motivation for believers to live righteously before God. It focuses on the present ongoing Christian walk with the cleansing of the justified sinners, as well as on the future with the resurrection.

The next stage of the redemptive cycle is the resurrection. At this point in our study, we are going to put everything together to see how the biblical doctrines relate to each other and how they clearly fit as a unified whole in the redemptive cycle. To view the chart for this section, go to https://rbeteach71.wixsite.com/justified-sinners/charts.

REDEMPTION CYCLE
(SHORT)

Introduction: At the beginning of this study, we looked at a bird's eye view of the redemptive cycle, which integrates the biblical doctrines around the Triune God's redeeming mankind, His image bearers. Today, we are going to put everything together.

Overview: Redeeming God's image-bearers. It is the restoration of lost fellowship between God and mankind as His image bearers[425] due to sin. The redemptive process is made up of a beginning and end, which have to do with fellowship between God and mankind, along with the four stages of the redemptive cycle: sin, the cross, the cleansing of justified sinners, and the resurrection. We are going to look at over twenty biblical doctrines that relate to the redemptive process where God, from the very beginning to the end of human history, is actively bringing fallen mankind back into relationship with Him. In the beginning, innocent mankind was made in the image of the Triune God,[426] living in full fellowship with Him.

---

[425]   Genesis 1:26–27; 2:7; 9:6

[426]   Genesis 1:26–27

Trinity: The Trinity is the foundation for the redemptive story. The work of the Trinity is seen throughout the redemptive cycle: sin, the cross, the cleansing of justified sinners, and the resurrection. The Triune God is the Trinity or one God in three persons. The Father,[427] Son,[428] and Holy Spirit[429] as distinct persons are each the one same God. Each one has His own distinct will,[430] mind,[431] and emotions.[432]

The Father[433] has certain roles that belong specifically to Him. He is the Source of all things.[434] He is the great initiator.[435] The Father is the Sovereign Ruler over all things,[436] and, in the end, all things return to Him so that He might be all in all.[437]

The Son (Jesus) is begotten of the Father[438] and has certain roles that belong specifically to Him. He is our

---

[427]   John 6:27

[428]   John 1:1–3, 18

[429]   Acts 5:3–4, 9

[430]   Father's will (John 6:38); Son's will (Luke 22:41–44); Holy Spirit's will (Acts 16:6)

[431]   Father's mind (1 Corinthians 2:11); Son's mind (1 Corinthians 2:16); Holy Spirit's mind (Romans 8:27)

[432]   Father's emotions (Luke 3:21–22); Son's emotions (Hebrews 5:7); Holy Spirit's emotions (Ephesians 4:30)

[433]   1 Corinthians 8:6

[434]   Acts 17:24–31

[435]   Matthew 28:18 (implied passively by coming from the Father: see John 17:1–2); Ephesians 1:17–23

[436]   1 Timothy 6:15–16

[437]   1 Corinthians 15:24–28

[438]   John 1:14, 18

Creator.[439] He holds the universe together.[440] He is the God-man.[441] He is our Savior,[442] and we will look at this more in-depth later on, but He is also our judge. The Father passed the judgment onto the Son.[443] Jesus is the judge of the righteous and the wicked.[444]

The Holy Spirit is the Spirit of the Father and of the Son,[445] yet is distinct from them, having His own will, mind, and emotions, and proceeds from the Father.[446] The Holy Spirit has certain roles that belong specifically to Him. He convicts the world of sin.[447] He seals the believers for the Day of Redemption.[448] He gives them assurance that they are children of God.[449] He intercedes for them to the Father.[450] And He uses the Bible to confront and speak to

---

[439] John 1:3; Colossians 1:16

[440] Hebrews 1:3; Colossians 1:17

[441] Philippians 2:6–7

[442] Matthew 1:21; John 3:17

[443] John 5:22, 27

[444] John 5:25–29

[445] Romans 8:9

[446] John 15:26

[447] He convicts believers and non-believers alike (John 16:8)

[448] Ephesians 1:13–14 (Upon believing in Jesus, the Holy Spirit is given to indwell the believer, waiting for the day when he is resurrected and conformed to the image of the Triune God. Being sealed by the Holy Spirit acts like a man giving his fiancé an engagement ring, with the future promise of marriage).

[449] Romans 8:15–16

[450] Romans 8:26–27

their innermost being, including the hidden thoughts and intentions of their hearts.[451]

The Father, Son, and Holy Spirit possess the same attributes. They are eternal.[452] They are all-knowing.[453] They are everywhere at once.[454] They are all-powerful.[455] They are holy.[456] They personify truth.[457] Each person of the Trinity is a giver and sustainer of life,[458] and they are worthy of the same glory.[459] The Trinity, one God in three persons is best stated in the Great Commission when Jesus told His disciples to baptize in the name of the Father, the Son, and the Holy Spirit.[460] Notice that the word "name" is singular, yet there are three persons.

God-man: Jesus (Son) is the second person of the Trinity, and we will look at Him more in-depth later on. Jesus is the God-man.

---

[451]   Hebrews 4:12

[452]   Father (Revelation 1:8); Son (Isaiah 9:6); Holy Spirit (Hebrews 9:14)

[453]   Father (1 John 3:20); Son (John 21:17); Holy Spirit (1 Corinthians 2:10)

[454]   Son (Matthew 18:20, 28:20); Father and the Holy Spirit (Psalm 139:1, 7–10)

[455]   Son (Matthew 28:18); Father and Spirit (Isaiah 40:13–18)

[456]   Plurality in one (Isaiah 6:3, 8); Father (Revelation 4:8); Son (Mark 1:24); Holy Spirit (Ephesians 4:30)

[457]   Son and Father (John 1:14); Son (John 14:6); Holy Spirit and Father (John 15:26)

[458]   Father and Son (John 5:21); Son (Hebrews 1:3); Holy Spirit (Romans 8:11)

[459]   Father and Son (John 17:1, 5); Holy Spirit (1 Peter 4:14)

[460]   Matthew 28:19 (one name = one essence, yet this one essence consists of three distinct persons)

Image-bearers: The image of God, the image of the Triune God, was breathed into man when he was created. When God made man and woman on the sixth day, He said, "Let us make man in Our image, after Our likeness. And let them..."[461] Genesis 2:7 says, "God formed the man of dust from the ground and breathed into his nostrils the breath of life, and man became a living being." God's very image resides in man, the image of the Father,[462] the image of the Son,[463] and the image of the Holy Spirit.[464] Man is God's highest creation.[465] When God made mankind, the world was perfect.[466] There was no sin. There was no concept of death.[467]

Let us look at the four phases of the redemptive cycle.

1. Sin: Sin and broken fellowship, the first stage of the redemptive process. But then man rebelled, sinning against God.[468] The image of God became distorted. The Fall resulted in a broken relationship between God and mankind. Because Adam disobeyed, he and Eve were removed from the Garden

---

461   Genesis 1:26

462   James 3:9

463   Romans 8:29; Philippians 3:20–21

464   2 Corinthians 3:18

465   Genesis 1:28

466   Genesis 1:31

467   Romans 5:12

468   Genesis 3:6

of Eden.[469] He took on a sin nature, corrupting the image of God within him. Adam passed on this sin nature, this natural tendency to do wrong and rebel against God,[470] to every one of his descendants throughout the entire human race.[471] This is called the *imputation of sin*. Every man, woman, and child from the time of Adam until the end of human history possesses a sin nature. They inherit this sin nature by birth[472] in the same way one inherits one's parents, one inherits one's last name. People are born with the tendency to sin, and people commit sins. Because of this, they have a broken relationship towards God and cannot come back to Him on their own terms.[473] God is holy, God is perfect, and God cannot tolerate sin in His presence. So, mankind is separated from God forever. There is no good work anyone can do to earn God's favor because God's standards are perfect. Romans 3:23 says, "For all have sinned and fallen short of the glory of God." No one meets God's holy standard. So, no one can come to God in and of himself. Mankind is condemned from birth. I believe there is an age of accountability. God will not hold people accountable for sins they commit until they develop the capacity to accept or reject truth about Him. But

---

[469]   Genesis 3:22–24

[470]   Isaiah 53:6; Romans 3:10–12

[471]   Romans 5:18–19

[472]   Psalm 51:5

[473]   Ephesians 2:8–9

everybody is born in sin, and everyone is going to hell unless God intervenes.[474] This is why people need a Savior.

2. Cross: The cross, the second stage of the redemptive process. The cross is the price of redemption. John 3:16 says, "God so loved the world that He gave His only begotten Son, that whosoever believeth in Him will not perish, but have everlasting life." God so loved the world that He had a plan. The Triune God had a plan to bring mankind back into restoration with Him.[475] His plan is carried out through the second person of the Trinity, Jesus. John 14:6 says, "I am the way, the truth, and the life. No one. No one comes to the Father but by Me." Every concept we will look at in salvation has to do with Jesus as the only way. And we are going to look at the different steps to see why this is true according to the Bible.

First, let's look at the *Atonement*. In the Old Testament, people were to bring animal sacrifices to God. They were to be healthy, they were to be of a certain age, they were to be without defect, and they were to be killed for sinful mankind. The idea is that the innocent shed its blood to pay for the sins of the guilty. As innocent, perfect sacrifices, animal blood was shed, killed to pay for people's wrongdoings.[476] That sums up the entire sacrificial system, and it

---

[474]   John 3:16

[475]   1 Peter 1:18–20

[476]   Leviticus 6:7

looks forward to Jesus, who would be the perfect sacrifice. His forerunner, John the Baptist, said, "Behold the Lamb of God who takes away the sins of the world."[477] He was the perfect, sinless sacrificial lamb who shed His blood to pay for the sins of the world.[478]

The Judge and Justifier. God is a holy and just God, and if He were to tolerate sin, He would not be righteous. He would not be holy. So He sent His Son Jesus as the answer. The Father sent the Son to be the Savior of the world.[479] The Holy Spirit impregnated Mary,[480] who gave birth to the Son of God.[481] Jesus grew up being fully human because of His mother, yet fully God at the same time.[482] He had a human nature like everyone else,[483] except without sin[484] and the natural tendency to sin. He had no sin nature. He became hungry like we do.[485] He became thirsty.[486] He grew tired.[487] He was lonely.[488] He struggled with temptation as much as

---

[477] John 1:29

[478] John 1:29 with Hebrews 9:26

[479] 1 John 4:14

[480] Matthew 1:18–23

[481] Luke 1:35

[482] Philippians 2:6–7

[483] Hebrews 2:14, 17

[484] Hebrews 4:15

[485] Matthew 4:2

[486] John 4:7

[487] John 4:6

[488] Luke 22:15

we have, yet He never sinned.[489] Because He was a sinless man, He could die in man's place.[490] As a sinless man, He redeemed mankind by completing the requirements of God's law for the human race.[491] As God simultaneously,[492] the sacrifice of Himself[493] at the cross paid for the sins of the world.[494] That is why He had to be fully God and fully man because that is the only man who would be born without sin. And the only one who could pay for the sins of the world from the time of Adam until the end of human history. That is why He is the only way. He is the only one who meets that standard of allowing God to be just and justify the sinner.

The *imputation of righteousness* is this. When we believe in Jesus, when we humble ourselves, recognizing we are sinners, believe Jesus died on the cross to take away our sins, and believe that Jesus rose from the dead, God the Father takes our sin nature and sins and places them on Jesus at the cross. God takes Jesus' righteousness and clothes us with it.[495] So God no longer sees us in our sin but Jesus' righteousness in our place.[496] This is how He can be our judge and simultaneously justify us.

---

489   Hebrews 4:15
490   Philippians 2:7–8; Hebrews 2:17
491   Galatians 4:4–5; Matthew 5:17
492   John 1:14; Philippians 2:6–7
493   Hebrews 7:26–27; 9:11–12
494   1 John 2:2
495   2 Corinthians 5:21
496   Philippians 3:9

Just as mankind was born into sin and has a sin nature without doing anything to earn it, in the same way, any person who believes in Jesus inherits Jesus' righteousness.[497] *They can do nothing to earn it but can only receive it by claiming it as a gift.*[498] This is how the imputation of sin and the imputation of righteousness are alike. They are inherited, but they cannot be earned. Anyone who tries to come to God on his own terms will fail because God is a Holy God, and He expects perfection. They can only be restored in relationship with God by receiving Jesus' gift of righteousness, not by earning it through good works. Because Jesus died and paid the punishment for sin, He met God's standard of perfection and can take mankind's place. As the God-man, He offered the perfect once-for-all sacrifice of Himself for mankind.[499] The biblical doctrines of the Atonement, Judge and Justifier, Imputation of Righteousness, and Gift, not Works, all point to why Jesus is the only way. It is the Holy Spirit who convicts people of sin and reveals their utter inability to earn God's righteous standard on their own terms.[500]

When we believe in Jesus, the Triune God safeguards our salvation, making sure it isn't lost.

---

[497]   Romans 5:17

[498]   Ephesians 2:8–9

[499]   Hebrews 10:10, 12, 14

[500]   He convicts believers and non-believers alike (John 16:8)

3. Cleansing (Justified Sinners): Part 3 in the redemptive process is the cleansing of justified sinners. There are two aspects to the cleansing of justified sinners: the Church and the individual believers. Let's look first at the *Church. What is its make-up?* When someone accepts Jesus' righteousness, he is baptized by the Holy Spirit into Jesus' body, the Church,[501] and indwelt by the Holy Spirit.[502] God the Father placed Jesus as head of the Church,[503] and the future reality is that the Church will become one, just as the Father and the Son are one, and the Church will be unified with the Trinity.[504] The Church is made up of everyone who believes that Jesus died for their sins and accepted His punishment for their sins in place of their own, that He rose from the dead, and that He is God. When they turn to Jesus, their sin nature is crucified with Him on the cross, and they are resurrected with Him.[505] This is their position spiritually.

Baptism portrays the beginning and end of the Christian life, where we died to sin at the cross and the resurrection, where we are raised with Jesus in the heavenly places,[506] our current position in Him, and our future reality. We are baptized in the name of the Triune God.[507]

---

501   1 Corinthians 12:13

502   1 Corinthians 6:19; Ephesians 1:13–14

503   Ephesians 1:17, 20–23

504   John 17:21–23

505   Romans 6:3–6

506   Ephesians 2:4–6

507   Matthew 28:19

Now that people are children of God, they are saints, but they are sinners simultaneously.[508] They have put on the nature of Jesus and the Triune God,[509] but they still retain the sin nature.[510] They are justified sinners, and they need to be cleansed continually to be able to be in fellowship with the Triune God.

Communion looks at the Christian life as an ongoing process or the middle. It is a corporate cleansing and an individual cleansing. As people take part in the bread and the cup, representing the body and blood of Jesus,[511] they remember His death and what it does for believers. And people who take Communion in an unworthy manner, when they are not in a right relationship with God and they are consciously sinning against other people, are eating and drinking judgment to themselves...[512] So, Communion acts as a cleansing process, where people need to settle accounts with God and settle accounts with their brothers and sisters in Jesus so they can come to God with a clean conscience and not be judged while participating. Communion also looks forward to God the Father setting up His earthly king-

---

508   Romans 3:22–24
509   2 Peter 1:4
510   Galatians 5:16–17; Romans 7:25b; 8:4
511   1 Corinthians 10:16; Luke 22:17
512   1 Corinthians 11:27–30

dom,[513] where Jesus is world ruler[514] and the Holy Spirit indwells God's people.[515]

Baptism and Communion are the two rituals practiced by the Church. The *functions of the Church* are to glorify God the Father[516] and build up Jesus' body to spiritual maturity,[517] empowered by the Holy Spirit. All the members, not just its leadership, are to serve the Church and to do ministry outside it, proclaiming the name of Jesus. The Holy Spirit at will gives spiritual gifts to people to build up the Church to maturity and to do the work of the ministry.[518]

We looked at the Church regarding cleansing to be in fellowship with Holy God. Now, let us look to individual believers concerning cleansing and justified sinners. As we talked about before, we have taken on Jesus' nature, the Triune nature, but we still possess the sin nature. We have a *battle of two natures* within us, and one is our master.[519] Whichever one we submit to takes control. We can submit to the works of the flesh, and we can be under its authority, or we can submit to the Holy Spirit and live out the fruit of the Spirit and be under the Spirit's authority,[520] but we are

---

513   Daniel 2:35, 44 with 7:13–14, 27
514   Zechariah 9:9–10; 14:9, 16–17
515   Ezekiel 36:26–27; 39:29
516   Ephesians 1:5–6, 12, 14; 3:21
517   Ephesians 4:7, 11–16
518   1 Corinthians 12:4–11
519   Romans 6:12–13, 16–20, 22
520   Galatians 5:16–23

not in control of ourselves. One of the two natures is going to control us, and we have to decide on a daily, hourly, even a minute basis at times who is going to be in control. This is part of the *sanctification* process when we are becoming conformed to the image of Jesus.[521]

The sanctification process is where we become increasingly dependent on God instead of our own efforts, attitudes, experiences, decisions, and will. In the same way, a debilitating disease takes over an individual, and they have to receive increasing care as time goes on. They have to give up more and more control of themselves. This is what God desires of us, to make us increasingly dependent on Him. This is how He can deal with the sin nature within us and conform us to Jesus' image, really the image of the Triune God.

In the sanctification process, *eternal rewards* are given as motivation to help believers strive under the empowerment of the Holy Spirit to do what is right and do good works. There is nothing anyone can do to earn God's favor and go to heaven on one's own terms.[522] It is not an issue of being good or bad. It is an issue of relying on Jesus' gift or rejecting His gift. Our good works do not earn our way to heaven, but our good works do determine the quality of life we will experience in heaven.[523] God says that we will be given eternal rewards. Over a hundred different verses and passages talk

---

[521]   2 Corinthians 3:18

[522]   Ephesians 2:8–9

[523]   Matthew 20:25–27; Mark 10:42–44

about eternal rewards. And while it is not the most import-ant topic in Scripture, it is a very important motivation to make us want to set our eyes on our future home instead of our temporary home, our current reality. One can earn five different crowns while living this life on earth. An imperishable crown is rewarded for running the spiritual race, disciplining oneself to serve Jesus for the duration of the race.[524] A crown of righteousness is for those who long for Jesus' return.[525] A crown of life is for those who endure trials because of their love for God[526] and for those who endure to the point of dying as a martyr.[527] A crown of glory is given to those who faithfully shepherd the flock of God.[528] A crown of rejoicing is given to those who win souls for Jesus.[529] There are many rewards that one can earn by how he lives, and his quality of life in heaven will be determined by how he serves God from the heart, not selfish gain.[530] This is an encouragement to strive to look to the future and not to the present because this battle of striving to be close to God and being cleansed as justified sinners is a battle that will be ongoing from the time we accept Jesus Christ as our Lord and Savior

---

[524]   1 Corinthians 9:24–27
[525]   2 Timothy 4:7–8
[526]   James 1:12
[527]   Revelation 2:10
[528]   1 Peter 5:2–4
[529]   1 Thessalonians 2:19–20
[530]   Matthew 6:2–4, 5–6, 16–18

until we die. It will never go away during our life because we will always have the two natures within us.

4. Resurrection: The last stage of the redemptive cycle is the resurrection. We revisit Baptism because it looks toward the future reality when we are resurrected and brought into conformity with the image of God when we have no more sin and we are free from our body of sin.

There are two general resurrections. Remember that Jesus is Judge.[531] He is the Savior[532] and the Judge. The *first resurrection* is the resurrection of the righteous, where Jesus will judge all the righteous. This is when they will receive eternal rewards. He will reward people according to how they lived.[533] He will expose the sin of the people who belong to Him if they have not confessed their sin[534] and He has confronted them,[535] but they will go to heaven. They will all be cleansed and brought into His presence. There will be a period of 1,000 years where Jesus will reign on earth. And then, there will be the *second resurrection*. This is the resurrection of the wicked, where everybody from the time of Adam until the end of the world will be judged for their evil deeds and for their rejection of God's message of salva-

---

531   John 5:22, 27–29
532   Matthew 1:21; John 3:17
533   1 Corinthians 3:10–15; 2 Corinthians 5:10
534   1 John 1:9
535   1 Corinthians 4:5; 2 Corinthians 5:10

tion. And every one of those will be thrown into hell[536] along with the demonic host and Satan himself,[537] who will be tormented forever.[538]

We saw an overview of the redemptive process, which is made up of a beginning and end, regarding the fellowship between God and mankind, along with the four stages of the redemptive cycle: sin, the cross, the cleansing of justified sinners, and the resurrection. We reviewed over twenty biblical doctrines that relate to the redemptive process of where God, from the very beginning to the end of human history, is actively bringing fallen mankind back into relationship with Him. <u>In the beginning, innocent mankind was made in the image of the Triune God, living in full fellowship with Him.</u>

End: <u>In the *Eternal State,* mankind is in restored fellowship with God.</u>[539] <u>The Triune God redeemed sinful mankind made in His image and restored fellowship with him.</u> In the Eternal State, all the righteous will be in heaven and the wicked in hell, humanity and the demonic host, death will be eliminated,[540] and Jesus will reign with perfected humanity who has been conformed to His image. There will be no more sorrow or pain, and God will dwell among

---

536   Revelation 20:11–15
537   Matthew 25:41
538   Revelation 20:10
539   Revelation 21:3
540   1 Corinthians 15:26

His people.[541] In the Garden of Eden, God dwelt among His people. Because of sin, that fellowship was broken, and God has been working throughout the entire human history to bring sinful mankind back to Himself. In the Eternal State, mankind will have the restored fellowship with the Triune God, living forever in His presence, free of any sin, free of any death, and it will be the most awesome time.

Conclusion: This lesson ties together the redemptive cycle of the restored fellowship between sinful mankind and the Triune God. Next, we will review the redemptive cycle, Baptism and Communion, as it gives us a snapshot of the redemptive cycle. God, thank you for loving us so much that you were willing to pay for the price of restoring our lost fellowship with you. To view the chart for this section, go to https://rbeteach71.wixsite.com/justified-sinners/charts.

---

[541] Revelation 21:3–4

REDEMPTIVE CYCLE: BAPTISM AND COMMUNION

As a snapshot, the two Church ordinances, Baptism and Communion, cover the entire redemptive cycle: sin, the cross, the cleansing of justified sinners, and the resurrection. They have to do with restoring lost fellowship between the Triune God and sinful mankind.

Baptism is a symbol of entrance into the family of God. It focuses on the *beginning and the end of the Christian walk* and deals with the redemptive stages of sin, the cross, and the resurrection. Baptism is a very concise illustration of a believer being united to Jesus in His death to sin on the cross and resurrection from the dead. Jesus' death to sin becomes our death to sin. Jesus' resurrection becomes our resurrection. This is our position in Christ and our future reality when we are transformed according to His image. Romans 6:3–5 proclaims, "Or do you not know that all of us who have been baptized into Christ Jesus have been baptized into His death? Therefore we have been buried with Him through baptism into death, so that as Christ was raised from the dead through the glory of the Father, so we too might walk in newness of life. For if we have become united with Him in the likeness of His death, certainly we shall also be in the likeness of His resurrection." Philippians 3:20–21 speaks of this resurrection.

"For our citizenship is in heaven, from which also we eagerly wait for a Savior, the Lord Jesus Christ; who will transform the body of our humble state into conformity with the body of His glory, by the exertion of the power that He has even to subject all things to Himself."

Communion acts as a heart cleansing or preparation for justified sinners to be in fellowship with Holy God. It focuses on the *ongoing Christian walk* and deals with sin, the cross, and the cleansing of justified sinners. It is about actively remembering Jesus' sacrifice on the cross for our sins. It also addresses how we as believers can fellowship with Holy God. We are to examine ourselves before taking part in the bread and the cup, for if we take it in an unworthy manner, we become guilty of the body and blood of Jesus, bringing judgment upon ourselves. Being conscious of this pushes us to settle accounts with God and people before taking Communion. This requires us to be continually cleansed to freely fellowship with Him. This goes on throughout our entire Christian walk from beginning to end.

The two ordinances that all Christians are to practice are concise, visual, and participatory illustrations covering the entire redemptive cycle: sin, the cross, the cleansing of justified sinners, and the resurrection. They have to do with restoring lost fellowship between the Triune God and sinful mankind.

Now that we see how Baptism and Communion combined provide a snapshot of the entire redemptive cycle, in the following lessons, we will examine the Tabernacle, the Old Testament Sacrifices, and the Seven Biblical Feasts. Then, we will see how these also relate to the biblical doctrines and fit as a unified whole in the redemptive cycle. To view the chart for this section, go to https://rbeteach71.wixsite.com/justified-sinners/charts.

STUDY A: TABERNACLE

T he Tabernacle. When God created mankind in the beginning, He was in fellowship with Adam and Eve. Sin entered the world, breaking fellowship between God and the human race. Since then, the Triune God has been actively working throughout history to restore sinful mankind to Himself. The Tabernacle illustrates this theme. In the Old Testament, the Tabernacle portrays God the Father dwelling with His people, Israel. This idea is carried into the New Testament. John 1:14 says, "And the Word (Jesus) became flesh and dwelt or tabernacled among us..." First Corinthians 6:19 says that the Holy Spirit indwells every believer, who is a temple of God. And the future Millennium furthers this idea when Jesus bodily rules in the midst of His people.

The Tabernacle is a replica, a copy, and shadow of the heavenly tent, according to the pattern God showed Moses on the mountain. The true tent was erected by God.[542] The Tabernacle is made up of three courts: the *Outer Court*,[543] the

---

[542]   Hebrews 8:2, 5; (See also Exodus 24:15–18 with 25:8–9, 40; 1 Chronicles 28:11–19)

[543]   Outer court (Ezekiel 42:14); court (Exodus 27:9). "Courts" refer to the outer court and the Holy Place (2 Kings 21:5).

Inner Court or the *Holy Place,*[544] and the *Holy of Holies.*[545] All the people of Israel were allowed to enter the Outer Court,[546] as well as any foreigner who joined the Lord and decided to follow His laws,[547] but any outsider who came into the Tabernacle and didn't join the Lord was to be killed.[548] Just the priests were allowed to enter the Inner Court.[549] Only the high priest was allowed to enter the Holy of Holies once a year.[550] In this place, God's presence dwelt, and anyone who entered would die.[551] The Veil separates the Inner Court from the Holy of Holies.

The seven pieces of the Tabernacle furniture[552] are positioned in the place of a cross.[553] We have the Brazen Altar, the Laver, the Altar of Incense, and the Ark of the Covenant and Mercy Seat, which make a straight line. To the left of the

---

[544] Holy Place (Exodus 26:33); Inner Court (Ezekiel 8:16); Tent of Meeting (Leviticus 1:1)

[545] Holy of Holies (Hebrews 9:3); Holy Place (Leviticus 16:2); Most Holy Place (1 Kings 6:16)

[546] Numbers 10:3

[547] Isaiah 56:6–7 (See also Mark 11:17).

[548] Numbers 3:38

[549] Numbers 18:22–23; 1 Chronicles 23:24 with 32

[550] Hebrews 9:7, 25

[551] Since only the high priest could enter once yearly or die trespassing, everyone else who tried would also die (Leviticus 16:2).

[552] Exodus 31:6–9

[553] The Ark of the Covenant with the Mercy Seat resting on top of it, and the Altar of Incense were facing each other, separated by the veil (Exodus 30:1, 6). The Brazen Altar was before the door (Exodus 40:6). the Laver was between the tent of meeting (Holy Place) and the Brazen Altar (Exodus 40:7). The Table of Shewbread was on the north side (Exodus 40:22) and the Candlestick was on the south side (Exodus 40:24). They were opposite each other (Exodus 26:35).

Altar of Incense is the Candlestick, and to the right is the Table of Shewbread. Jesus is the only way to heaven.[554] The Tabernacle portrays this through the shape of a cross. In this study, we will see that each piece represents how God is working in the Old and New Testament to redeem sinful mankind to Himself and dwell among His people.

The theme of the Tabernacle is throughout the redemptive process from the beginning to the end. The Tabernacle simultaneously reveals the theme of how sinful mankind can approach Him as Holy God and God dwelling among His people. We will look at its different parts: one gate, the Brazen Altar and the Laver in the Outer Court, the Candlestick, Altar of Incense, and the Table of Shewbread in the Inner Court, the Veil separating the Inner Court from the Holy of Holies, the Ark of the Covenant and the Mercy Seat in the Holy of Holies, and the High priest.

Tabernacle—One Gate

The Tabernacle is made of the Outer Court, the Inner Court, and the Holy of Holies. There is only one entrance to each,[555] signifying there is only one way to God the Father, which was provided at the cross through Jesus. The Taber-

---

[554]   John 14:6

[555]   Gate entrance to Tabernacle and outer court (Exodus 27:16). Screen as entrance from outer court to inner court/Holy Place (Exodus 26:36–37). Entrance from Inner court/Holy Place to Holy of Holies separated by the veil (Exodus 26:31–33).

nacle's one gate looks at the cross and illustrates how Jesus is the only way to God the Father.

Tabernacle—Brazen Altar

The Brazen Altar[556] is in the Outer Court of the Tabernacle. It was made of shittim or acacia wood, overlaid with bronze. It was a square shape with a horn on each corner.[557] Animal sacrifices were offered on this altar, and its fire was to never go out.[558] If it was a sin, offering the blood of the sacrifices was sprinkled on its four horns.[559] In all the sacrifices, the shed blood was poured out at its base.[560] The bloodshed from the innocent animals without defect was God's payment for the sinner, a substitution of the innocent for the guilty. It was one altar for the entire nation, the only place God designated for offering sacrifice.[561] In the New Testament, the Brazen Altar represents the cross of Jesus, the place of sacrifice.[562]

In the redemptive process, the Tabernacle's Brazen Altar looks at the cross and illustrates how Jesus is the only way.

---

[556] Altar of Burnt Offering (Exodus 38:1), Altar of Shittim (acacia) wood (Exodus 27:1)

[557] Exodus 27:1–8; 38:1–7

[558] Leviticus 6:13

[559] Leviticus 4:25

[560] Leviticus 4:25

[561] Leviticus 17:1–9

[562] John 1:29 with I Peter 2:24

He is the only acceptable sacrifice to God the Father, as His death paid for all the sins of the world. [563]

Tabernacle—Laver

The Laver[564] is in the Outer Court of the Tabernacle. It was a basin of bronze resting on a stand of bronze made from the brass mirrors of women who ministered in the court.[565] It contained water for just the priests to wash their hands and feet, probably as a ceremonial washing before they went to the tent of meeting or altar to minister.[566] In the New Testament, the Laver stands for cleansing or sanctifying believers through the washing of water by the Word. Ephesians 5:25–27 declares, "Christ loved the church and gave Himself up for her, that He might sanctify her, having cleansed her by the washing of water with the word, so that He might present the church to Himself in splendor, without spot or wrinkle or any such thing, that she might be holy and without blemish." Jesus is the Word of God[567] who cleanses us through the Word and work of the Holy Spirit to be presented holy and blameless as a Church before God the Father. In the redemptive cycle, the Laver illustrates how

---

[563]   Ephesians 5:2; Hebrews 9:26; 1 John 2:2
[564]   Bronze Basin (Exodus 30:18)
[565]   Exodus 38:8
[566]   Exodus 30:18–21
[567]   John 1:1–2, 14

Jesus cleanses us as justified sinners to be in fellowship with Holy God.

Tabernacle—Candlestick

The Candlestick, sometimes called the lampstand,[568] is in the Inner Court of the Tabernacle, also called the Holy Place. The Candlestick has seven lamps,[569] made up of one main shaft and three branches on each side of the main shaft. Every branch includes the three stages of the almond plant, unopened, bud/knob, and flower/fruit. The material was of beaten gold.[570] Every morning and evening, the priests were to light its lamps using pure olive oil. The light was never to go out.[571] In the New Testament, the Candlestick represents Jesus, the Light of God[572] and the only way to God the Father. This comes through conviction of sin by the Holy Spirit.

In the redemptive process, the Tabernacle's Candlestick looks at the cross, illustrating how Jesus is the light of the world and the only way to God.

---

[568]   Golden Lampstand (2 Chronicles 13:11); Lampstand (Exodus 37:20)

[569]   Exodus 25:37

[570]   Exodus 25:31–40

[571]   Leviticus 24:1–4

[572]   John 8:12. Jesus fulfills Old Testament promises of the coming of the "light" of salvation and the "light" of God (Isaiah 49:6; Acts 13:47; 26:23)

Tabernacle—Altar of Incense

The Altar of Incense[573] is in the Inner Court of the Tabernacle. It was made of shittim or acacia wood, overlaid with pure gold. It was a square shape with a horn on each corner.[574] It was placed directly in front of the veil before the Ark of the Covenant.[575] Every morning and evening, the high priest was to offer fragrant or sweet incense to the Lord, to burn continuously before Him.[576] No unauthorized incense, burnt offering, grain offering, drink offering, or any other offering was to ever be offered on it.[577] Once a year, blood from the sin offering of the bull and goat was to be sprinkled on its horns for atonement on the Day of Atonement.[578] In the New Testament, the Altar of Incense represents Jesus, our Intercessor who advocates for us to God the Father when we sin.[579] Psalm 141:2 says incense are the prayers of the

---

573   The Altar (Leviticus 16:18); The Incense Altar (1 Chronicles 6:49); The Golden Altar (1 Kings 7:48); The Whole Altar that belonged to the inner sanctuary (1 Kings 6:22); The Altar of Sweet (fragrant) incense (Leviticus 4:7)

574   Exodus 37:25–29

575   Exodus 30:6

576   Exodus 30:7–8

577   Exodus 30:9

578   Exodus 30:10 with Leviticus 16:18–19

579   Jesus is our intercessor (advocate) before the Father (Romans 8:34; 1 John 2:1)

saints.[580] When believers pray, they are to pray to God the Father[581] through the Holy Spirit,[582] in the name of Jesus.[583]

In the redemptive cycle, the Altar of Incense illustrates how we as believers have an advocate to the Father when we sin through Jesus. This is important as it shows how justified sinners can be cleansed to be in fellowship with Holy God.

Tabernacle—Table of Shewbread

The Table of Shewbread[584] is in the Inner Court of the Tabernacle. It was made of Shittim or acacia wood and overlaid with pure gold.[585] Every Sabbath, twelve loaves, one for each tribe of Israel, were baked and set on the Table of Shewbread. Only the high priest and his sons could eat it.[586] Bread was to always be placed before the Lord.[587] In the New Testament, the Table of Shewbread represents Jesus, the Bread of God.[588] Jesus is our daily bread, and we are dependent

---

[580] See also Revelation 8:3–4 with 5:8

[581] Matthew 6:9–13

[582] Romans 8:26

[583] John 14:13–14

[584] Showbread Table (Exodus 25:30); Table of Shittim (acacia) Wood (Exodus 25:23); Table of Gold (1 Kings 7:48); The Table (Exodus 25:27)

[585] Exodus 25:23–30

[586] Leviticus 24:5–9

[587] Bread = Bread of Presence (holy bread—1 Samuel 21:4), mentioned in Exodus 25:30 & 1 Samuel 21:6

[588] John 6:30–33, **35, 48–51**

on Him for our daily needs.[589] We are dependent on Him in place of ourselves to live the Christian life.

In the redemptive cycle, the Table of Shewbread illustrates how believers need to continually depend on Jesus in place of themselves as justified sinners.

Tabernacle—Veil

In the Tabernacle, the Veil[590] separates the Inner Court from the Holy of Holies.[591] The Veil was made of blue, purple, and scarlet yarns and fine twined linen. Cherubim were worked into the material[592] and hung on four pillars of acacia wood, overlaid with gold. At Jesus' death, it was torn in two,[593] indicating that believers now have direct access to God the Father[594] through His sacrificial death.[595]

In the redemptive process, the Tabernacle's Veil looks at the cross and illustrates that Jesus is the only way to enter God the Father's presence. The writer of Hebrews says that the Veil is Jesus' flesh.[596]

---

[589] Matthew 6:11

[590] Also called curtain

[591] Exodus 26:31–33

[592] Cherubim are the angels with the closest access to God (Ezekiel 10:3–5; 28:14) and one of their tasks is to act as guardians (Genesis 3:24). In regards to the veil, their figures woven into it signifies the Holy of Holies is being carefully protected.

[593] Matthew 27:51

[594] Hebrews 10:19–20

[595] Hebrews 9:11–14, 24–28

[596] Hebrews 10:19–20

Tabernacle—Ark of the Covenant

In the Tabernacle, the Ark of the Covenant[597] is in the Holy of Holies, behind the Veil.[598] The Ark of the Covenant was made of shittim or acacia wood and overlaid inside and out with gold.[599] Inside it were three things:[600] manna[601], Aaron's rod that budded,[602] and the two tablets of the Ten Com-

---

[597]   The Ark of the Covenant (Joshua 3:6); The Ark of the Testimony (Exodus 25:22); testimony (Exodus 30:36); The Ark of the Covenant of the Lord (Numbers 10:33); The Ark of the Lord God (1 Kings 2:26); The Ark of the Lord, the Lord of all the earth (Joshua 3:13); The Ark of God (1 Samuel 3:3); The Holy Ark (2 Chronicles 35:3); The Ark of Thy Strength (Psalm 132:8); The Ark of the Covenant of God (Judges 20:27); The Ark of the Lord (Joshua 4:11); The Ark of God, the God of Israel (1 Samuel 5:7); The Ark of Shittim [acacia] Wood (Exodus 25:10).

[598]   Exodus 26:33

[599]   Exodus 25:10–16

[600]   Hebrews 9:4

[601]   God fed Israel manna ("It was like coriander seed, white, and the taste of it was like wafers made with honey [Exodus 16:31]) for forty years while wandering in the wilderness between the time they left Egypt and entered the Promised Land (Exodus 16:35 with Joshua 5:10–12). It was later placed in a golden jar inside the Ark of the Covenant as a reminder of God's provision for His people (Exodus 16:31–34).

[602]   Korah (a Levite) led a rebellion of 250 influential, senior leaders among the Israelite community against Moses and Aaron's leadership, complaining it was their fault the people of Israel were brought out of Egypt to wander in the wilderness, waiting to die. It was their fault they were unable to enter the Promised Land. In response God opened the ground to swallow Korah, all the people who belonged to Him, and all their possessions. He sent down fire, incinerating the 250 leaders who sided with Korah. Then the whole congregation of Israel blamed Moses and Aaron for their deaths and God sent a plague to kill some of them (Numbers chapter 16). Then to prove to the people of Israel that God backed Aaron, and to warn the congregation not to rebel and complain against Him, He instructed Moses to assemble the leader of each tribe with their staff. The man whom God chose, his staff would sprout. Aaron's staff (of the tribe of Levi) "sprouted and put forth buds and produced blossoms, and it bore ripe almonds" (Numbers 17:8). Aaron's staff was to be put in the Ark of the Cove-

mandments.[603] Beside it was placed the Book of the Law.[604] God's presence dwelt there,[605] and anyone who approached it would immediately die.[606] The Ark of the Covenant represents God's presence dwelling in the midst of His people.

In the redemptive process, the Tabernacle's Ark of the Covenant is at the beginning and end of the redemption cycle when the Triune God is in fellowship with mankind.

Tabernacle—Mercy Seat

In the Tabernacle, the Ark of the Covenant is in the Holy of Holies, behind the Veil. The Mercy Seat rests on top of the Ark of the Covenant.[607] It was made of pure gold. There was a cherub[608] of beaten gold on both ends. The whole unit was one single piece.[609] Exodus 25:20 describes, "The cherubim shall spread out their wings above, overshadowing the mercy seat with their wings, their faces one to another; toward the mercy seat shall the faces of the cherubim be."

---

nant as a reminder of Aaron's (and his descendants') authority and position as priests, and more so as warning against those who rebel and complain against God (Numbers 17:10 – See also Numbers chapter 17).

603   Deuteronomy 10:2–5

604   Deuteronomy 31:24–26; It was to be placed read to the entire congregation of Israel, young to old and foreigners living among them, every seven years (Deuteronomy 31:9–13).

605   Exodus 25:21–22

606   2 Samuel 6:6–7

607   Exodus 26:34

608   None

609   Exodus 37:6–8

God's presence dwelt above the Mercy Seat between the cherubim, and He spoke from there.[610] At times, He is mentioned as being "enthroned" upon the cherubim,[611] where He rules.[612] And in the Millennium, Jesus' throne is in the Holy of Holies, where the cherubim sat. The Mercy Seat was the meeting place between Holy God and sinful man. When the high priest entered the Holy of Holies once yearly, he sprinkled the blood of sin offerings for himself and God's people on the Mercy Seat to cover their sins.[613] Jesus is the Mercy Seat.[614] [615] Because God the Father sees Jesus' blood covering sinners,[616] believers have direct access to the Mercy Seat in God's presence.[617]

In the redemptive process, the Tabernacle's Mercy Seat in the Holy of Holies looks at the cross. The Mercy Seat[618] illustrates how Jesus is the only way for sinful man to meet

---

[610] Exodus 25:22

[611] 2 Kings 19:15; Psalm 99:1; Ezekiel 10:1

[612] His throne, or place of rule is in the Holy of Holies. It is at the Mercy Seat between the cherubim. (Ezekiel 43:4–8 [vs 7])

[613] Leviticus 16:2, 14–15 (Hebrews 9:7, 25), 30, 34

[614] Wallace, Dan. "Class Notes," NT 105 Exegesis of Romans, Dallas: Dallas Theological Seminary, Fall 2009. (His notes on Romans 3:21–26 says that the correct translation for propitiation means Mercy Seat)

[615] As the Mercy Seat (Romans 3:25), He is the place for the sin offering of the people in the Holy of Holies (Leviticus 16:2, 14–15).

[616] Hebrews 9:12, 25–26

[617] Hebrews 10:19–20

[618] Also called the throne of grace in Hebrews 4:16 (God's throne is associated with the Mercy Seat)

Holy God and, as a sinner at the same time, be declared righteous before God[619] and enter His presence.[620]

Tabernacle—High Priest

The high priest was in charge of the Tabernacle. Once a year, on the Day of Atonement, he sprinkled the blood of sin offerings for himself and God's people on the Mercy Seat to cover their sins.[621] Jesus is also the high priest[622] who offered the sacrifice for the sins of the people and sprinkled its blood on the Mercy Seat.[623] The difference is that Jesus, as the high priest, completed the Day of Atonement when He not only offered the sacrifice, *but the sacrifice He presented to God the Father was Himself.*[624] It was a sacrifice one time, forever paying for the sins of the world.[625]

In the redemptive process, the Tabernacle's high priest looks at the cross and illustrates that Jesus is the only way to God. The next lesson is about the Old Testament sacrifices.

---

619 Romans 3:23–24; 5:18–19; 2 Corinthians 5:21

620 Hebrews 10:19–20

621 Leviticus 16:2, 14–15 [Hebrews 9:7], 30, 34

622 Hebrews 2:17; 8:1. Because he was fully man He was a merciful and high priest who could understand people's struggle with sin's temptations (Hebrews 4:14–15)

623 Hebrews 9:25–26 ("blood of another" was the blood of the bull and goat sprinkled on the Mercy Seat [Leviticus 16:14–15])

624 Hebrews 7:26–27; 9:11–12

625 Propitiation is sacrifice (1 John 4:10). His sacrifice of Himself takes away the sins of the world (Hebrews 9:26; 1 John 2:2).

To view the chart for this section, go to https://rbeteach71.wixsite.com/justified-sinners/charts.

STUDY B: OLD TESTA-MENT SACRIFICES

I t is assumed that Old Testament sacrifices have to do with earning one's way to heaven. But really, it is about how God's people, who are simultaneously sinners, can live in a relationship with Holy God. In the Redemptive process, the sacrificial system is much more focused on the Cleansing of justified sinners than it is on the cross. In this lesson, we will look at the purpose for the Old Testament sacrifices, where they are to be offered, how they are made up, a description of what they are, and when they are offered.

Why Offer Sacrificial Offerings?

Animal sacrifices were not offered to save one's soul but for God's people to live in relationship with their Creator, who is holy. The sin offerings could never take away sin.[626] All they could do was point to one who could. But they illustrated a very important point: the death of an innocent life is required to satisfy a Holy God's wrath against sinners. Every year, the Israelites celebrated the Passover. In preparation for the first Passover, God told the people of Israel to kill

---

[626]   Hebrews 10:4, 11

an unblemished lamb and smear blood on the door frame, then have all household inhabitants inside so He would pass over the house and not kill the firstborn. When God brought the final plague on the Egyptians so Pharaoh would let His people go, the death angel came to every household in Egypt to kill the firstborn. Whenever the death angel saw the blood of the acceptable sacrifice over the door frame, he passed over it.[627] In the same way, Old Testament sins were passed over when people offered acceptable sacrifices to God by faith.

This is how God could "pass over the sins previously committed"; only by looking forward to the actual payment for sins by His own Son. It is, in fact, only in the cross where God fully satisfies His own righteousness against sin and thus demonstrates His righteousness.[628] Through the work of the cross, God the Father transfers our sins to Jesus and credits Jesus' righteousness to our account.[629] He demonstrates His righteousness by exacting full payment for sin through offering Jesus' sinless, perfect body and shedding blood as a **sin offering payment**[630] for it. This payment is sufficient one time, forever, for all who take hold of it through faith in Jesus.[631]

---

[627] Exodus 12:3, 5–7, 11–13, 21–23, 27

[628] Romans 3:21–26

[629] 2 Corinthians 5:21

[630] John 1:29 with 1 John 2:1. See also Isaiah 53:10

[631] Hebrews 9:26; 10:10, 12, 14

Where Is the Place of Offering?

All the sacrificial offerings were to be offered on the Brazen Altar. It is one altar for the entire nation and the only place God designated for offering sacrifice.[632] The Brazen Altar represents the cross of Jesus, the place of sacrifice.[633] Jesus was also the sin offering,[634] which, through the sacrifice of Himself, paid for all the sins of the world.[635] He is the only way to God.[636]

The Sacrificial Offerings

Burnt, grain, drink, peace, sin, and guilt offerings.

What are the sacrificial offerings, and what are they for? The food offerings were the burnt, grain, drink, and peace offerings, which were to be presented as a pleasing aroma to the Lord,[637] and the burnt offering also involved atonement.[638] In the offerings, the Lord had His portion,

---

[632] Leviticus 17:1–9

[633] John 1:29 with 1 Peter 2:24

[634] John 1:29 with 1 John 2:1; 4:10. See also Isaiah 53:10

[635] Propitiation is sacrifice (1 John 2:2; 4:10). His sacrifice of Himself takes away the sins of the world (Hebrews 9:26; 1 John 2:2).

[636] John 14:6

[637] Burnt (Leviticus 1:9); grain (Numbers 28:8); drink (Numbers 15:10); peace (Leviticus 3:9, 16)

[638] Leviticus 1:4

which was everything burned up on the altar; the priests had their portion, which they ate, and at times, the one who brought the offering had his portion. The burnt offerings were to be completely burned up[639] as a dedication offering to the Lord.

The sin and guilt offerings were not offered to be a pleasing aroma to the Lord but to make atonement in order that the offender's sin(s) would be forgiven.[640] Leviticus 17:11 reveals, "For the life of the flesh is in the blood, and I have given it to you upon the altar to make atonement for your souls; for it is the blood that makes atonement for the soul." Atonement is shedding innocent blood to pay for the sins of the guilty. As innocent, perfect sacrifices, animal blood was shed, killed to pay for people's wrongdoings.[641] The idea is that the innocent was substituting the place of the guilty so that the guilty were forgiven because the innocent paid their punishment.

---

[639]   Leviticus 1:9

[640]   Sin (Leviticus 4:20, 26); guilt (Leviticus 5:16, 18)

[641]   Leviticus 6:6–7

Description of the Offerings

Let's look at a description of each of the offerings: burnt, grain, drink, peace, sin, and guilt offerings. Burnt offerings[642] were dedication offerings to be presented as a pleasing aroma to the Lord[643] and to make atonement for the individual's sin.[644] They were to be from a male without defect,[645] either a bull,[646] sheep, goat,[647] turtledove, or pigeon,[648] depending on the wealth of the offender. The animal was to be brought outside the entrance to the Holy Place.[649] The priest would lay his hand on the animal's head, kill it, and throw the blood against the sides of the Brazen Altar.[650] The entire animal would be burned on the altar.[651] This was to demonstrate that the whole offering belonged to the Lord.

Grain offerings[652] were made of fine flour (baked in the oven as unleavened bread,[653] baked on a griddle,[654] or

---

[642]   Leviticus chapter 1
[643]   Leviticus 1:9, 13, 17
[644]   Leviticus 1:4
[645]   Leviticus 1:3, 10
[646]   Leviticus 1:5
[647]   Leviticus 1:10
[648]   Leviticus 1:14
[649]   Leviticus 1:3
[650]   Leviticus 1:4–5, 11, 15
[651]   Leviticus 1:9
[652]   Leviticus chapter 2
[653]   Leviticus 2:4
[654]   Leviticus 2:5

cooked in a pan[655]), then they were seasoned with salt[656] and accompanied with oil[657] and frankincense.[658] They could come from the first harvest of the crop, crushed heads of new grain.[659] The priest would burn a memorial portion on the Brazen Altar as a pleasing aroma to the Lord,[660] and the rest would be for the priests to eat.[661] They were to be given along with the burnt offering, and their amount depended on what animal it was offered with. A tenth of an ephah (3 ½ bushels or 22 liters) of fine flour mixed with oil was to be presented with a lamb,[662] two-tenths of an ephah of fine flour mixed with oil with a ram,[663] and three-tenths of an ephah of fine flour mixed with oil with a bull.[664]

Drink offerings made of wine were part of the food offerings,[665] as a pleasing aroma to the Lord.[666] They were to be given along with the burnt offering, and their amount depended on what was offered with it. A quarter of a hin of wine, which was about 4 quarts or 3.5 liters, was to be pre-

---

[655]   Leviticus 2:7
[656]   Leviticus 2:13
[657]   Leviticus 2:2, 4–7
[658]   Leviticus 2:1–2
[659]   Leviticus 2:14
[660]   Leviticus 2:2, 9, 16
[661]   Leviticus 2:3, 10
[662]   Numbers 15:4–5
[663]   Numbers 15:6
[664]   Numbers 15:8–9
[665]   Numbers 15:3, 5–10
[666]   Numbers 15:10

sented with a lamb,[667] a third of a hin of wine with a ram,[668] and half a hin of wine with a bull.[669]

Peace offerings[670] were a thanksgiving,[671] vow, or free-will offering.[672] It could be an ox,[673] lamb,[674] or goat,[675] male or female without defect,[676] offered as a pleasing aroma to the Lord.[677] The one who brought the peace offering was to lay his hand on the animal's head, kill it at the entrance to the Holy Place, and the priests would throw the blood on the sides of the Brazen Altar.[678] All the fat, kidneys, and liver were to be placed on the altar and burned.[679] The one who offered the peace offering could eat the rest of the meat,[680] minus the blood,[681] but the breast and right thigh were for the priests.[682] The peace offerings were accompanied with

---

667   Numbers 15:5
668   Numbers 15:7
669   Numbers 15:10
670   Leviticus chapter 3
671   Leviticus 7:12–13, 15
672   Leviticus 7:16
673   Leviticus 4:10
674   Leviticus 3:7
675   Leviticus 3:12
676   Leviticus 3:6
677   Leviticus 3:5, 16
678   Leviticus 3:2, 8, 13
679   Leviticus 3:3–5, 9–11, 14–16
680   Leviticus 7:15–16
681   Leviticus 7:26–27
682   Leviticus 7:31–35

unleavened bread and wafers with oil and leavened bread.[683] The thanksgiving offering had to be eaten the same day,[684] but if it was a vow or a free-will offering, he could take two days to eat it.[685] Everything not eaten after that time had to be burned.[686]

Sin offerings[687] were presented for unintentionally committed sins[688] when the offender(s) later became aware of them.[689] The priest would use the sin offering to make atonement for the offender(s)' committed sin, and he would be forgiven.[690] If the offender(s) was a priest,[691] the whole congregation,[692] one of their leaders,[693] or any individual,[694] he was to offer an animal. A priest[695] or a whole congregation[696] would offer a bull, a leader would offer a male goat,[697] and an individual would offer a female goat or a lamb.[698] This

---

683   Leviticus 7:11–13, 16
684   Leviticus 7:15
685   Leviticus 7:16
686   Leviticus 3:17
687   Leviticus chapter 4
688   Leviticus 4:2
689   Leviticus 4:13–14, 22–23, 27–28
690   Leviticus 4:20, 26, 31, 35
691   Leviticus 4:3
692   Leviticus 4:13–14
693   Leviticus 4:22–23
694   Leviticus 4:27–28
695   Leviticus 4:3
696   Leviticus 4:15
697   Leviticus 4:22–23
698   Leviticus 4:28, 32

would be offered outside the entrance to the Holy Place.[699] If the offender(s) was a priest or the whole congregation, the priest or elders of the congregation would lay hands on the animal and kill it before the Lord.[700] The priest would take some of the animal's blood, enter the Holy Place, dip his finger in the blood, and sprinkle part of it before the Lord in front of the veil of the sanctuary. He would put some of the blood on the horns of the Altar of Incense and pour out the rest of the blood at the base of the Brazen Altar.[701] The rest of it (skin, flesh, head, legs, entrails, and poop) had to be carried outside the camp to the ash heap and burned.[702]

If the offender was a leader or individual, the priest would take some of the animal's blood, dip his finger in the blood, and put it on the horns of the Brazen Altar.[703] The rest of the blood would be poured at the base of the altar.[704] All the fat was to be removed, along with the kidneys and liver, and burned on the altar.[705] The rest of it was for the priests to eat.[706] If the individual couldn't afford to bring a female lamb

---

[699] Leviticus 4:4, 14, 23–24 (see also 1:3), 29 (see also 1:3), 33 (see also 1:3)

[700] Leviticus 4:4, 15

[701] Leviticus 4:5–7, 16–18

[702] Leviticus 4:11–12, 21

[703] Leviticus 4:25, 30, 34

[704] Leviticus 4:7, 18, 25, 30, 34

[705] Leviticus 4:8–9, 19, 26, 31, 35

[706] Leviticus 6:26, 29 (If the blood of the sin offering was taken inside the Holy Place to make atonement (for a priest [4:3–5] or the whole congregation [4:13, 16], all of it was to be burned [4:11–12, 21; 6:30], but if it wasn't taken into the Holy Place, the rest was for the priests to eat (6:26, 29–30].

or goat, he could offer pigeons or turtledoves.[707] If those were too costly, he could bring a tenth of an ephah of flour.[708]

Guilt offerings[709] were for deliberate sins or unknowingly failing to do something that was required. If he chose not to reveal the truth as a witness in a court case,[710] if he became unclean by touching a dead animal[711] or human uncleanness,[712] or made a thoughtless oath and forgot about it,[713] when he realized his guilt, he was to confess his sin[714] and bring a sin offering[715] so that the priest could make atonement for his wrongdoing.[716] It was to be offered on the Brazen Altar.[717] Just like the sin offering, the priests received their portion. A guilt offering was also required for unintentional violation of sacred property,[718] unintentionally doing something the Lord's commandment told him not to do,[719]

---

[707]   Leviticus 5:7

[708]   Leviticus 5:11

[709]   Leviticus 5:1–6:7

[710]   Leviticus 5:1

[711]   Leviticus 5:2

[712]   Leviticus 5:3

[713]   Leviticus 5:4

[714]   Leviticus 5:5; Numbers 5:6–7

[715]   Offer a female lamb or goat (Leviticus 5:6). If too poor, he was to bring two turtledoves or two pigeons (Leviticus 5:7). If still too poor, he was to bring a tenth of an ephah of fine flour. As it is a sin offering, no oil or frankincense is to accompany it (Leviticus 5:11)

[716]   Leviticus 5:6, 10, 13

[717]   Leviticus 5:6 (see 4:27–31), 12

[718]   Leviticus 5:15–16

[719]   Leviticus 5:17

stealing,[720] taking something by force,[721] deceiving his neighbor in a financial matter,[722] recovering a lost item and lying about it,[723] or swearing falsely.[724] When his offense caused a financial loss, he was to fully restore it plus 20 percent.[725] He also needed to bring a ram without defect or its equivalent value to the priest for a guilt offering. The priest would make atonement for him before the Lord, and he would be forgiven for his sins that were committed unintentionally or deliberately.[726]

---

[720]   Leviticus 6:2, 4

[721]   Leviticus 6:2, 4

[722]   Leviticus 6:5

[723]   Leviticus 6:5

[724]   Leviticus 6:5

[725]   Leviticus 5:16; 6:5

[726]   Leviticus 5:18; 6:1–7

When Are the Sacrifices Offered?

The calendar offerings were daily, on the Sabbath, at the new moon, monthly, and each of the Seven Biblical Feasts.

Daily

The daily offering was a burnt offering of two year-old male lambs without defect, one in the morning and one at sundown, both with their grain and drink offerings.[727]

Sabbath

On every Sabbath, daily offerings were presented, *plus* a burnt offering of two year-old male lambs without defect, accompanied by their grain and drink offerings.[728]

On the New Moon

Unspecified burnt offerings were sacrificed on the new moon, *plus* the daily offerings.[729]

Monthly

On the first day of every month, daily offerings were presented, *plus* a burnt offering of two bulls, one ram, seven one-year-old lambs, all without defect, along with their grain and drink offerings and a sin offering of one goat.[730]

Seven Feasts

---

[727]   Numbers 28:1–8
[728]   Numbers 28:1–8
[729]   Numbers 29:6; 1 Chronicles 23:31; 2 Chronicles 8:13
[730]   Numbers 28:11–15

The Seven Biblical Feasts were offered during the Spring and Fall Feasts and the Feast of Weeks. The Spring Feasts are the Passover, Feast of First Fruits, and Unleavened Bread. The Fall Feasts are the Trumpets, the Day of Atonement, and the Tabernacles. The Feast of Weeks, also known as the Day of Pentecost, is between the Spring and Fall Feasts.

The *Passover* is the fourteenth of the first month at sundown.[731] On the Passover, daily offerings were presented, *plus* each family would sacrifice and eat one male year-old lamb without defect.[732]

The Feast of *First Fruits* is the Sunday after Passover.[733] On this day, daily offerings were presented, *plus* each family was to bring a sheaf of the first fruits of their harvest to the priest, who would wave it before the Lord, along with a burnt offering of a male, year-old lamb without defect with its grain and drink offering.[734]

The Feast of *Unleavened Bread* is from the 14th at sundown to the 21st at sundown.[735] During this week, daily offerings were presented, *plus* the Sabbath offerings, *plus* the Passover lamb on its day, *plus* the offering of First Fruits on its day, *plus* for the Feast of Unleavened Bread, a burnt offering of two bulls, one ram, and seven one-year-old male lambs

---

[731]   Exodus 12:6; Leviticus 23:5

[732]   Exodus 12:3–14, 21–27

[733]   Leviticus 23:11

[734]   Leviticus 23:9–14

[735]   Exodus 12:18

without defect with their grain and drink offerings, and a sin offering of one goat. These were offered each day for seven days.[736]

The Feast of the *Feast of Weeks, known as the Day of Pentecost,*[737] is seven weeks after the feast of First Fruits[738] and is celebrated one day.[739] They presented daily offerings, *plus* the burnt offering of two bulls, one ram, and seven male year-old lambs, all without defect and with their grain and drink offerings, and a sin offering of one goat.[740]

The Feast of *Trumpets* was celebrated on the first day of the seventh month,[741] Tishri, which is now the Jewish New Year.[742] Daily offerings were presented, *plus* the new moon offerings, *plus* Feast of Trumpets burnt offerings of one bull, one ram, seven male year-old lambs, all without defect and with their grain and drink offerings, and a sin offering of one goat.[743]

---

[736]   Numbers 28:17–26

[737]   The Feast of Weeks (Exodus 34:22) was called the Day of Pentecost in the New Testament (Acts 2:1). The Feast of Weeks was also called Feast of Harvest (Exodus 34:22 with 23:16) and the Day of First Fruits (Numbers 28:26 – also called the Feast of Weeks). *It is not to be confused with the Feast of First fruits.*

[738]   Leviticus 23:16

[739]   Leviticus 23:21

[740]   Numbers 28:26–31

[741]   Leviticus 23:24

[742]   It is called Rosh Hashanah

[743]   Numbers 29:1–6

The *Day of Atonement* was celebrated on the tenth of the seventh month,[744] the holiest day of the year. Daily offerings were presented, *plus* burnt offerings of one bull, one ram, seven one-year-old male lambs without defect with their grain and drink offerings, and the sin offerings of a bull for the high priest and two goats for the congregation. One goat was killed, and the other was sent away as the scapegoat.[745] A sin offering of a bull and goat is to make atonement for the Holy of Holies, the Holy Place, and the Brazen Altar.

The Feast of *Tabernacles (also known as the Feast of Booths)* was observed on the fifteenth of the seventh month for eight days.[746] Daily offerings were presented, *plus* the Sabbath offering, *plus* for the Feast of Tabernacles, burnt offerings of bulls, rams, and lambs without defect and their grain and drink offerings, and the sin offering.[747] Take a look at this chart of offerings. Every single day, there was a sin offering of one goat. But, there were different amounts of burnt offerings depending on the day.

---

744   Leviticus 23:27; Numbers 29:7
745   Numbers 29:7–11 with Leviticus 16:2–34
746   Leviticus 23:34; Numbers 29:12
747   Numbers 29:12–38

Burnt offerings	Bull	Ram	Year-old male lamb	Sin offering–goat
Day 1	13	2	14	1
Day 2	12	2	14	1
Day 3	11	2	14	1
Day 4	10	2	14	1
Day 5	9	2	14	1
Day 6	8	2	14	1
Day 7	7	2	14	1
Day 8	1	1	7	1

Non-Calendar Offerings

Along with the calendar offerings, there were also non-calendar offerings. People presented peace offerings of thanksgiving, vow, and freewill[748] and sin and guilt offerings[749] at any time.

---

[748] Numbers 29:39 with Leviticus 7:15–16

[749] Sin offering (Leviticus 4:13–14, 22–24, 27–28); Guilt offering (Leviticus 6:1–6)

Thanksgiving Offering

The sacrifice of a peace offering was presented with thanksgiving along with unleavened bread and wafers with oil and leavened bread.[750]

Vow Offering

The sacrifice of a peace offering was presented with a vow along with unleavened bread and wafers with oil and leavened bread.[751]

Freewill Offering

The sacrifice of a peace offering was presented with a freewill offering along with unleavened bread and wafers with oil and leavened bread.[752]

Sin Offering

The type of sin offering depended on who had committed the sin, whether it was a priest, the whole congregation, a leader, or an individual. The more prominent people or congregation paid a higher-priced offering, and the poorer individuals paid a lower-priced offering.[753]

Guilt Offering

The guilt offering depended on the offense. If it caused monetary value, the offender had to fully pay back the

---

[750] Leviticus 7:11–15
[751] Leviticus 7:16–18
[752] Leviticus 7:16–18
[753] Leviticus 4 & 5:6–7, 11

amount plus 20 percent.[754] He also had to offer an animal without defect, its value according to how wealthy he was.[755]

We have looked at the purpose for the Old Testament Sacrifices, where they are to be offered, how they are made up, a description of what they are, and when they are offered. As stated before, the Old Testament sacrifices were not carried out to earn one's way to heaven, but the way for God's people who are sinful to have fellowship with Holy God. In the redemptive process, the focus is much more on the cleansing of justified sinners than on the cross. The following lesson is about the Seven Biblical Feasts. To view the chart for this section, go to https://rbeteach71.wixsite.com/justified-sinners/charts.

---

[754]   Leviticus 5:16; 6:5
[755]   Leviticus 5:6–7, 11; 6:6

STUDY C: SEVEN BIBLICAL FEASTS

M oses wrote the first five books of the Old Testament. They instructed the people of Israel to celebrate seven yearly feasts.[756] **These Seven Biblical Feasts point toward the 1st and 2nd Coming of Jesus. The first three feasts look forward to His 1st Coming.** The *Passover* looks towards Jesus as the Passover lamb. The *Feast of Unleavened Bread* is about the removal of sin. Leaven is associated with sin. Jesus is the unleavened bread, who lived a sinless life, and believers take part in His life. The *Feast of First Fruits* looks forward to Jesus' resurrection. He is the first of all believers who will be resurrected and will be transformed to be like Him.

The Feast of Weeks anticipates the inauguration of the Church. The *Feast of Weeks* is also called the Day of Pentecost. It is when the Holy Spirit indwelt the believers.

The last three feasts point toward His 2nd Coming. The *Feast of Trumpets* looks forward to Israel's future regathering at the end of the Tribulation period. The *Day of Atonement* is Israel's national repentance, conversion, and cleansing when Jesus returns, based on His death at His 1st

---

[756] Leviticus chapter 23

Coming. The *Feast of Tabernacles* is also called the *Feast of Booths*. It pictures the restoration of Israel's kingdom God has prepared for them when their Messiah returns and they receive Him.[757] It is their millennial joy and peace after cleansing[758] when Jesus, the second person of the Triune God, bodily lives among His people[759] and the Holy Spirit indwells Israel.[760]

Seven Biblical Feasts—Passover

The three Spring Feasts are interrelated: the Passover, the Feast of Unleavened Bread, and the Feast of First Fruits. The Passover[761] is the first feast, the feast of Israel's deliverance from slavery.

It is celebrated every year at sundown on the 14th day of the first month,[762] Nisan. On the tenth of the month, every man would take a lamb for his household, a year-old male without defect. On sundown of the fourteenth, everyone in the nation was to kill it and prepare it. The lamb would

---

[757] Zechariah 12:10–13:1 (Israel's response to Jesus' return); see Isaiah 35 (millennial blessings). The feast will be celebrated with Jews and Gentile nations (Zechariah 14:16–19).

[758] Zechariah 14 (vs. 1–7 and 12–15 talk about Jesus 2nd Coming and judgment, and the rest talks about the millennial blessings amidst Jesus' rule).

[759] Ezekiel 37:23, 27; Zechariah 2:10 with Psalm 2:6 & Zechariah 14:16–17

[760] Ezekiel 36:26–27; 39:29

[761] Lord's Passover (Leviticus 23:5); Feast of the Passover (Exodus 34:25)

[762] Exodus 12:6; Numbers 28:16

be roasted whole over the fire,[763] and no bones could be broken.[764] It was to be eaten with bitter herbs and unleavened bread.[765] If any of the lamb was leftover the next morning, it had to be burned.[766]

When God was delivering the people of Israel from Egypt, He brought ten plagues on the Egyptians. The tenth plague was the death of the firstborn. Before the final plague, Moses told each household of the people of Israel to take a year-old lamb without defect and kill it. They were to smear its blood on the two sides and top of their front doorway. Then, the inhabitants were to be inside the house.[767] God traveled throughout the land of Egypt that night, killing all the firstborn in the land of Egypt, both of man and livestock. He passed over the households that had the blood of the Passover lamb over the front doorways and whose inhabitants were inside the house.[768] The Passover was celebrated the night the people of Israel came out of Egypt under cover of darkness.[769] Pharaoh let them go because God had killed all the firstborn of the Egyptians and their livestock.[770] That night and the next day, a great multitude who had been

---

763   Exodus 12:3, 5–6, 8–9
764   Exodus 12:46
765   Exodus 12:8
766   Exodus 12:10
767   Exodus 12:3, 5–7, 21–23
768   Exodus 11–13, 26–27, 29–32
769   Exodus 12:41–42
770   Exodus 11:1, 4–8; 12:29–32

slaves left Egypt triumphantly as the Egyptians were burying the dead bodies of their firstborn.[771]

Jesus is the Passover lamb,[772] who years later was crucified on the Passover.[773] Like the lamb, Jesus was without defect,[774] and when sacrificed,[775] none of His bones were broken.[776] His act of sacrificing Himself[777] paid for the sins of the world.[778] It is the acceptance of His death for us that causes God to **pass over** people's sins[779] because He sees the blood of Jesus covering them instead of their sins.[780]

In the redemptive cycle, the Passover looks at the cross and illustrates how Jesus is the only way. He is the only acceptable sacrifice to God the Father, as His death alone paid for all the sins of the world.

Seven Biblical Feasts—Feast of Unleavened Bread

The Feast of Unleavened Bread is the second of the Spring feasts. The Feast of Unleavened Bread and the Pass-

---

[771] Numbers 33:3–4; Exodus 12:37–38
[772] 1 Corinthians 5:7 with John 1:29
[773] Matthew 26:2; John 19:14–16
[774] Exodus 12:5 with 2 Corinthians 5:21; 1 Peter 1:18–19
[775] John 11:49–53
[776] Exodus 12:46 with John 19:31–33, 36
[777] Hebrews 7:26–27; 9:11–12
[778] Hebrews 9:26; 1 John 2:2
[779] Romans 3:21–26 (**25**)
[780] Hebrews 9:12, 25–26

over are associated with the deliverance from Egypt and the death of the firstborn. At times, they are considered part of the same feast,[781] even though they are distinct. Both remind Israel what God did, liberating them from slavery in the land of Egypt by His strong hand.[782]

The feast begins on sundown, the 14th of the first month, the same time as the Passover, and lasts for seven days, until sundown, the 21st. During this time, people eat unleavened bread,[783] but nothing leavened.[784] On the first day, all the leaven is to be removed from one's house.[785] The first and last day of the feast, they were to do no ordinary work but to gather together.[786] Each day, a food offering was to be presented as a pleasing aroma to the Lord,[787] and a sin offering of one male goat was offered to make atonement for their sin.[788]

The Feast of Unleavened Bread tells how they were thrust out of Egypt at a moment's notice without time to prepare any food for the journey. While traveling, they had to bake

---

781   Luke 22:1

782   Exodus 13:3, 8–9; 23:15

783   Exodus 12:18

784   Exodus 12:20

785   Exodus 12:15, 19

786   Exodus 12:16

787   Numbers 28:24

788   Numbers 28:22

and eat unleavened cakes from the unprepared dough they brought out of Egypt.[789]

Leaven is associated with sin.[790] As the people of Israel were to remove leaven from their houses during this feast, believers are to continuously remove sin from their lives as cleansing to be in fellowship with the Triune God. Eating unleavened bread gives a picture of believers breaking from their previously sinful life and walking holy before God.[791] Jesus is the unleavened bread who lived a sinless life,[792] and believers take part in His life.[793]

In the redemptive cycle, the Feast of Unleavened Bread illustrates that believers need to continually remove sin from their lives as cleansing to be in fellowship with the Triune God.

Seven Biblical Feasts—
Feast of First Fruits

The Feast of First Fruits[794] is the third of the Spring Feasts. Israel was to celebrate and dedicate the entire harvest to

---

[789] Exodus 12:33–34, 37–39

[790] Leaven is like sin, which spreads throughout a person and organization (1 Corinthians 5:6–8). Leaven is likened to malice and wickedness (1 Corinthians 5:8), hypocrisy (Luke 12:1), false doctrine (Galatians 5:7–9), and compared to the wrong teaching of the Pharisees and Sadducees (Matthew 16:6, 12).

[791] 1 Corinthians 5:7–8

[792] knew no sin (2 Corinthians 5:21), did no sin (1 Peter 2:22), and in Him is no sin (1 John 3:5).

[793] John 6:30–33, 35, 48–51

[794] Leviticus 23:9–14

God as His blessing from them. It was to be celebrated the Sunday after the Passover[795] during the Feast of Unleavened Bread. It was the day after the Sabbath,[796] normally considered the sixteenth of the month.

The Feast was carried out in two stages. First, the sheaf or bundle of the barley harvest was to be brought to the priest, and he would wave it before the Lord as a wave offering. People were commanded not to eat of the harvest until the first fruits had been given to the Lord.[797] This symbolized that the first and best belonged to God before Israel reaped the harvest for themselves. Second, a burnt offering of a male lamb without defect was presented to the Lord with its grain and drink offerings.[798] These offerings represented the entire harvest. The first sheaf of barley represents the beginning of the whole harvest and that everything else to come was like the first sheaf.

In the same way that God accepted the first fruits for the entire harvest,[799] Jesus is the first fruit of all believers, whom God also accepted. Jesus' resurrection, by the power of the Holy Spirit, is the first fruits of believers,[800] who will be resurrected and will be transformed to be like Him.[801] As the

---

795   Exodus 23:18–19; 34:25–26 with Leviticus 23:11

796   Leviticus 23:11, 15

797   Leviticus 23:14

798   Leviticus 23:9–14

799   Leviticus 23:10; Deuteronomy 18:4; Nehemiah 10:28–29, 35–37

800   1 Corinthians **15:20**, 23

801   Philippians 3:20–21; 1 John 3:2

Feast of First Fruits is on a Sunday, Jesus' resurrection was on a Sunday. That is why believers worship on Sunday.

In the redemption cycle, the Feast of First Fruits looks toward the resurrection. Jesus' resurrection is the first fruit of all believers who will be resurrected and will be transformed to be like Him.

Seven Biblical Feasts—Feast of Weeks (Day of Pentecost)

The Feast of Weeks is known as the Day of Pentecost.[802] It is not part of the Spring Feasts or the Fall Feasts. It is in between, just as the Church Age is between the 1st and 2nd Coming of Jesus.

The Day of Pentecost is seven weeks[803] after the Feast of First Fruits[804] and is celebrated for one day.[805] All the people of the nation[806] were to gather together and do no work.[807]

---

[802] The Feast of Weeks (Exodus 34:22) was called the Day of Pentecost in the New Testament (Acts 2:1). The Feast of Weeks was also called Feast of Harvest (Exodus 34:22 with 23:16) and the Day of First Fruits (Numbers 28:26 – also called the Feast of Weeks). *It is not to be confused with the Feast of First Fruits.*

[803] Pentecost is the Feast of Weeks, or seven sevens. From when the Passover lamb was offered, the day after the following Sabbath when the Feast of the first fruits was celebrated (Exodus 23:18–19; 34:25–26 with Leviticus 23:11), count seven full weeks to the Day of Pentecost (Leviticus 23:15). It is called Pentecost because "you shall count 50 days to the day after the seventh Sabbath…" (Leviticus 23:16).

[804] Leviticus 23:16

[805] Leviticus 23:21; Numbers 28:26

[806] Deuteronomy 16:10–11

[807] Leviticus 23:21; Numbers 28:26

The congregation was to bring various offerings. They were to bring a grain offering[808] of two loaves of leavened bread,[809] a burnt offering of seven one-year-old male lambs, one bull, and two rams, all without defect, along with their grain and drink offerings as a pleasing aroma to the Lord.[810] They were to offer a peace offering of two lambs. Also, a sin offering of a male goat was to be offered to make atonement for their sins.[811]

The Law was given to the people of Israel at about this time.[812] The birth of the Church began on the Day of Pentecost.[813] Just as Israel has become a nation through the gift of the Law, the Church came to exist through the gift of the Holy Spirit.[814] While with His disciples, Jesus said He had to leave so God the Father would send the Spirit to come upon them.[815]

In the redemptive cycle, the Day of Pentecost looks towards the Cleansing of Justified Sinners and the birth of the Church.

---

808   Leviticus 23:21; Numbers 28:26
809   Leviticus 23:17
810   Leviticus 23:18
811   Leviticus 23:19
812   Exodus 19:1, 9–11, 16–20; 20:1–21
813   Acts 1:4–5, 8; chapter 2
814   Acts 2, Joel 2:28
815   John 14:26; 16:7

Seven Biblical Feasts—Feast of Trumpets

The Feast of Trumpets is the first of the Fall feasts. It is celebrated on the first day of the seventh month,[816] which is now the Jewish New Year.[817] Trumpets were used to assemble the congregation of Israel.[818] It was a one-day feast where the congregation of Israel was to gather together. They were not to do any work that day but to present offerings.[819] The burnt offerings were to be one bull, one ram, and seven one-year-old male lambs without defect, with their grain and drink offerings as a pleasing aroma to the Lord. The sin offering was to be a male goat as an atonement for their sin.[820]

The future fulfillment of the Feast of Trumpets was prophesied various times in the Old Testament. It is when God the Father set the time to regather the people of Israel at Jesus' 2nd Coming, at the end of the Tribulation period.[821] The Holy Spirit then brings conviction of sin and acceptance of their Messiah and King whom they rejected and killed at His 1st Coming. It explicitly says it is the gathering of God's elect, or chosen, at this time,[822] which, in context with the other two

---

[816] Leviticus 23:24

[817] It is called Rosh Hashanah

[818] Numbers 10:2

[819] Leviticus 23:24–25

[820] Numbers 29:2–5; 15:8–12 (drink offering)

[821] Matthew 24:29–31

[822] Jeremiah 31:7–13, 17; 32:8, 10, 37

latter feasts, strongly supports the claim it is referring to the nation of Israel.

Seven Biblical Feasts—Day of Atonement

The Day of Atonement[823] is the second of the Fall Feasts. It is celebrated on the tenth day of the seventh month,[824] the holiest day of the year. The purpose of the Day of Atonement is to cleanse the high priest, his family,[825] and the people of Israel from their sins[826] and to cleanse the Tabernacle.[827] All the congregation of Israel is to assemble and do no work.[828] It is the only feast day where the people are required to fast.[829]

This day, once a year, the high priest enters the Holy of Holies to offer atonement on the Mercy Seat for the whole congregation's sins. The high priest bathes in water, then puts on the high priest's garments. First, he offers a bull without

---

[823] Atonement is shedding innocent blood to pay for the sins of the guilty. "For the life of the flesh is in the blood, and I have given it to you upon the altar to make atonement for your souls; for it is the blood that makes atonement for the soul" (Leviticus 17:11). As innocent, perfect sacrifices, animal blood was shed, killed to pay for people's wrong doings (Leviticus 6:7), resulting in forgiveness (Matthew 26:27–28; Ephesians 1:7).

[824] Leviticus 23:27: Numbers 29:7

[825] Leviticus 16:6, 17

[826] Leviticus 16:17, 30

[827] Leviticus 16:16, 20, 33

[828] Numbers 29:7

[829] Leviticus 16:29, 31

defect as a sin offering to make atonement for himself and his household. Then, he brings two goats without defect from the people to the entrance of the Holy Place. He casts lots to see which will be killed as a sin offering and which one will be sent out into the wilderness bearing the sins of the people.

Then, he enters the Holy of Holies three times. First, he takes a censer full of coals of fire from the Altar of Incense with incense and brings it inside the veil so that the cloud of incense covers the Mercy Seat. He enters a second time to sprinkle some of the blood of the bull and sprinkle it with his finger over the Mercy Seat, and in the front of it, he sprinkles some of the blood with his finger seven times. Then, he kills the goat of the sin offering that is for the people and brings its blood inside the veil and does the same as the bull. In this way, he makes atonement for the Holy of Holies because of the congregation's uncleanness and all their sins.

Then, he takes some of the bull's and goat's blood to the Altar of Incense and puts it on the four horns of the altar. He sprinkles some of the blood on it with his finger seven times, cleansing and consecrating it from the uncleanness of the people of Israel. After he atones the Holy Place and the Holy of Holies, he lays both his hands on the live goat. He then confesses over it all the sins of the people of Israel, puts their sins on the goat's head, and sends it away into the wilderness. The goat bears all their sins. The fat of the bull and goat offered as a sin offering is burned on the Brazen Altar, and the rest is carried outside the camp and completely burned.[830] Then, the high priest offers a burnt offering to the Lord as a pleasing aroma.[831] He sacrifices a bull, a ram, and seven one-year-old male lambs. All the animals are to be without defect with their grain and drink offerings.[832]

In the same way the high priest placed the sins of Israel on the scapegoat, God the Father placed the sins of the world on Jesus at the cross. First Corinthians 5:21 says, "He (God the Father) made Him (Jesus) who knew no sin to be sin on our behalf..." You see, God made Jesus guilty by transferring the world's sins to Him. Isaiah explicitly declares this. God took man's sin and put it on His Servant (Jesus).[833]

At His 1st Coming, Jesus partially completed the Day of Atonement as an acceptable sacrifice to God the Father when He, as high priest, entered the Holy of Holies in the heavenly Tabernacle with His blood.[834] He offered Himself there as a sacrifice one time, forever paying for the sins of the world.[835] The future fulfillment of the Day of Atonement

---

[830]   Leviticus 16:3–27

[831]   Numbers 29:8

[832]   Numbers 29:8–10; 15:8–12 (drink offering)

[833]   Isaiah 53:4–6, 10–11

[834]   Hebrews 9:11–12. The blood is the life of a creature (Leviticus 17:11), so Jesus shedding His blood was the innocent Son of God offering the sacrifice of Himself for the sins of the guilty world.

[835]   Hebrews 9:26; 1 John 2:2

is Israel's national conversion and following cleansing at Jesus' 2nd Coming, based on His death at His 1st Coming.[836]

In the redemption cycle, the Day of Atonement looks at the cross, illustrating that Jesus was the perfect sacrifice, paying for the sins of the world.

Seven Biblical Feasts—Feast of Tabernacles

The Feast of Tabernacles, also known as the Feast of Booths,[837] is the last Fall feast. It is observed on the fifteenth of the seventh month for eight days[838] to celebrate the bringing in of the harvest.[839] The people of Israel are to rejoice, remembering how God has provided for them by blessing their crops.[840] During that time, the whole nation is to dwell in tents, also called booths,[841] made from fresh branches of leafy trees.[842] It is to remind the people of Israel that God took care of them in the wilderness after He brought them out of Egypt.[843] Throughout those forty years, Israel lived

---

[836] Hebrews 9:23–**28** with Matthew 23:37–39 (Jesus won't return until the nation of Israel as a whole acknowledges and turns to Him as their King and Savior they previously rejected and killed); Zechariah 12:10–13:1

[837] The Feast of Tabernacles (Leviticus 23:34; Zechariah 14:16) is also called Feast of Booths in some translations. Feast of ingathering (Exodus 23:16).

[838] Leviticus 23:34

[839] Leviticus 23:39

[840] Deuteronomy 16:15; Leviticus 23:40

[841] Leviticus 23:42

[842] Leviticus 23:40

[843] Leviticus 23:43

in tents,[844] and God lived in their midst in a tent, too, the Tabernacle.[845]

Every seven years, all the people of Israel and any foreigners in their midst are to assemble for the feast so the Law can be publicly read to them.[846] Daily offerings are presented. Burnt offerings were offered daily of bulls, rams, and lambs without defect and their grain and drink offerings. A goat was offered for the sin offering.[847]

According to the chart, we can see that the sin offering is the same every single day, but the burnt offerings change depending on the day. First, let's look at the bull. On the first day, they offered thirteen bulls, but every day, they took away one bull; towards on the seventh day, they just had seven bulls, and on the eighth day, they offered one. With the ram, the first seven days, they offered two rams, and on the last day, they offered one. Same with the male year-old lambs. They offered fourteen-year-old male lambs the first seven days, and on the last day, they offered seven.

---

844   Leviticus 23:43
845   Leviticus 26:11 with Numbers 2:2–31
846   Deuteronomy 31:10–13
847   Numbers 29:12–38

Burnt offerings	Bull	Ram	Year-old male lamb	Sin offering–goat
Day 1	13	2	14	1
Day 2	12	2	14	1
Day 3	11	2	14	1
Day 4	10	2	14	1
Day 5	9	2	14	1
Day 6	8	2	14	1
Day 7	7	2	14	1
Day 8	1	1	7	1

The future fulfillment of the Feast of Tabernacles is during the Millennium[848] after the 2nd Coming of Jesus. It has to do with cleansing. It looks forward to sinful saints living among Holy God. At this time, Jesus, the second person of the Triune God, bodily lives among His people, and the Holy Spirit indwells Israel. Every year, all the nations of the world will be required to worship Jesus in Jerusalem and bring their sacrifices to Him at the Feast of Tabernacles. If

---

[848] Ezekiel 45:25

they do not, God will withhold rain from their land.[849] Even though redeemed mankind is in close fellowship with Holy God during this time, he is still a sinner and needs to be continually cleansed to be in fellowship with Holy God.

In the redemption cycle, the Feast of Tabernacles illustrates how justified sinners need to be continually cleansed to be in fellowship with Holy God. Now that we have examined the Tabernacle, the Old Testament Sacrifices, and the Seven Biblical Feasts, we will see how these also relate to the biblical doctrines and fit as a unified whole in the redemptive cycle. To view the chart for this section, go to https://rbeteach71.wixsite.com/justified-sinners/charts.

---

[849] Zechariah 14:16–19

REDEMPTION CYCLE
(LONG)

Introduction: At the beginning of this study, we looked at a bird's eye view of the redemptive cycle, which integrates the biblical doctrines around the Triune God's redeeming mankind, His image-bearers. Today, we are going to put everything together to see how the biblical doctrines, the Tabernacle, the Old Testament Sacrifices, and the Seven Biblical Feasts relate to each other and how they clearly fit as a unified whole in the redemptive cycle. Let's begin.

Overview: Redeeming God's image-bearers. It is the restoration of lost fellowship between God and mankind as His image-bearers[850] due to sin. The redemptive process is made up of a beginning and end, which have to do with fellowship between God and mankind, along with the four stages of the redemptive cycle: sin, the cross, the cleansing of justified sinners, and the resurrection. We are going to look at over twenty biblical doctrines, the Old Testament Sacrifices, the Tabernacle, and Biblical Feasts that relate to the redemptive process of where God, from the very beginning to the end of human history, is actively bringing fallen mankind back into

---

[850]   Genesis 1:26–27; 2:7; 9:6

relationship with Him. In the beginning, innocent mankind was made in the image of the Triune God,[851] living in full fellowship with Him.

Theme of God dwelling with mankind: The theme of God living in fellowship or dwelling among His people is repeated throughout the Bible and climaxes in Revelation 21:3 when everything is made new, with sin and death removed. God dwelling with His people is portrayed by the *Tabernacle* and the *Ark of the Covenant.* The Tabernacle depicted God living among His people in the Old Testament. Jesus, as God, also dwelt among His people. "And the Word became flesh and dwelt or tabernacled among us..." (John 1:14)." In the New Testament, the Holy Spirit indwells every believer.[852] As part of the Tabernacle, the Ark of the Covenant was placed in the Holy of Holies. God's presence dwelt there[853] in the midst of His people.[854]

Trinity: The Trinity is the foundation for the redemptive story. The work of the Trinity is seen throughout the redemptive cycle: sin, the cross, the cleansing of justified sinners, and the resurrection. The Triune God is the Trinity

---

[851]   Genesis 1:26–27

[852]   Romans 8:9

[853]   Exodus 25:21–22

[854]   Numbers 2, 3:14–39

or one God in three persons. The Father,[855] Son,[856] and Holy Spirit[857] as distinct persons are each the one same God. Each one has His own distinct will,[858] mind,[859] and emotions.[860]

The Father[861] has certain roles that belong specifically to Him. He is the Source of all things.[862] He is the great initiator.[863] The Father is the Sovereign Ruler over all things,[864] and in the end, all things return to Him so that He might be all in all.[865]

The Son (Jesus) is begotten of the Father[866] and has certain roles that belong specifically to Him. He is our Creator.[867] He holds the universe together.[868] He is the God-man.[869] He is our Savior,[870] and we will look at this more

---

855   John 6:27

856   John 1:1–3, 18

857   Acts 5:3–4, 9

858   Father's will (John 6:38); Son's will (Luke 22:41–44); Holy Spirit's will (Acts 16:6)

859   Father's mind (1 Corinthians 2:11); Son's mind (1 Corinthians 2:16); Holy Spirit's mind (Romans 8:27)

860   Father's emotions (Luke 3:21–22); Son's emotions (Hebrews 5:7); Holy Spirit's emotions (Ephesians 4:30)

861   1 Corinthians 8:6

862   Acts 17:24–31

863   Matthew 28:18 (implied passively by coming from the Father: see John 17:1–2); Ephesians 1:17–23

864   1 Timothy 6:15–16

865   1 Corinthians 15:24–28

866   John 1:14, 18

867   John 1:3; Colossians 1:16

868   Hebrews 1:3; Colossians 1:17

869   Philippians 2:6–7

870   Matthew 1:21; John 3:17

in-depth later on, but He is also our Judge. The Father passed the judgment onto the Son.[871] Jesus is the judge of the righteous and the wicked.[872]

The **Holy Spirit** is the Spirit of the Father and of the Son,[873] yet is distinct from them, having His own will, mind, and emotions, and proceeds from the Father.[874] The Holy Spirit has certain roles that belong specifically to Him. He convicts the world of sin.[875] He seals the believers for the day of redemption.[876] He gives them assurance that they are children of God.[877] He intercedes for them to the Father.[878] And He uses the Bible to confront and speak to their innermost being, including the hidden thoughts and intentions of their hearts.[879]

The Father, Son, and Holy Spirit possess the same attributes. They are eternal.[880] They are all-knowing.[881] They are

---

[871] John 5:22, 27

[872] John 5:25–29

[873] Romans 8:9

[874] John 15:26

[875] He convicts believers and non-believers alike (John 16:8)

[876] Ephesians 1:13–14 (Upon believing in Jesus, the Holy Spirit is given to indwell the believer, waiting for the day when he is resurrected and conformed to the image of the Triune God. Being sealed by the Holy Spirit acts like a man giving his fiancé an engagement ring, with the future promise of marriage).

[877] Romans 8:15–16

[878] Romans 8:26–27

[879] Hebrews 4:12

[880] Father (Revelation 1:8); Son (Isaiah 9:6); Holy Spirit (Hebrews 9:14)

[881] Father (1 John 3:20); Son (John 21:17); Holy Spirit (1 Corinthians 2:10)

everywhere at once.[882] They are all-powerful.[883] They are holy.[884] They personify truth.[885] Each person of the Trinity is a giver and sustainer of life,[886] and they are worthy of the same glory.[887] The Trinity, one God in three persons, is best stated in the Great Commission when Jesus told His disciples to baptize in the name of the Father, the Son, and the Holy Spirit.[888] Notice that the word "name" is singular, yet there are three persons.

God-man: Jesus (Son) is the 2nd person of the Trinity, and we will look at Him more in-depth later on. Jesus is the God-man.

Image-bearers: The image of God, the Image of the Triune God, was breathed into man when he was created. When God made man and woman on the sixth day, He said, "Let us make man in Our image, after Our likeness. And let them..."[889] Genesis 2:7 says, "God formed the man of dust from the ground and breathed into his nostrils the breath of life, and man became a living being." God's very image resides

---

882   Son (Matthew 18:20, 28:20); Father and the Holy Spirit (Psalm 139:1, 7–10)

883   Son (Matthew 28:18); Father and Spirit (Isaiah 40:13–18)

884   Plurality in one (Isaiah 6:3, 8); Father (Revelation 4:8); Son (Mark 1:24); Holy Spirit (Ephesians 4:30)

885   Son and Father (John 1:14); Son (John 14:6); Holy Spirit and Father (John 15:26)

886   Father and Son (John 5:21); Son (Hebrews 1:3); Holy Spirit (Romans 8:11)

887   Father and Son (John 17:1, 5); Holy Spirit (1 Peter 4:14)

888   Matthew 28:19 (one name = one essence, yet this one essence consists of three distinct persons)

889   Genesis 1:26

in man, the image of the Father,[890] the image of the Son,[891] and the image of the Holy Spirit.[892] Man is God's highest creation.[893] When God made mankind, the world was perfect.[894] There was no sin. There was no concept of death.[895]

Let us look at the four phases of the redemptive cycle.

1. Sin: Sin and broken fellowship, the first stage of the redemptive process. But then man rebelled, sinning against God.[896] The image of God became distorted. The Fall resulted in a broken relationship between God and mankind. Because Adam disobeyed, he and Eve were removed from the Garden of Eden.[897] He took on a sin nature, corrupting the image of God within him. Adam passed on this sin nature, this natural tendency to do wrong and rebel against God[898] to every one of his descendants throughout the entire human race.[899] This is called the *imputation of sin*. Every man, woman, and child from the time of Adam until the end of human history possesses a sin nature. They inherit this sin nature

---

890   James 3:9
891   Romans 8:29; Philippians 3:20–21
892   2 Corinthians 3:18
893   Genesis 1:28
894   Genesis 1:31
895   Romans 5:12
896   Genesis 3:6
897   Genesis 3:22–24
898   Isaiah 53:6; Romans 3:10–12
899   Romans 5:18–19

by birth[900] in the same way one inherits one's parents, one inherits one's last name. People are born with the tendency to sin, and people commit sins. Because of this, they have a broken relationship towards God and cannot come back to Him on their own terms.[901] God is holy, God is perfect, and God cannot tolerate sin in His presence. So, mankind is separated from God forever. There is no good work anyone can do to earn God's favor because God's standards are perfect. Romans 3:23 says, "For all have sinned and fallen short of the glory of God." No one meets God's holy standard. So, no one can come to God in and of himself. Mankind is condemned from birth. I believe there is an age of accountability. God will not hold people accountable for sins they commit until they develop the capacity to accept or reject truth about Him. But everybody is born in sin, and everyone is going to hell unless God intervenes.[902]

2. Cross: The cross, the second stage of the redemptive process. The cross is the price of redemption. John 3:16 says, "God so loved the world that He gave His only begotten Son, that whosoever believeth in Him will not perish, but have everlasting life." God so loved the world that He had a plan. The Triune God had a plan to bring mankind back

---

[900]   Psalm 51:5

[901]   Ephesians 2:8–9

[902]   John 3:16

into restoration with Him.[903] His plan is carried out through the second person of the Trinity, Jesus. John 14:6 says, "I am the way, the truth, and the life. No one. No one comes to the Father but by Me." Every concept we will look at in salvation has to do with Jesus as the only way. And we are going to look at the different steps to see why this is true according to the Bible.

First, let's look at the *Atonement*. In the Old Testament, people were to bring animal sacrifices to God. They were to be healthy, they were to be of a certain age, they were to be without defect, and they were to be killed for sinful mankind. The idea is that innocent life shed its blood to pay for the sins of the guilty. As innocent, perfect sacrifices, animal blood was shed, killed to pay for people's wrongdoings.[904] That sums up the entire *sacrificial system,* and it looks forward to Jesus, who would be the perfect sacrifice. Jesus is the *Passover* lamb,[905] who was crucified on the Passover.[906] His act of sacrificing Himself[907] paid for the sins of the world.[908] It is the acceptance of His death for us that causes God the Father to **pass over** people's sins[909] because He sees the

---

903 1 Peter 1:18–20
904 Leviticus 6:7
905 1 Corinthians 5:7 with John 1:29
906 Matthew 26:2; John 19:14–16
907 Hebrews 7:26–27; 9:11–12
908 Hebrews 9:26; 1 John 2:2
909 Romans 3:21–26 (**25**)

blood of Jesus covering them instead of their sins.[910] This was foreshadowed in the Old Testament when God delivered the enslaved people of Israel from the Egyptians. God traveled throughout the land of Egypt, killing all the firstborn, but passed over the households that had the Passover lamb's blood smeared on their doorway and whose inhabitants were inside the house.[911]

The Atonement is further illustrated by the *Day of Atonement* and the *Brazen Altar.* Once a year in Israel on the Day of the Atonement, the high priest shed the blood of sin offerings for himself and God's people.[912] He entered the Holy of Holies and sprinkled the blood on the Mercy Seat in God's presence to cover their sins.[913] A scapegoat was also chosen, and the high priest would lay his hands on it, confessing the sins of Israel over it and transferring their sins to it. The goat would carry all their sins. Then, the goat would be cast out into the wilderness. By bearing the sins of the people, the goat would make atonement for their sins.[914] In the same way the high priest placed the sins of Israel on the scapegoat, God the Father placed the sins of the world on Jesus at the cross. "He (God the Father) made Him (Jesus)

---

[910]   Hebrews 9:12, 25–26
[911]   Exodus 12:3, 6–7, 12–13, 22–23
[912]   Hebrews 9:7
[913]   Leviticus 16:14–15
[914]   Leviticus 16:10, 20–22

who knew no sin to be sin on our behalf..."[915] God made Jesus guilty by transferring the world's sins to Him. Isaiah explicitly declares this. God took man's sin and put it on His Servant (Jesus).[916] The Brazen Altar represents the cross of Jesus, the place of sacrifice.[917]

The Judge and Justifier. God is a holy and just God, and if He were to tolerate sin, He would not be righteous. He would not be holy. So, He sent His Son Jesus as the answer. The Father sent the Son to be the Savior of the world.[918] The Holy Spirit impregnated Mary,[919] who gave birth to the Son of God.[920] Jesus grew up being fully human because of His mother, yet fully God at the same time.[921] He had a human nature like everyone else,[922] except without sin[923] and the natural tendency to sin. He had no sin nature. He became hungry like we do.[924] He became thirsty.[925] He grew tired.[926] He was lonely.[927] He struggled with temptation as much as

---

[915]   2 Corinthians 5:21
[916]   Isaiah 53:4–6, 10–11
[917]   John 1:29 with 1 Peter 2:24
[918]   1 John 4:14
[919]   Matthew 1:18–23
[920]   Luke 1:35
[921]   Philippians 2:6–7
[922]   Hebrews 2:14, 17
[923]   Hebrews 4:15
[924]   Matthew 4:2
[925]   John 4:7
[926]   John 4:6
[927]   Luke 22:15

we have, yet He never sinned.[928] Because He was a sinless man, He could die in man's place.[929] As a sinless man, He redeemed mankind by completing the requirements of God's law for the human race.[930] As God simultaneously,[931] the sacrifice of Himself[932] at the cross paid for the sins of the world.[933] That is why He had to be fully God and fully man because that is the only man who would be born without sin. And the only one who could pay for the sins of the world from the time of Adam until the end of human history. That is why He is the only way. He is the only one who meets that standard of allowing God to be just and justify the sinner.

The *imputation of righteousness* is this. When we believe in Jesus, when we humble ourselves, recognizing we are sinners, believe Jesus died on the cross to take away our sins, and believe that Jesus rose from the dead, God the Father takes our sin nature and sins and places them on Jesus at the cross. God takes Jesus' righteousness and clothes us with it.[934] So God no longer sees us in our sin but Jesus' righteousness in our place.[935] This is how He can be our judge, and He can simultaneously justify us.

---

[928]   Hebrews 4:15

[929]   Philippians 2:7–8; Hebrews 2:17

[930]   Galatians 4:4–5; Matthew 5:17

[931]   John 1:14; Philippians 2:6–7

[932]   Hebrews 7:26–27; 9:11–12

[933]   1 John 2:2

[934]   2 Corinthians 5:21

[935]   Philippians 3:9

Just as mankind was born into sin and has a sin nature without doing anything to earn it, in the same way, any person who believes in Jesus inherits His righteousness.[936] *No one can do anything to earn it but can only receive it by claiming it as a gift.*[937] This is how the imputation of sin and the imputation of righteousness are alike. They are inherited, but they cannot be earned. Anyone who tries to come to God on his own terms will fail because God is a holy God, and He expects perfection. He can only be restored in relationship with God by receiving Jesus' gift of righteousness, not by earning it through good works. Because Jesus died and paid the punishment for sin, He met God's standard of perfection and can take mankind's place. As the God-man, He offered the perfect once-for-all sacrifice of Himself for mankind.[938] It is the Holy Spirit who convicts people of sin and reveals their utter inability to earn God's righteous standard on their own terms.[939]

Jesus as the only way is revealed in various Tabernacle elements: *one gate*, the Candlestick, the Veil, the Mercy Seat, and the High Priest. The temple is made of the outer court, inner, court, and Holy of Holies. There is only one entrance to each,[940] signifying there is only one way to God

---

936   Romans 5:17

937   Ephesians 2:8–9

938   Hebrews 10:10, 12, 14

939   He convicts believers and non-believers alike (John 16:8)

940   Gate entrance to Tabernacle and outer court (Exodus 27:16). Screen as entrance from outer court to inner court/Holy Place (Exodus 26:36–37). Entrance

the Father, which was provided at the cross through Jesus. The *Candlestick* represents Jesus, the light of God.[941] The *Veil* separated the Holy Place from the Holy of Holies,[942] where God's presence dwelt. At Jesus' death, it was torn in two,[943] demonstrating believers have direct access to God the Father's presence[944] through His sacrificial death.[945] The *Veil* is Jesus' flesh.[946] The *Mercy Seat* was the meeting place between Holy God and sinful man. The *Mercy Seat*[947] in the Holy of Holies represents Jesus as the only way for sinful man to meet Holy God and, as a sinner at the same time, be declared righteous before God[948] and enter His presence.[949] Once a year, the high priest sprinkled the blood of sin offerings for himself and God's people on the Mercy Seat to cover

---

from Inner court/Holy Place to Holy of Holies separated by the veil (Exodus 26:31–33).

[941] John 8:12. Jesus fulfills Old Testament promises of the coming of the "light" of salvation and the "light" of God (Isaiah 49:6; Acts 13:47; 26:23)

[942] Exodus 26:31–33

[943] Matthew 27:51

[944] Hebrews 10:19–20

[945] Hebrews 9:11–14, 24–28

[946] Hebrews 10:19–20

[947] Also called the throne of grace in Hebrews 4:16 (God's throne, or place of rule is in the Holy of Holies. It is at the Mercy Seat between the cherubim. [Ezekiel 43:4–8 {**vs 7**}])

[948] Romans 3:23–24; 5:18–19; 2 Corinthians 5:21

[949] Hebrews 10:19–20

their sins.[950] Jesus is the Mercy Seat.[951] [952] He is also the *high priest*[953] who offered the sacrifice for the sins of the people and sprinkled its blood on the Mercy Seat.[954] *The sacrifice He presented to God was Himself.*[955] It was a sacrifice one time, forever paying for the sins of the world.[956]

When we believe in Jesus, the Triune God safeguards our salvation, making sure it isn't lost.

3. Cleansing (Justified Sinners): Part 3 in the redemptive process is the cleansing of justified sinners. There are two aspects to the cleansing of justified sinners: the Church and the individual believers. Let's look first at the *Church. What is its make-up?* When someone accepts Jesus' righteousness, he is baptized by the Holy Spirit into Jesus' body, the Church,[957] and indwelt by the Holy Spirit.[958] God the

---

950   Leviticus 16:2, 14–15 (Hebrews 9:7, 25), 30, 34

951   Wallace, Dan. "Class Notes," NT 105 Exegesis of Romans, Dallas: Dallas Theological Seminary, Fall 2009. (His notes on Romans 3:21–26 says that the correct translation for propitiation means Mercy Seat)

952   As the Mercy Seat (Romans 3:25), He is the place for the sin offering of the people in the Holy of Holies (Leviticus 16:2, 14–15).

953   Hebrews 2:17; 8:1. Because he was fully man He was a merciful and high priest who could understand people's struggle with sin's temptations (Hebrews 4:14–15)

954   Hebrews 9:25–26 ("blood of another" was the blood of the bull and goat sprinkled on the Mercy Seat [Leviticus 16:14–15])

955   Hebrews 7:26–27; 9:11–12

956   Propitiation is sacrifice (1 John 4:10). His sacrifice of Himself takes away the sins of the world (Hebrews 9:26; 1 John 2:2).

957   1 Corinthians 12:13

958   1 Corinthians 6:19; Ephesians 1:13–14

Father placed Jesus as head of the Church,[959] which began on the *Day of Pentecost*.[960] The future reality is that the Church will become one, just as the Father and the Son are one, and the Church will be unified with the Trinity.[961] The Church is made up of everyone who believes that Jesus died for their sins and accepted His punishment for their sins in place of their own, that He rose from the dead, and that He is God. When they turn to Jesus, their sin nature is crucified with Him on the cross, and they are resurrected with Him.[962] This is their position spiritually.

Baptism portrays the beginning and end of the Christian life, where we died to sin at the cross and the resurrection, where we are raised with Jesus in the heavenly places,[963] our current position in Him and our future reality. We are baptized in the name of the Triune God.[964]

Now that people are children of God, they are saints, but they are sinners simultaneously.[965] They have put on the nature of Jesus and the Triune God,[966] but they still retain the sin nature.[967] They are justified sinners, and they need

---

[959] Ephesians 1:17, 20–23

[960] Acts 1:4–5; chapter 2

[961] John 17:21–23

[962] Romans 6:3–6

[963] Ephesians 2:4–6

[964] Matthew 28:19

[965] Romans 3:22–24

[966] 2 Peter 1:4

[967] Galatians 5:16–17; Romans 7:25b; 8:4

to be cleansed continually to be able to be in fellowship with the Triune God.

Communion looks at the Christian life as an ongoing process or the middle. It is a corporate cleansing and an individual cleansing. As people take part in the bread and the cup, representing the body and blood of Jesus,[968] they remember His death and what it does for believers. And people who take Communion in an unworthy manner, when they are not in a right relationship with God and they are consciously sinning against other people, are eating and drinking judgment to themselves.[969] So Communion acts as a cleansing process, where people need to settle accounts with God and settle accounts with their brothers and sisters in Jesus so they can come to God with a clean conscience and not be judged while participating. Communion also looks forward to God the Father setting up His earthly kingdom,[970] where Jesus is world ruler[971] and the Holy Spirit indwells God's people.[972]

Baptism and Communion are the two rituals practiced by the Church. The *functions of the Church* are to glorify God the Father[973] and build up Jesus' body to spiritual maturity,[974]

---

[968] 1 Corinthians 10:16; Luke 22:17

[969] 1 Corinthians 11:27–30

[970] Daniel 2:35, 44 with 7:13–14, 27

[971] Zechariah 9:9–10; 14:9, 16–17

[972] Ezekiel 36:26–27; 39:29

[973] Ephesians 1:5–6, 12, 14; 3:21

[974] Ephesians 4:7, 11–16

empowered by the Holy Spirit. All the members, not just its leadership, are to serve the Church and to do ministry outside it, proclaiming the name of Jesus. The Holy Spirit at will give *spiritual gifts* to people to build up the Church to maturity and to do the work of the ministry.[975]

We looked at the Church regarding cleansing to be in fellowship with Holy God. Now, let us look to individual believers concerning cleansing and justified sinners. As we talked about before, we have taken on Jesus' nature, the Triune nature, but we still possess the sin nature. We have a battle of two natures within us, and one is our master.[976] Whichever one we submit to takes control. We can submit to the works of the flesh, and we can be under its authority, or we can submit to the Holy Spirit and live out the fruit of the Spirit and be under the Spirit's authority,[977] but we are not in control of ourselves. One of the two natures is going to control us and we have to decide on a daily, hourly, even a minute basis at times who is going to be in control. This is part of the sanctification process when we are becoming conformed to the image of Jesus.[978]

The sanctification process is where we become increasingly dependent on God instead of our own efforts, attitudes, experiences, decisions, and will. In the same way, a debilitat-

---

[975]   1 Corinthians 12:4–11

[976]   Romans 6:12–13, 16–20, 22

[977]   Galatians 5:16–23

[978]   2 Corinthians 3:18

ing disease takes over an individual, and they have to receive increasing care as time goes on. They have to give up more and more control of themselves. This is what God desires of us, to make us increasingly dependent on Him. This is how He can deal with the sin nature within us and conform us to the image of Jesus, really the image of the Triune God.

As seen in the chart, there are various subjects that sanctification addresses: dependence, removal of sin, cleansing, an advocate, and motivation, along with their biblical topics.

Under dependence, the *Table of Shewbread* represents Jesus, the Bread of God.[979] Jesus is our daily bread, and we are dependent on Him for our daily needs.[980] We are dependent on Him in place of ourselves to live the Christian life. In regards to removal of sin, the *Feast of Unleavened Bread* was a yearly feast that would last a week. Eating unleavened bread gives a picture of believers breaking from their previously sinful life and walking holy before God.[981] This is visualized by an absence of leaven, as associated with sin.[982] Jesus is the unleavened bread who lived a sinless life,[983] and

---

[979]   John 6:30–33, **35, 48–51**

[980]   Matthew 6:11

[981]   1 Corinthians 5:7–8

[982]   Leaven is like sin, which spreads throughout a person and organization (1 Corinthians 5:6–8). Leaven is likened to malice and wickedness (1 Corinthians 5:8), hypocrisy (Luke 12:1), false doctrine (Galatians 5:7–9), and compared to the wrong teaching of the Pharisees and Saducees (Matthew 16:6, 12).

[983]   Knew no sin (2 Corinthians 5:21), did no sin (1 Peter 2:22), and in Him is no sin (1 John 3:5).

believers take part of or participate in His life.[984] Concerning the subject of cleansing, we see four topics: the Laver, Communion, the Old Testament Sacrifices, and the Feast of Tabernacles. One of the Tabernacle's furniture was the **Laver**. It contained water for just the priests to wash their hands and feet, probably as a ceremonial washing before they went to the tent of meeting or altar to minister.[985] In the New Testament, the Laver stands for cleansing or sanctifying believers through the washing of water by the Word. Jesus is the Word of God[986] who transforms believers through His Word and the Holy Spirit so that He may present the Church as holy and blameless before God the Father.[987] **Communion**, as before mentioned is used as a heart cleansing to be in fellowship with Holy God. The *Old Testament sacrifices* were offered for God's people to live in relationship with their Creator, who is holy. The sin offerings could never take away sin.[988] 'All they could do was to point to one who could. But they illustrated a very important point: the death of an innocent life is required to satisfy a Holy God's wrath against sinners. Old Testament sins were passed over when people offered acceptable sacrifices to God by faith because they

---

984   John 6:30–33, 35, 48–51
985   Exodus 30:18–21
986   John 1:1–2, 14
987   Ephesians 5:25–27
988   Hebrews 10:4, 11

looked forward to Jesus' perfect sacrifice of Himself.[989] In the redemptive process, the sacrificial system is much more focused on the Cleansing of Justified Sinners than it is on the cross.

The ***Feast of Tabernacles*** also has to do with cleansing, for its future fulfillment is during the Millennium.[990] It looks forward to sinful saints living among Holy God. At this time, Jesus, the second person of the Triune God, bodily lives among His people, and the Holy Spirit indwells them. Every year, all the nations of the world will be required to worship Jesus in Jerusalem and bring their sacrifices to Him at the Feast of Tabernacles. If they don't, God will withhold rain from their land.[991] Even though redeemed mankind is in close fellowship with Holy God during this time, he is still a sinner and needs to be continually cleansed to be in fellowship with Holy God.

Involving an advocate, the ***Altar of Incense*** represents Jesus, our Intercessor who advocates for us to God the Father when we sin.[992] Psalm 141:2 says incense are the prayers of the saints.[993]When believers pray, they are to pray

---

[989]   Romans 3:21–26

[990]   Ezekiel 45:25

[991]   Zechariah 14:16–19

[992]   Jesus is our intercessor (advocate) before the Father (Romans 8:34; 1 John 2:1)

[993]   See also Revelation 8:3–4 with 5:8

to God the Father[994] through the Holy Spirit,[995] in the name of Jesus.[996]

And the last subject of Sanctification is motivation. **_Eternal rewards_** are given as motivation to help believers strive under the empowerment of the Holy Spirit to do what is right and do good works. There is nothing anyone can do to earn God's favor and go to heaven on one's own terms.[997] It is not an issue of being good or bad. It is an issue of relying on Jesus' gift or rejecting His gift. Our good works do not earn our way to heaven, but our good works do determine the quality of life we will experience in heaven.[998] The Bible says that we will be given eternal rewards. Over a hundred different verses and passages talk about eternal rewards. And while it is not the most important topic in Scripture, it is a very important motivation to make us want to set our eyes on our future home instead of our temporary home, our current reality. One can earn five different crowns while living this life on earth. An imperishable crown is rewarded for running the spiritual race, disciplining oneself to serve Jesus for the duration of the race.[999] A crown of righteousness is for those who long for Jesus' return.[1000] A crown of

---

[994]   Matthew 6:9–13

[995]   Romans 8:26

[996]   John 14:13–14

[997]   Ephesians 2:8–9

[998]   Matthew 20:25–27; Mark 10:42–44

[999]   1 Corinthians 9:24–27

[1000]   2 Timothy 4:7–8

life is for those who endure trials because of their love for God[1001] and for those who endure to the point of dying as a martyr.[1002] A crown of glory is given to those who faithfully shepherd the flock of God.[1003] A crown of rejoicing is given to those who win souls for Jesus.[1004] There are many rewards that one can earn by how he lives, and his quality of life in heaven will be determined by how he serves God from the heart, not selfish gain.[1005] This is an encouragement to strive to look to the future and not to the present because this battle of striving to be close to God and being cleansed as justified sinners is a battle that will be ongoing from the time we accept Jesus Christ as our Lord and Savior until we die. It will never go away during our life because we will always have the two natures within us.

4. Resurrection: The last stage of the redemptive cycle is the resurrection. We revisit Baptism because it looks toward the future reality when we are resurrected and brought into conformity with the image of God when we have no more sin and we are free from our body of sin.

The Feast of First Fruits very clearly reveals how believers' resurrection follows Jesus' resurrection. The Feast of First Fruits was to celebrate and dedicate the entire harvest

---

[1001] James 1:12

[1002] Revelation 2:10

[1003] 1 Peter 5:2–4

[1004] 1 Thessalonians 2:19–20

[1005] Matthew 6:2–4, 5–6, 16–18

to God as His blessing from them. In the same way that God accepted the first fruits for the entire harvest,[1006] Jesus is the first fruits of all believers, whom God also accepted. Jesus' resurrection is the first fruits of believers,[1007] who will be conformed to His image[1008] and the image of the Triune God.

There are *two general resurrections*. Remember that Jesus is Judge.[1009] He is the Savior[1010] and the judge. The *first resurrection* is the resurrection of the righteous, where Jesus will judge all the righteous. This is when they will receive eternal rewards. He will reward people according to how they lived.[1011] He will expose the sin of the people who belong to Him if they have not confessed their sin[1012] and He has confronted them,[1013] but they will go to heaven. They will all be cleansed and brought into His presence. There will be a period of 1,000 years where Jesus will reign on earth. And then there will be the *second resurrection*. This is the resurrection of the wicked, where everybody from the time of Adam until the end of the world will be judged for their evil deeds and for their rejection of God's message of salva-

---

[1006] Leviticus 23:10; Deuteronomy 18:4; Nehemiah 10:28–29, 35–37
[1007] 1 Corinthians **15:20**, 23
[1008] Philippians 3:20–21; 1 John 3:2
[1009] John 5:22, 27–29
[1010] Matthew 1:21; John 3:17
[1011] 1 Corinthians 3:10–15; 2 Corinthians 5:10
[1012] 1 John 1:9
[1013] 1 Corinthians 4:5; 2 Corinthians 5:10

tion. And every one of those will be thrown into hell[1014] along with the demonic host and Satan himself,[1015] who will be tormented forever.[1016]

End: In the *Eternal State,* mankind is in restored fellowship with God.[1017] The Triune God redeemed sinful mankind made in His image and restored fellowship with him. In the Eternal State, all the righteous will be in heaven and the wicked in hell, humanity and the demonic host, death will be eliminated,[1018] and Jesus will reign with perfected humanity who has been conformed to His image. There will be no more sorrow or pain, and God will dwell among His people.[1019] In the Garden of Eden, God dwelt among His people. Because of sin, that fellowship was broken, and God has been working throughout the entire human history to bring sinful mankind back to Himself.

This is what the *Tabernacle* represents: God dwelling among His people. We see this in the Eternal State when mankind will have the restored fellowship with the Triune God, living forever in His presence, free of any sin, free of any death. The redemptive cycle is Sin, the Cross, the Cleansing of Justified Sinners, and the Resurrection. It is where the

---

1014   Revelation 20:11–15
1015   Matthew 25:41
1016   Revelation 20:10
1017   Revelation 21:3
1018   1 Corinthians 15:26
1019   Revelation 21:3–4

Triune God is working to restore lost fellowship with sinful mankind, His image-bearers, so He can dwell with them throughout eternity. This is redeeming God's image-bearers.

Where does an understanding of *redeeming God's image-bearers* take us? The realization that, as justified sinners, we need to be increasingly conformed to the image of the Triune God. This leads us to our final lesson in part one: *be sanctified.* To view the chart for this section, go to https://rbeteach71.wixsite.com/justified-sinners/charts.

BE SANCTIFIED

S anctification is an essential theme in the Christian life, and many biblical topics address it. But before we examine these, we need to understand what sanctification is and why it matters. First, sanctification is becoming conformed to the image of Jesus. The sanctification process is where we become increasingly dependent on God instead of our own efforts, attitudes, experiences, decisions, and will. In the same way, a debilitating disease takes over an individual, and they have to receive increasing care as time goes on. They have to give up more and more control of themselves. This is what God desires of us, to make us increasingly dependent on Him.

Second, why does sanctification matter? We, as Christians, are not in control of ourselves. As believers, we have taken on Jesus' nature, the Triune nature, but we still possess the sin nature. We have a *battle of two natures* within us, and one is our master.[1020] Whichever one we submit to takes control. We can submit to the works of the flesh, and we can be under its authority, or we can submit to the Holy Spirit and live out the fruit of the Spirit and be under the

---

[1020]   Romans 6:12–13, 16–20, 22

Spirit's authority,[1021] but we are not in control of ourselves. One of the two natures is going to control us, and we have to decide on a daily, hourly, even a minute basis at times who is going to be in control. This is why we need the sanctification process to become conformed to the image of Jesus.[1022]

In this study, redeeming God's image-bearers, sanctification plays out in five areas: dependence, removal of sin, cleansing, advocate, and motivation. First, our need for dependence on God is illustrated through the Tabernacle furniture, the Table of Shewbread. Second, our call for the removal of sin is demonstrated through the Biblical Feast of Unleavened Bread. Third, our status as justified sinners in the presence of Holy God requires cleansing, as portrayed through the Tabernacle furniture, the Laver, Communion, Old Testament sacrifices, and the Biblical Feast of Tabernacles. Fourth, our sin necessitates an advocate, as illustrated in the Tabernacle furniture, the Altar of Incense. And fifth, while our motivation for becoming conformed to the image of God primarily comes from our love for God, it is also fueled by Eternal Rewards, which is investing in our heavenly home over our earthly home. Sanctification is an essential theme to the Christian life because God is holy, and His people, who are justified sinners, need to be in a right relationship to be in fellowship with Him.

[1021] Galatians 5:16–23

[1022] 2 Corinthians 3:18

Sanctification is an ongoing battle from the beginning until the end of the Christian walk. Paul encourages us in this struggle when he writes in Philippians 1:6, "He who began a good work in you will continue it until the day of Christ Jesus." This is when we are in heaven with Him.

In this study, we will shift our focus from the four stages of the redemptive cycle to the end times. Before looking at the following lessons, we will briefly look at a framework on how to view the end times. To view the chart for this section, go to https://rbeteach71.wixsite.com/justified-sinners/charts.

END TIMES FRAMEWORK

T his study is separated into two sections: the *redemptive process* and the *end times framework*. First, we will look at the redemptive process, then see how the end times framework relates to it. The redemptive process has four stages: Sin, the Cross, the Cleansing of Justified Sinners, which have to do with the Church and individual believers, and the Resurrection. Let's look at it a little more in-depth.

In the redemptive process, we are going to look at redeeming God's image-bearers, which is the restoration of lost fellowship between God and mankind due to sin. In the beginning, God made mankind perfect, without sin.[1023] He had full fellowship with the Triune God. But then the Fall came. Adam and Eve disobeyed God[1024] and brought sin into the world,[1025] breaking fellowship, not only between themselves and God but between God and all of humankind, all of their descendants throughout human history.[1026] Because God loves mankind, He did not want them to be separated

---

[1023] Genesis 1:31
[1024] Genesis 3:6
[1025] Romans 5:12
[1026] Romans 5:18–19

from Him forever and go to hell.[1027] So, He worked to save mankind at the cross. The cross was the price of redemption. Once mankind believes in God's provision of salvation through Jesus Christ, he becomes part of the family of God.[1028] He is a saint, and he is a sinner, and he needs to be continually cleansed to be in fellowship with Holy God. We see this in the Church, and we see this in individual believers. After the stage of the Cleansing of Justified Sinners comes the Resurrection. And mankind again is in fellowship with Holy God, without any sin, and death is gone.[1029] The fellowship is fully restored.[1030] We have looked at the redemptive process through the previous lessons. But now we are going to look at how it fits with the end times.

We are going to study the end times through the following framework that you see on this chart and, at the same time, understand how it relates to the redemptive cycle. First, we are going to take a look at Daniel's seventy weeks, as this puts all the major events of the end times on a timeline. Then, we are going to look at the concept of the 1st Coming when Jesus came at the cross. In the end times framework, we are going to ask five key questions that define one's position on future biblical events.

[1027]   John 3:16

[1028]   John 1:12

[1029]   1 Corinthians 15:26

[1030]   Revelation 21:3

First, is Jesus' return literal? Is Jesus physically returning to the earth or not? And second, if He is physically returning, is His return future, or has it already happened? Your position on Jesus' literal return and future return determines whether or not you are part of Orthodox Christianity, which means what all Christians everywhere at all times believe. If you do not believe that Jesus' return is literal and you do not believe that Jesus' return is future, then you believe false doctrine. Having looked at these first two questions, this brings us to two concepts: the 2nd Coming and the two general resurrections. If Jesus is physically returning and He is returning in the future, that's the 2nd Coming. And when He returns, He will return to judge the righteous and the wicked. These are the two general resurrections. At the judgment of the righteous, He will give eternal rewards.

If He is literally returning in the future, the third question we ask is: Is Jesus' return premillennial? Your view on the nature of the Millennium determines your answer on this question. Do you believe that there is no Millennium? Do you believe in Postmillennialism, in which the Church will bring in a glorious age through gradually making it a Christian world, or do you believe that Jesus will literally reign for 1,000 years? The study of the New Covenant supports the Millennial view, for this is when its complete fulfillment takes place. If you believe that Jesus' return is pre-millennial, this brings us to the fourth question. Is the Tribulation going to happen in the future? Are the Old and New Testament prophecies about the Tribulation still awaiting future fulfillment, or have they mainly happened? If you don't believe in the future Tribulation, there is no point in talking about the Rapture because the Rapture is being removed before God pours out His wrath on earth. So the fifth question is, is the Rapture Pre-Tribulation? Does the Rapture happen in the middle of the Tribulation, the end of the Tribulation, or before it starts? We believe it happens before the Tribulation. The Rapture marks the end of the Church Age, which is between Daniel's 69th and 70th week.

These five questions—is Jesus' return literal, is Jesus' return future, is Jesus' return Pre-millennial, is the Tribulation future, and is the Rapture Pre-Tribulation—define one's position on future Biblical events. So, we are going to look at key biblical concepts through this framework. At the end is the Eternal State when mankind is in fellowship with the Triune God again, without sin and without death. The two concepts, the Fall results in spiritual death and the Eternal State, together make up the two bookends in the redemptive cycle. Because the first one is where sin and death are introduced into the world, breaking fellowship with God and mankind, and the second one is where sin and death are removed and mankind is in full fellowship with the Triune God again. As we look at each of these key concepts through the end times, we will see where they fall on the redemptive cycle. To view the chart for this section, go to https://rbe-teach71.wixsite.com/justified-sinners/charts.

STUDY D: DANIEL'S SEVENTY WEEKS

To understand the end times, it helps to see it on a time-line. The timeline we will use is the prophetic clock: Daniel's seventy weeks. First, we will study its purpose. Second, we will understand how it works. Third, we will place the end times biblical concepts of the 1st Coming, the 2nd Coming, the Two General Resurrections, the Millennium, the Tribulation, the Rapture, and the Eternal State on the timeline. Fourth, we will reveal how the Trinity is actively working through it. And fifth, we will look at how under-standing this helps believers today.

The prophetic clock: Daniel's seventy weeks. **First, the purpose of the seventy weeks prophesied in Daniel is God's appointed time of judgment for the nation of Israel.** Because they rebelled against God and broke His covenant with them, He judged them by casting them out of the land and putting foreign rulers over them.[1031] He took away their kingdom. The prophet Jeremiah prophesied they would be in exile for seventy years until the land had recovered its un-kept Sabbaths.[1032]

[1031] Leviticus 26:14–15, 17, 31–33, 38–39; Daniel 9:4–15 (**verses 11 and 13**)

[1032] 2 Chronicles 36:21. See also Leviticus 26:33–35

Near the end of the Babylonian exile, Daniel prayed, confessing the sins of his nation, Israel, and asking God to return His people to their land at the end of seventy years according to God's promise through Jeremiah the prophet.[1033] Daniel prayed to God for three things: to forgive the sins of the nation of Israel, rebuild the city of Jerusalem, and restore the temple.[1034] God sent His messenger Gabriel to tell Daniel that "seventy weeks" of judgment would be decreed for his people, Israel, and their city of Jerusalem. During that time, the nation of Israel and its city, Jerusalem, would be under the control of foreign rulers, called the "Times of the Gentiles."

The "Times of the Gentiles"[1035] is that period of time in which the Promised Land, given by God to Abraham and his descendants, is controlled by foreign rulers, and the Davidic throne is empty of any rightful heir in the line of David.[1036] The "Times of the Gentiles," beginning with Nebuchadnezzar's invasion of Jerusalem in 605 B.C., will continue until the Messiah returns to the earth at the end of the Tribulation Period. During this time, four world empires rule over the nation of Israel: the Babylonian Empire, the Medo-Per-

---

[1033]   Daniel 9:2; Jeremiah 25:11–12
[1034]   Daniel 9:16–19
[1035]   Luke 21:24
[1036]   Hosea 3:4–5

sian Empire, the Greek Empire, and the Roman Empire, including the Revived Roman Empire.[1037]

As stated in Daniel 9:24, God's purpose in decreeing these "seventy weeks" of judgment for the Jews and Jerusalem is six-fold in order to restore the kingdom of Israel and the city of Jerusalem. The first three of these three purposes have to do with sin. First, it will end the transgression, the people of Israel's sin of disobedience against God.[1038] Second, it will end Israel's national sins.[1039] Third, there would be reconciliation for their iniquity. This would be accomplished by offering a sacrifice that would pay for their sins, which was Jesus' death on the cross.[1040] The future fulfillment of the Day of Atonement completes this. It's Israel's national conversion to Jesus, their Messiah, and following cleansing at His 2nd Coming, based on His sacrifice and death at His 1st Coming.[1041] The second three have to do with the kingdom. Fourth, it will inaugurate a new world

---

[1037] Daniel chapters 2, 7

[1038] He will internalize His laws in their hearts (Jeremiah 31:33; Ezekiel 11:19) and place the Holy Spirit within them (Ezekiel 36:26–27; 39:29), enabling them to obey His laws (Ezekiel 36:26–27), and they shall all know the Lord (Isaiah 11:9; Jeremiah 31:34).

[1039] Zechariah 13:1; Romans 11:26–27

[1040] While Jesus died for the sins of the whole world (John 1:29; 1 John 2:2), and the Church (Acts 20:28), He also died for the people of Israel (John 11:44–52).

[1041] Hebrews 9:23–28 with Matthew 23:37–39 (Jesus won't return until the nation of Israel as a whole acknowledges and turns to Him as their king and Savior they previously rejected and killed); Zechariah 12:10–13:1

society known for its everlasting righteousness.[1042] Fifth, the Old Testament prophecies concerning Israel's awaited kingdom will be fulfilled, and Jesus will physically reign over the earth, so there will be no more need for prophets or visions. And sixth, it will result in the anointing of **the most holy**. According to HALOT (the Hebrew Aramaic Lexicon of the Old Testament), the Hebrew phrase קֹדֶשׁ קָדָשִׁים refers to the anointing of the temple.[1043] Since this temple will be restored after the "seventy weeks" of judgment, this is the future Millennial temple.[1044] All six are in answer to Daniel's prayer that His people be forgiven, Jerusalem rebuilt, and the temple restored. This six-fold purpose for the nation of Israel and Jerusalem is completed at the 2nd Coming of Jesus. It establishes Israel's future Millennial kingdom under the authority of her promised King (Jesus), as prophesied through His covenants.[1045] The kingdom of the nation of Israel was lost during the Babylonian exile due to their disobedience towards God's covenant and their rebellion against Him. Their kingdom is restored at Jesus' 2nd Coming

---

[1042] This era of righteousness and justice (Isaiah 9:7; 42:1–4) is because Jesus will enact swift judgment (Malachi 3:5) and rule with a rod of iron over the nations (Psalm 2:8–9 with Revelation 19:15–16).

[1043] Ludwig Koehler et al., *The Hebrew and Aramaic Lexicon of the Old Testament* (Leiden: E.J. Brill, 1994–2000), 1078.

[1044] Ezekiel 37:26, 28; Haggai 2:6–9; Zechariah 6:12–13, 15

[1045] Abrahamic (Genesis 15:18–21), Palestinian - Mosaic (Leviticus 26 with Deuteronomy 30:1–10), Davidic (2 Samuel 7:12–13, 16), and New (Jeremiah 31:31–34) Covenants.

when the entire nation repents of their sin[1046] and embraces their Messiah whom they previously rejected and killed.[1047]

Now that we have comprehended the need for God's appointed time of judgment, we will understand how Daniel's seventy weeks works. **The "seventy weeks" is divided into three sections: seven weeks, sixty-two weeks, and one week.** Each week is not a week of days. It is a week of years. Each week represents seven years, so the seventy weeks represent 490 years of judgment. *The seven* weeks (or forty-nine years) began in 444 B.C. with the decree to rebuild and restore Jerusalem.[1048] Scripture records four decrees concerning the rebuilding of Jerusalem. The first was Cyrus' decree to rebuild the temple in 538 B.C.[1049] The second was Darius I's decree in 512 B.C., confirming Cyrus' earlier one.[1050] The third, Artaxerxes' decree in 457 B.C., provided for animal sacrifices in the temple.[1051] The fourth was Artaxerxes' decree authorizing Nehemiah to rebuild Jerusalem's walls in 444 B.C.[1052] This fourth decree is when Daniel's seventy weeks began. The first "seven weeks" (or forty-nine years) probably refer to the time in which the rebuilding of the city of Jerusalem was completed (444–395 B.C.). While

---

[1046]   Isaiah 59:20; Ezekiel 36:31–32

[1047]   Acts 3:14–15

[1048]   Daniel 9:25

[1049]   2 Chronicles 36:22–23; Ezra 1:1–4

[1050]   Ezra 6:1–12

[1051]   Ezra 7:11–26

[1052]   Nehemiah 2:1–8

the wall was rebuilt in fifty-two days,[1053] many years may have been needed to clean up the city's debris after lying desolate for many years, and restore it to good conditions. The Scripture does not give a reason for the division of the "seven weeks."[1054]

The "sixty-two weeks" (434 years) is the time when the Jews live in the land and occupy Jerusalem during troubled times. When Alexander the Great died, his Greek Empire was divided among his four generals. The two most powerful groups were the Ptolemies (the Greeks ruling Egypt and, at times, territory to the north and around parts of the Mediterranean Sea) and the Seleucids (Syria, Mesopotamia, and parts of Asia Minor). These two groups on the north and the south fought over the land of Palestine, and during this time, the nation of Israel and Jerusalem changed hands between their rulers six times. The Roman Empire took control of Palestine in 63 B.C.[1055] The end of the 'sixty-two weeks' to the day was Jesus' triumphal entry into Jerusalem.[1056] [1057] Daniel 9:26 reads, "After these 'sixty-two weeks, ' an anointed one

---

[1053] Nehemiah 6:15

[1054] 7. Pentecost, Dwight, "Daniel" in the *Bible Knowledge Commentary: An Exposition of the Scriptures, vol. 1. Edited by* Walvoord, John F. Walvoord, Roy B. Zuck (Wheaton, Ill.: Victor Books, 1983), 1363.

[1055] Thomas V. Brisco, *Holman Bible Atlas,* Holman Reference (Nashville, TN: Broadman & Holman Publishers, 1998), 186–187.

[1056] Zechariah 9:9 with Matthew 21:1–11

[1057] Hoehner, Harold. *Chronological Aspects of the Life of Christ* (Dallas: Dallas Theological Seminary, 1973), 139

shall be cut off and shall have nothing." [1058] This brings us to the redemptive stage, the cross. The Jews would reject Jesus as their king and hand Him over to the Romans to be crucified. [1059] Because Israel rejected Him at this time, the kingdom could not be put into place, as He did not receive the royal glory as the King on David's throne over Israel.

There is a gap between the end of the sixty-ninth week and the beginning of the 70th week. [1060] The "sixty-nine weeks" were completed exactly on the day of Jesus' triumphal entry, 483 years from the decree to rebuild Jerusalem. [1061] The day of Jesus' triumphal entry happened when He came riding into Jerusalem on a donkey. That same day, He prophesied over Jerusalem that because the nation of Israel rejected Him, He would not return until they embraced Him as their

---

[1058] Daniel 9:26

[1059] John 19:6–16

[1060] Daniel 9:26–27

[1061] "When one investigates the calendars of ancient India, Persia, Babylonia and Assyria, Egypt, Central and South America, and China it is interesting to note that they uniformly had twelve thirty day months, making a total of 360 days for the year, and they had various methods of intercalculating days so the year would come out correctly. Although it may be strange to present day thinking it was common in those days to think of a 360 day year" (Hoehner, Harold. *Chronological Aspects of the Life of Christ* [Dallas: Dallas Theological Seminary, 1973], 135–136). The prophet Daniel and apostle John did this in calculating the second half of the Tribulation, the second half of the "70th week" (Time, times, & half a time [Daniel 7:25; 12:7] = 42 months [Revelation 11:2; 13:5] = 1,260 days [Revelation 11:3]). "From the time Artaxerxes decree authorized Nehemiah to rebuild Jerusalem's walls in 444 B.C. (Nehemiah 2:1–8) until the day of Jesus' triumphal entry into Jerusalem (Zechariah 9:9 with Matthew 21:1–11) was exactly '69 weeks,' or 483 years according to the 360 day year calendar" (Ibid, 138).

king and Messiah.[1062] Between the end of the 69th and the beginning of the 70th week, the Jews sent Jesus to His death. Then, thirty-seven years later, the Roman emperor Titus destroyed Jerusalem in 70 A.D.[1063] Jesus predicted this destruction, saying the city would become desolate because His people rejected Him. [1064] He said the temple would be completely torn down.[1065] At the beginning of the 70th week, the Anti-Christ makes a strong peace treaty with Israel,[1066] and they offer sacrifices in their rebuilt temple.[1067]

Paul declared that this time was a spiritual hardening of Israel[1068] when all but a remnant of the Jews[1069] are broken off and Gentiles are grafted into the olive tree, the people of God.[1070] The majority of God's saving work would be with the Gentiles, not the Jews, until the fullness of the Gentile believers has come in.[1071] Apart from the undefined gap of

---

[1062] He would not return until they embraced Him as their king and Messiah (Matthew 23:37–**39**). When they see Him at His return (Revelation 1:7), they will nationally repent (Isaiah 59:20; Ezekiel 36:31–33a) and individually mourn over their king and Messiah whom they had previously rejected and killed (Zechariah 12:10–14).

[1063] Daniel 9:26

[1064] Luke 19:41–44

[1065] Daniel 9:26; Matthew 24:1–2

[1066] Daniel 9:27a

[1067] Daniel 9:27a with 8:11–14 and 12:11

[1068] Romans 11:7–10, 25

[1069] God has not rejected the people of Israel, but has kept a remnant of believing Jews during this time period (Romans 11:1–6).

[1070] Romans 11:11–24

[1071] Romans 11:25

time in Daniel 9:26–27, this gap of time is also clearly seen in various Old Testament prophecies that refer to Jesus' 1st and 2nd Coming as a one-time event.[1072]

The "70th week" (Daniel 9:27) is the Tribulation, after the Church is removed. This time has not yet been fulfilled. It is to complete the seventy weeks of judgment under foreign rule for Israel's disobedience against God's covenant.[1073] This judgment prepares them, as a spiritually hardened people,[1074] to nationally repent of their sin[1075] and accept their King and Messiah whom they rejected at His 1st Coming when they see Him return a second time. He will deliver them[1076] and forgive and cleanse them from their sins.[1077] At that time, He will conquer all nations,[1078] deliver the land of Israel from its foreign ruling oppressors,[1079] and bring the

---

[1072] The following are some passages that include both Jesus' first and second coming together with a large gap of time in between their fulfillment (Isaiah 61:1–2 [See Jesus' commentary on Isaiah 61:1–2 in Luke 4:16–21]; Zechariah 9:9–10)

[1073] Daniel 9:24, 27. See also Daniel chapter 9 as context in which Daniel confessed the sins of Israel because they did not keep God's covenant and how God responded.

[1074] Romans 11:7–10, 25

[1075] Isaiah 59:20; Ezekiel 36:31–33a

[1076] Jeremiah 30:7–8, 11

[1077] Zechariah 13:1; Romans 11:26–27

[1078] Joel 3:9–16; Revelation 19:11–21

[1079] Jeremiah 30:8–9 says that Israel will no longer be ruled by foreigners and David will be their king. This is in the context of Israel (30:3–4, 10) being restored to the land (30:3, 10), without the rule of foreign leaders over them (30:8) after the Tribulation (30:7).

nation of Israel into her covenantal blessings in the Millennial Kingdom.[1080]

Third, we will place the end times biblical concepts on the timeline. The 1st Coming is at the end of the 69th week. The 2nd Coming is at the end of the Tribulation, the 70th week. The Church Age is between the 69th and 70th week. The end of the Church Age is the Rapture before the Tribulation. From the Rapture through the Tribulation period is also the time of the 1st general resurrection, the Resurrection of the Righteous. Jesus' 2nd Coming ends the Tribulation and begins the Millennium. At the end of the Millennium is the 2nd general resurrection, Resurrection of the Wicked. After this comes the Eternal state.

Fourth, we will reveal how the Trinity is actively working in Daniel's seventy weeks. This is God the Father's plan to judge and later restore Israel to its future kingdom. The anointed one between the 69th and the 70th week is Jesus. The everlasting righteousness that comes after this time of judgment is when Jesus will bodily rule the earth and the Holy Spirit will indwell the people of God.

Fifth, how does knowing what God is doing with the nation of Israel throughout history help believers today?

[1080]   Ezekiel 37:15–28

Application

1. God is a God of redemption. He will redeem His stubborn, rebellious people who walk away from Him.

2. God is in control of nations and times. He not only knows what is going to happen. He plans it out.

3. God is prophetic. Because He accurately predicts the future, we know the Bible can be trusted.

4. God keeps His promises no matter what the obstacles or who opposes Him.

Daniel's seventy weeks reveals Israel's past, present, and future history. It helps create a framework to see how God is working throughout history and what we can expect to happen in the end times. This timeline sets the stage for understanding when the end times biblical concepts occur. The next lesson will deal with the later part of Daniel's seventy weeks, the 1st Coming. To view the chart for this section, go to https://rbeteach71.wixsite.com/justified-sinners/charts.

21. 1ST COMING

Concept: Last session, we looked at Daniel's seventy weeks, which sets the framework for the end times. Using the timeline, we see that the 1st Coming is at the end of Daniel's 69th week, coming to an end at Jesus' triumphal entry into Jerusalem before the crucifixion. The 2nd Coming is at the end of the Tribulation, Daniel's 70th week. The 1st and 2nd Coming act as bookends in Jesus' work on earth as Savior and Judge. Before looking at the five key questions that define one's position on future biblical events, we are going to examine the 1st Coming.

In the Old Testament, the coming of the Messiah was understood as a one-time event, where He would come to save people from their sin[1081] and restore the kingdom of Israel to them,[1082] reigning as their king[1083] and king over the earth.[1084] One reason many people didn't receive Jesus as the promised one was because He did not try to set up an earthly kingdom. Even His forerunner, John the Baptist, had

---

[1081]   Isaiah 53:5–6; 10–12

[1082]   It was expected the kingdom would be restored to Israel (Ezekiel 37:15–28). The Old Testament predicted this coming kingdom (Zechariah 9:9–10; 14:9) and New Testament passages confirm they were waiting for it (Matthew 19:28; Luke 19:11; **Acts 1:6**).

[1083]   Isaiah 9:6–7; Micah 5:2

[1084]   Zechariah 9:9–10; 14:9, 16–17

his own doubts while in prison as to whether or not Jesus was the Messiah.[1085] Before ascending to heaven, His disciples asked Him when He, as their promised Messiah, was going to restore the kingdom to Israel.[1086] Today, we know there is a 1st and 2nd Coming, but the Old Testament prophecies didn't reveal that. It didn't differentiate between the two.[1087] In His 1st Coming, Jesus came to save people from their sins, and in His 2nd Coming, He will return to judge mankind and physically rule the earth.

Here are some prophecies concerning His 1st Coming that apply to His family line and identity. Concerning His family line, He will be born of the seed of a woman,[1088] of the seed of Abraham[1089] and Isaac,[1090] come from Jacob[1091] through the tribe of Judah,[1092] and be a descendant of

---

[1085] Luke 7:**20**–22

[1086] Acts 1:6. The "Times of the Gentiles" (Luke 21:24) is that period of time in which the promised land, given by God to Abraham and his descendants, is controlled by Gentile powers (Daniel chapter 2, 7) and the Davidic throne is empty of any rightful heir in the Davidic line (Hosea 3:4–5). The "Times of the Gentiles" beginning with Nebuchadnezzar's invasion of Jerusalem in 605 B.C. will continue until the Messiah returns to the earth at the end of the Tribulation Period. Then Israel will be restored in the land with David as king (**Hosea 3:5**).

[1087] The following are some passages that include both Jesus' first and second coming together with a large gap of time in between their fulfillment (Isaiah 61:1–2 [See Jesus' commentary on Isaiah 61:1–2 in Luke 4:16–21]; Zechariah 9:9–10)

[1088] Genesis 3:15; Galatians 4:4

[1089] Genesis 12:7 with Galatians 3:16; Matthew 1:1

[1090] Genesis 21:12 with Romans 9:7

[1091] Numbers 24:17–19 with Matthew 2:2

[1092] Genesis 49:10 with Hebrews 7:14

David.[1093] He will be born in Bethlehem[1094] of a virgin,[1095] and the king of the land will massacre all the infants in His village and surrounding area, trying to kill him.[1096] He will flee to Egypt[1097] and live there for a time. Concerning His identity, He will be preceded in His ministry by a forerunner. [1098] He will be declared the Son of God,[1099] a prophet like Moses,[1100] a priestly king[1101] according to the order of Melchizedek, [1102] not the Levitical priesthood (after the order of Aaron),[1103] and as a direct descendant of David, king of Israel. This establishes David's kingdom forever through His rule.[1104] Even though He is a descendant of David, Jesus, as the pre-existent God,[1105] is David's Lord at God's right hand.[1106] He is

---

[1093] 2 Samuel 7:12–13 with Matthew 1:1

[1094] Micah 5:2 with Matthew 2:1–6

[1095] Isaiah 7:14 with Luke 1:26–35

[1096] Jeremiah 31:15 with Matthew 2:16–18

[1097] Hosea 11:1 with Matthew 2:13–15

[1098] Malachi 3:1 with Matthew 11:7–10

[1099] Psalm 2:7 with Luke 1:35; Hebrews 1:5

[1100] Deuteronomy 18:15, 18–19 with Acts 3:17–23 (**22–23**)

[1101] Zechariah 6:12–13 with Hebrews 8:1–2

[1102] Psalm 110:4 with Hebrews 5:6, 10; 7:1–22

[1103] Hebrews 7:11

[1104] 2 Samuel 7:12–13, 16 with Luke 1:31–33

[1105] Exodus 3:14–15 with John 8:57–59

[1106] Psalm 110:1 with Matthew 22:41–45

the promised Redeemer[1107] and a light to the Gentiles.[1108] His name will be called Immanuel, God with us.[1109]

One of the clearest examples of how Jesus' 1st and 2nd Coming were seen as one event is the prophecy predicting His triumphal entry into Jerusalem as king.[1110] A week later, the Jews rejected and killed Him,[1111] their king[1112] and Savior.[1113] You can find this in Zechariah 9:9–10 with Matthew 21:1–10. At the end of His earthly ministry, Luke talks about Jesus fulfilling the Old Testament prophecies concerning Him. Luke 24:44–47 reads, 'Then He said to them, "These are the words which I spoke to you while I was still with you, that all things must be fulfilled which were written in the Law of Moses and the Prophets and the Psalms concerning Me." Then, He opened their understanding that they might comprehend the Scriptures. Then He said to them, "Thus it is written, and thus it was necessary for the Christ to suffer and to rise from the dead the third day, and that repentance and remission of sins should be preached in His name to all nations, beginning in Jerusalem."'

[1107] Job 19:25–27 with Galatians 4:4–5
[1108] Isaiah 49:6 with Acts 13:47
[1109] Isaiah 7:14 with Matthew 1:21–23
[1110] Zechariah 9:9–10 with Matthew 21:1–10
[1111] Acts 3:14–15
[1112] John 18:33–37; 19:19–22
[1113] Acts 13:23; 1 John 4:14

The Old Testament is filled with the things Jesus suffered. He was hated without reason,[1114] sold for thirty pieces of silver,[1115] and betrayed by a friend.[1116] He was the shepherd that was struck with the sheep scattered[1117] while His friends stood afar off.[1118] He was accused by false witnesses,[1119] silent when accused,[1120] rejected and insulted,[1121] and scourged and spat upon.[1122] He was crucified with transgressors,[1123] hands and feet pierced with nails,[1124] and lifted up on the cross as the serpent in the wilderness was lifted up.[1125] He was cursed by God on the tree.[1126] Jesus was mocked and insulted,[1127] stung by reproaches,[1128] felt forsaken by God,[1129] was thirsty,[1130] and given gall and vinegar to drink.[1131] He was

---

[1114]   Psalm 35:19 with John 15:24–25
[1115]   Zechariah 11:12–13 with Matthew 26:14–15
[1116]   Psalm 41:9; 55:12–14 with Matthew 26:14–16, 20–25, 47–50
[1117]   Zechariah 13:7 with Matthew 26:31, 56
[1118]   Psalm 38:11 with Matthew 27:55
[1119]   Psalm 27:12 with Matthew 26:59–61
[1120]   Isaiah 53:7 with Matthew 27:12–14
[1121]   Isaiah 53:3 with Luke 18:31–33
[1122]   Isaiah 50:6 with Matthew 26:67
[1123]   Isaiah 53:12 with Mark 15:27–28
[1124]   Psalm 22:16 with John 20:20, 25, 27
[1125]   Numbers 21:8–9 with John 3:14–15
[1126]   Deuteronomy 21:22–23 with Galatians 3:13
[1127]   Psalm 22:7–8 with Matthew 27:39–43
[1128]   Psalm 69:9 with Romans 15:3
[1129]   Psalm 22:1 with Matthew 27:46
[1130]   Psalm 22:15 with John 19:28
[1131]   Psalm 69:21 with Matthew 27:34, 48

the Lamb slain for us,[1132] His body was pierced for our transgressions,[1133] and not one of His bones was broken.[1134]

Besides suffering, it was prophesied that He would be buried with the rich,[1135] rise from the dead[1136] and ascend to heaven.[1137] The Old Testament also prophesied that *repentance and forgiveness of sins should be preached in His name to all the nations.* He bore mankind's iniquities and offered them forgiveness.[1138] His message was not only for Israel but also the Gentiles[1139] throughout all the world.[1140] The nations would walk in His light.[1141] There are other prophecies that Jesus fulfilled, all proving that He was the Messiah, the promised Redeemer who would save people from their sin. In the redemptive process, we would place the 1st Coming at the cross. How does understanding Jesus' 1st Coming affect the way we approach Him and the Word of God?

[1132] Isaiah 53:7 with Acts 8:27–35

[1133] Isaiah 53:5 with John 19:34, 37; Romans 4:25

[1134] Psalm 34:20 with John 19:31–33, 36

[1135] Isaiah 53:9 with Matthew 27:57–60

[1136] Psalm 16:8–10 with Acts 13:30, 33–**35, 37**

[1137] Psalm 68:18 with Ephesians 4:**8**–10

[1138] Isaiah 53:11 with 1 Peter 2:24; Ephesians 1:7

[1139] Isaiah 55:4–5 with Romans 9:24–26

[1140] Isaiah 49:6 with Acts 13:47

[1141] Isaiah 60:1–3 with Luke 2:32

Application

1. First, John 5:22, 27–29 says Jesus is our Judge, but He offers salvation before He condemns. He does not want anyone to go to hell. Second Peter 3:9 declares, "The Lord is not slow about His promise, as some count slowness, but is patient toward you, not wishing for any to perish, but for all to come to repentance."

2. Second, Jesus completes the Old Testament prophecies of a coming Messiah, a Savior. This is proof that He is who He says He is and gives clear, compelling evidence that the Bible is true.

In this lesson, we looked at the first of the two bookends in Jesus' work on earth as Savior and Judge. In the next lesson, we will focus on the 2nd Coming. To view the chart for this section, go to https://rbeteach71.wixsite.com/justified-sinners/charts.

22. 2ND COMING

T he 2nd Coming. We are looking at the end times biblical concepts through the lens of five key questions
that define one's position on future biblical events. We will
look at the initial two questions now. First, is Jesus' return
literal? Is He physically returning to the earth or not? And
second, if He is physically returning, is His return future, or
has it already happened? The first two questions have to do
with whether or not one's position on the end times is part
of Christian Orthodoxy, which means what Christians everywhere at all times believe. If one does not believe Jesus'
return is literal and in the future, then one believes false
doctrine. Using the timeline from Daniel's seventy weeks,
we see that the 1st Coming is at the end of Daniel's 69th week,
coming to an end at Jesus' triumphal entry into Jerusalem
before the cross. The 2nd Coming is at the end of the Tribulation, Daniel's 70th week. In the last lesson, we looked at
the first two bookends of Jesus' work on earth as Savior and
Judge, His 1st Coming. In this lesson, we will focus on the 2nd
Coming, which addresses His literal and future return.

Concept: In the Old Testament, the coming of the promised king and Messiah was understood as a one-time event,

where He would come to save people from their sin[1142] and restore the kingdom of Israel to them,[1143] reigning as their king[1144] and king over the earth.[1145] Today, we know there is a 1st and a 2nd Coming, but the Old Testament prophecies didn't reveal that. It didn't differentiate between the two.[1146] In His 1st Coming, Jesus came to save people from their sins, and in His 2nd Coming, He will judge mankind and physically rule the earth as its king. At His return, He will bodily descend in the same way He ascended into heaven.[1147]

At Jesus' 1st Coming, He and John the Baptist preached that the people of Israel should repent, for the kingdom was very near.[1148] However, the Jewish leaders vigorously opposed Him. Then, Jesus prophesied that the people of Israel would reject and kill him,[1149] which they did.[1150] He said that because of their response, He would not return again

---

[1142] Isaiah 53:5–6; 10–12

[1143] It was expected the kingdom would be restored to Israel (Ezekiel 37:15–28). The Old Testament predicted this coming kingdom (Zechariah 9:9–10; 14:9) and New Testament passages confirm they were waiting for it (Matthew 19:28; Luke 19:11; **Acts 1:6**).

[1144] Isaiah 9:6–7; Micah 5:2

[1145] Zechariah 9:9–10; 14:9, 16–17

[1146] The following are some passages that include both Jesus' first and second coming together with a large gap of time in between their fulfillment (Isaiah 61:1–2 [See Jesus' commentary on Isaiah 61:1–2 in Luke 4:16–21]; Zechariah 9:9–10)

[1147] Acts 1:11

[1148] Matthew 3:2; 4:17; In Mark 1:14–15 Jesus said the time of the seventy weeks in Daniel 9:24–27 was to be fulfilled.

[1149] Matthew 20:17–19; 21:33–39, 45

[1150] Mark 14:60–64; Matthew 26:62–66 with 27:1

until the nation of Israel embraced Him as their King and Savior.[1151] The Tribulation is to prepare the surviving Jews to repent and accept Him at His return, which completes Daniel's seventy weeks.

We are going to look at key events about Jesus' 2nd Coming. These have to do with the nations, Israel, and heaven. Concerning the key events of all nations, at the beginning of His return, signs will appear in the earth and sky announcing His coming.[1152] Nations will gather against Jerusalem in battle, and the city will be ravaged.[1153] During the worst part, Jesus, the Son of Man in power,[1154] will return with the armies of heaven for the whole world to see.[1155] The Anti-Christ will unite the armies of the nations at Armageddon against Him and His heavenly armies.[1156] Jesus will bodily descend onto the Mt. of Olives.[1157] When His feet land on Mt. of Olives, it will split in two from east to west with a very wide valley between. The Jews will flee Jerusalem,

---

[1151] The day of Jesus' triumphal entry when he came riding into Jerusalem on a donkey (Matthew 21:1–11), He prophesied over Jerusalem saying that because the nation of Israel rejected Him as king and Messiah, He would not return until they embraced Him as their king and Messiah (Matthew 23:37–39). When they see Him at His return (Revelation 1:7), they will nationally repent (Isaiah 59:20; Ezekiel 36:31–32) and individually mourn over their king and Messiah whom they had previously rejected and killed (Zechariah 12:10–14).

[1152] Matthew 24:29; Luke 21:25–26

[1153] Zechariah 14:1–2

[1154] Daniel 7:13–14 with Matthew 24:30; Luke 21:27

[1155] Matthew 24:30; Revelation 1:7

[1156] Revelation 16:13–14, 16; 19:19

[1157] Zechariah 14:4 with Acts 1:9–11

enabled by the sudden major topographical changes.[1158] Great panic will seize the armies, and they will attack one another.[1159]While still living, a plague will cause their bodies to rot, and the birds and the beasts of the field will gorge on their flesh and blood.[1160] Jesus will destroy them.[1161] The Anti-Christ and false prophet will be thrown alive into the lake of fire.[1162]

Concerning the events with Israel, at Jesus' 2nd Coming, Israel's final regathering will take place.[1163] Upon seeing His return, the surviving people of Israel[1164] will nationally repent.[1165] Individually, they will bitterly mourn over their king and Messiah whom they had previously rejected and killed.[1166] He will deliver them[1167] and forgive and cleanse them from their sins.[1168] This national repentance will fulfill the seventy weeks prophesied in Daniel.[1169]

At His return, Jesus will judge everyone. Jewish and Gentile followers of Jesus will enter the Millennial

---

[1158]   Zechariah 14:4–5
[1159]   Zechariah 14:13
[1160]   Zechariah 14:12; Ezekiel 39:17–20; Revelation 19:17–18, 21
[1161]   Revelation 19:19, 21
[1162]   Daniel 7:11; Revelation 19:20
[1163]   Isaiah 11:11–12; Ezekiel 37:1–14; Matthew 24:31
[1164]   Two thirds will die (Zechariah 13:7–9)
[1165]   Isaiah 59:20; Ezekiel 36:31–33a
[1166]   Zechariah 12:10–14 with Revelation 1:7
[1167]   Jeremiah 30:7–8, 11
[1168]   Zechariah 13:1; Romans 11:26–27
[1169]   Daniel 9:24

kingdom, and the rest will be cast into hell.[1170] Satan will be thrown into the bottomless pit for 1,000 years.[1171] Let's look at the key event in heaven. The marriage supper of the Lamb will be celebrated,[1172] where the Bride of Christ, the Church, has made herself ready.[1173] After Jesus has come to conquer His enemies and judge, He will begin His physical reign on earth.[1174]

How should understanding Jesus' 2nd Coming govern believers' lives today?

Application

1. First, according to Luke 12:4–5, Jesus said, "...Do not be afraid of those who kill the body and after that they have no more that they can do. But I will warn you whom to fear: fear the One who, after He has killed, has authority to cast into hell; yes, I tell you, fear Him!" Jesus came to save at His 1st Coming but comes to judge at His 2nd Coming. Those who do not follow Him by this point will have no more chances to repent. They will be judged and cast into hell. Praise God. *Our Judge is **also** our Savior!*

1170   Matthew 25:31–46
1171   Revelation 20:1–3
1172   Revelation 19:6–9
1173   Revelation 19:7b with 2 Corinthians 11:2; Titus 2:14
1174   Daniel 2:24, 31–35 & 44–45 with 7:13–14

2. Second, Jesus is a conquering king who will overcome all His enemies. Philippians 2:10–11 says that at some point in time, every person in the human race and the entire demonic host, Satan included, will bow his knee and worship Jesus as Lord. Take Him seriously!

In this lesson, we have looked at the 2nd Coming of Jesus as a literal, future return. This leads us into the following lesson, the Two General Resurrections, where we grow in understanding of who Jesus is as Judge. To view the chart for this section, go to https://rbeteach71.wixsite.com/justified-sinners/charts.

23. TWO GENERAL RESURRECTIONS

Concept: In the redemptive process, the Two General Resurrections are in the final stage, the Resurrection after the Cleaning of Justified Sinners. Using the chart, we see where we would place the Two General Resurrections in relation to the other biblical concepts, along with Eternal rewards. In the previous lesson, we looked at the initial two questions that define one's position on future biblical events. Is Jesus' return literal, and is it in the future? These lead to the end times biblical concepts, the 2nd Coming, and the Two General Resurrections.

In the Old Testament, the resurrection was understood to be a single event, just like the coming of the Messiah. The righteous would awake to everlasting life, and the wicked would arise to eternal punishment,[1175] as confirmed by Jesus.[1176] The Resurrection of the Righteous includes all the true believers throughout history. The Resurrection of the Wicked comprises all of the unsaved in the human race. But like the coming of Jesus, the Resurrection of the Righteous and the wicked is not a single event, but two sep-

---

[1175]   Daniel 12:1–2

[1176]   John 5:29

arate resurrections, the Living and the Dead separated by His 1,000-year earthly reign, the Millennium.[1177] Jesus, the second person of the Trinity, will judge the righteous and the wicked, not God the Father.[1178]

Using the timeline of Daniel's seventy weeks, we can see that the 1st general resurrection is the Resurrection of the Righteous, occurring between the Rapture, which comes before the Tribulation, and the 2nd Coming of Jesus when He bodily reigns on earth. The 1st general resurrection involves five different classes of judgments: the New Testament believers, Old Testament saints, Tribulation martyrs, Jewish Tribulation survivors, and Gentile Tribulation survivors. There are the New Testament believers who will be judged at the judgment seat of Jesus. There, everyone will give an account for how he lived.[1179] One's good and bad deeds will be publicly brought to light.[1180] I personally believe the bad deeds are only the unconfessed sin the believer didn't deal with because of what 1 John 1:9 says. Then, he will receive the eternal rewards he has earned.[1181] The Old Testament saints will be rewarded for their faith in God.[1182] The Tribulation saints who are martyred will be

---

[1177]   Revelation 20:4–5
[1178]   John 5:25–29
[1179]   Romans 14:10, 12
[1180]   1 Corinthians 4:5; 2 Corinthians 5:10
[1181]   1 Corinthians 3:10–15; Revelation 22:12
[1182]   Daniel 12:1–3

rewarded for their faith in Jesus and faithfulness to Him. They will reign with Him during the Millennium.[1183] The Jews who survived the Great Tribulation will be judged in the wilderness. The rebels will be purged, and the believers will enter the Millennial kingdom because of their faith in Jesus.[1184] The Gentiles who survive the Great Tribulation will be judged in the Valley of Jehoshaphat. Those who have faith in Jesus, demonstrated by their works, will be believers in the Millennial kingdom, and the rest will be cast into hell.[1185]

Looking at the timeline of Daniel's seventy weeks, we can see that the 2nd general resurrection is the Resurrection of the Wicked[1186] at the end of the Millennium. At the Great White Throne judgment, Jesus will judge all of the unsaved from the beginning of the world until its end according to their works and because their name is not found in the Book of Life. They will be thrown into the lake of fire.[1187] Satan and all the disobedient angels who rebelled against God Almighty by following him will be thrown into the Lake of Fire, which was prepared specifically for them.[1188] Satan will not be the king of hell but will be tormented forever.[1189]

[1183]   Revelation 20:4–6

[1184]   Ezekiel 20:33–38

[1185]   Joel 3:1–2, 11–12; Matthew 25:31–46

[1186]   Daniel 12:2b; John 5:29b

[1187]   Revelation 20:11–15

[1188]   Matthew 25:41

[1189]   Revelation 20:10

Everyone will bow before the name of Jesus and confess He is Lord, including Satan and the demons.[1190]

The 1st and 2nd general resurrections dictate our future destiny. How we as believers choose to live directly affects how Jesus evaluates us at the Judgment of the Righteous. Let's see how this applies to our personal lives in three areas.

Application

1. First, you are accountable to God for your actions. If you don't confess your sins in this life, they will be publicly brought to light at the judgment seat of Christ. Second Corinthians 5:10 declares, "For we must all appear before the judgment seat of Christ, so that each one may be recompensed for his deeds in the body, according to what he has done, whether good or bad."

2. Second, honor the name of Jesus. Philippians 2:9–11 says that everyone, even His enemies and the demonic host, will declare He is their Master or Lord and worship Him.

3. Third, whether one spends forever in heaven or hell depends on their relationship to God the Father and Jesus Christ. John 17:3 reveals, "This

---

[1190] Philippians 2:9–11

is eternal life, that they may know You, the only
true God, and Jesus Christ whom You have sent."

In this lesson, we have looked at the Two General Resurrections when Jesus literally returns in the future. The
third question that defines one's position on future biblical
events is whether or not Jesus' return is premillennial. This
leads us to the following lesson: the Millennium. To view the
chart for this section, go to https://rbeteach71.wixsite.com/
justified-sinners/charts.

24. MILLENNIUM

We are looking at the end times biblical concepts through the lens of five key questions that define one's position on future biblical events. We already covered the initial two questions. First, is Jesus' return literal? Second, is He physically returning to the earth or not? These led to the end times biblical concepts, the 2nd Coming, and the Two General Resurrections. The third question that defines one's position on future biblical events is whether or not Jesus' return is premillennial. Will He literally reign for 1,000 years? This leads us to the following biblical concept: the Millennium.

Purpose

What is the purpose of the Millennium? *The Millennium is the fulfillment of the Abrahamic Covenant.* The Abrahamic Covenant promised a land, a seed, and a blessing. Three separate covenants fulfill this promise. The Land Covenant promised a land with specific land boundaries. The Davidic Covenant promised a seed: an eternal king and an everlasting kingdom. The New Covenant promised blessings: national, physical, and spiritual.

Fulfillment of "Daniel's Seventy Weeks" and "The Times of the Gentiles"

What does the fulfillment of "The Times of the Gentiles" and "Daniel's Seventy Weeks" have to do with the Millennium? *The Millennium is the 1,000-year earthly reign of Jesus,*[1191] *taking place between the 1st and 2nd general resurrections.* It takes place at the end of "The Times of the Gentiles" and "Daniel's Seventy Weeks." The seventy weeks prophesied in Daniel are God's appointed time of judgment for the nation of Israel. Because they rebelled against God and broke His covenant with them, He judged them by casting them out of the land and putting foreign rulers over them.[1192] Near the end of the Babylonian exile, Daniel prayed, confessing the sins of his nation, Israel, and asking God to return his people to their land at the end of seventy years according to God's promise through Jeremiah the prophet.[1193] Daniel prayed to God for three things: to forgive the sins of the nation of Israel, rebuild the city of Jerusalem, and restore the temple.[1194] God sent His messenger, Gabriel, to tell Daniel that seventy weeks of judgment would be decreed for his people, Israel, and their city, Jerusalem. During that time, the nation of Israel and the city of Jerusa-

---

[1191]   Revelation 20:4–6
[1192]   Leviticus 26:14–15, 17, 31–33, 38–39; Daniel 9:4–15 (**verses 11 and 13**)
[1193]   Daniel 9:2; Jeremiah 25:11–12
[1194]   Daniel 9:16–19

lem would be under the control of foreign rulers, called "The Times of the Gentiles." "The Times of the Gentiles"[1195] is that period of time in which the Promised Land, given by God to Abraham and his descendants, is controlled by foreign rulers, and the Davidic throne is empty of any rightful heir in the line of David.[1196] "The Times of the Gentiles," beginning with Nebuchadnezzar's invasion of Jerusalem in 605 B.C., will continue until the Messiah returns to the earth at the end of the Tribulation Period. During this time, four world empires rule over the nation of Israel: the Babylonian Empire, the Medo-Persian Empire, the Greek Empire, and the Roman Empire, including the Revived Roman Empire.[1197]

Catalyst

What is the catalyst to finally bring about the Millennium? The "70th week" (Daniel 9:27) is the Tribulation after the Church is removed. This time has not yet been fulfilled. It is to complete the seventy weeks of judgment under foreign rule for Israel's disobedience against God's covenant.[1198] This judgment prepares them, as a spiritually

---

[1195] Luke 21:24

[1196] Hosea 3:4–5

[1197] Daniel chapters 2, 7

[1198] Daniel 9:24, 27. See also Daniel chapter 9 as context in which Daniel confessed the sins of Israel because they did not keep God's covenant and how God responded.

hardened people,[1199] to nationally repent of their sin[1200] and accept their King and Messiah whom they rejected at His 1st Coming when they see Him return a second time.[1201] He will deliver them[1202] and forgive and cleanse them from their sins.[1203] At that time, He will conquer all nations,[1204] deliver the land of Israel from its foreign ruling oppressors,[1205] and bring the nation of Israel into her covenantal blessings in the Millennial Kingdom.[1206] *After Jesus has come to conquer His enemies and judge, He will begin His physical reign on earth.*[1207]

[1199] Romans 11:7–10, 25

[1200] Isaiah 59:20; Ezekiel 36:31–33a

[1201] The day of Jesus' triumphal entry when he came riding into Jerusalem on a donkey (Matthew 21:1–11), He prophesied over Jerusalem saying that because the nation of Israel rejected Him as king and Messiah, He would not return until they embraced Him as their king and Messiah (Matthew 23:37–**39**).

[1202] Jeremiah 30:7–8, 11

[1203] Zechariah 13:1; Romans 11:26–27

[1204] Joel 3:9–16; Revelation 19:11–21

[1205] Jeremiah 30:8–9 says that Israel will no longer be ruled by foreigners and David will be their king. This is in the context of Israel (30:3–4, 10) being restored to the land (30:3, 10), without the rule of foreign leaders over them (30:8) after the Tribulation (30:7).

[1206] Ezekiel 37:15–28

[1207] Daniel 2:24, 31–35 and 44–45 with 7:13–14

Millennium: Fulfillment of the Abrahamic Covenant

The Millennium is the fulfillment of the Abrahamic Covenant, which was given to Abraham,[1208] Isaac,[1209] and Jacob.[1210] It is unconditional[1211] and everlasting.[1212] The Abrahamic Covenant is referenced throughout the Old[1213] and New Testament[1214] of God's promise[1215] and oath[1216] to Israel and promises a land, seed, and blessing.

Land

Let's look at the land fulfillment. In the Land Covenant, Moses wrote that the land promised to Abraham and his descendants[1217] would be established, from the river of Egypt on the south to the great river Euphrates on the north, from the Mediterranean Sea on the west to the wilderness

---

[1208]   Genesis 12:1–3, 6–7;15:1–21

[1209]   Genesis 26:1–5

[1210]   Genesis 28:3–4, 12–14

[1211]   Genesis 15:7–11, 17 (It is unconditional because the only one who has to keep the terms of the covenant is God [15:17–18]); Jeremiah 33:23–26

[1212]   Genesis 17:7–8

[1213]   Exodus 2:23–25 *with Genesis 15:13–14, 16, 18*; Leviticus 26:40–45; Joshua 1:2–4 (conquest in Joshua based on the Abrahamic covenant); 2 Kings 13:22–23; Nehemiah 9:7–8; Ezekiel 20:41–42.

[1214]   Luke 1:67 with 72–75; Galatians 3:13–18

[1215]   Genesis 12:1–3, 6–7

[1216]   Genesis 15:1–20 (**17–18**)

[1217]   Genesis 15:18–21

on the east.[1218] The land boundaries were not fulfilled when Israel entered the Promised Land and conquered it, during the United Kingdom under Saul, David, or Solomon, or any time since then. Ezekiel prophesied how these land boundaries would be fulfilled, being divided among the tribes of Israel, along with the portion for the Levites during the Millennium.[1219] At Jesus' Second Coming, the separate houses of Israel and Judah will be gathered from the surrounding countries and given this land,[1220] where they will be joined as one nation. The houses of Israel and Judah have been separated since the kingdom split under King Solomon's son more than 900 years before Jesus was born.

Seed (Eternal King and Everlasting Kingdom)

Next, let's look at the fulfillment of the seed, an eternal king and an everlasting kingdom. The Davidic Covenant[1221] clarified Abraham's seed. David was promised a descendant to rule forever and an everlasting kingdom.[1222] This promise is unconditional.[1223] It will be fulfilled through Jesus, the promised Messiah and King, at His 1st Coming through His

---

[1218]   Exodus 23:31; Numbers 34:2–12

[1219]   Ezekiel 47:13–23; 48:1–29

[1220]   Ezekiel 37:21, **25–26**

[1221]   2 Samuel 7:10–16; Psalm 89:30–37 (**36–37**)

[1222]   2 Samuel 7:12–13, 16

[1223]   Jeremiah 33:17, 20–21, 25–26

family line,[1224] and at His 2nd Coming *with His earthly reign and everlasting kingdom.*[1225] At its fulfillment, Jesus will be on the throne of David,[1226] where He reigns over Israel[1227] and the whole earth,[1228] judging them[1229] from Jerusalem.[1230] An era of justice and righteousness will prevail[1231] because Jesus will enact swift judgment[1232] and rule with a rod of iron over the nations.[1233] King David,[1234] also referred to as the prince in Ezekiel,[1235] will physically rule over the nation of Israel,[1236] and Jesus' twelve disciples will rule over its twelve tribes.[1237] The resurrected Tribulation martyrs[1238] and saints[1239] will reign with Jesus.

[1224]   2 Samuel 7:12–13 with Matthew 1:1; Luke 1:32
[1225]   2 Samuel 7:12–13, 16 with Luke 1:31–33
[1226]   2 Samuel 7:11–16; Luke 1:31–33
[1227]   Isaiah 9:6–7; Micah 5:2
[1228]   Zechariah 9:9–10; 14:9, 16–17
[1229]   Isaiah 11:3–5; 16:5
[1230]   Zechariah 14:16–17
[1231]   Isaiah 9:7; 42:1–4
[1232]   Malachi 3:5
[1233]   Psalm 2:8–9 with Revelation 19:15–16
[1234]   Jeremiah 30:9
[1235]   Ezekiel 37:25
[1236]   Ezekiel 37:22, 24–25; Hosea 3:5
[1237]   Matthew 19:28
[1238]   Revelation 20:4–6
[1239]   Daniel 7:22, 27

Blessing

Let's see how the blessing will be fulfilled. According to the New Covenant, the Abrahamic blessings are national, physical, and spiritual.

National

These are the national blessings. The separate houses of Israel and Judah will be joined as one nation.[1240] In peace and safety,[1241] David will rule as their king[1242] in Jerusalem[1243] with the Millennial temple in their midst.[1244] God will dwell among them,[1245] promising never to turn away from them again.[1246] They will be distinct from the surrounding nations.[1247] They will have a great reputation,[1248] receive no more threats or insults from other nations,[1249] and their cities will be rebuilt and inhabited.[1250]

[1240]   Ezekiel 37:22 with 37:15–19

[1241]   Jeremiah 32:37; Ezekiel 37:26

[1242]   Ezekiel 37:22, 24–25; Hosea 3:4–5

[1243]   Jeremiah 30:4, 8–9, 17–18, 21; Jerusalem will be rebuilt and never destroyed again (Jeremiah 31:38–40)

[1244]   Ezekiel 37:26, 28

[1245]   Ezekiel 37:23, 27; Zechariah 2:10

[1246]   He will never turn away from them again, and they will never turn away from Him as a nation (Jeremiah 32:40)

[1247]   Isaiah 61:9

[1248]   Zechariah 8:22–23

[1249]   Ezekiel 34:28–29

[1250]   Ezekiel 36:33, 36, 38

Physical

These are the physical blessings. God will bless the nation of Israel.[1251] During this time, the terrain and geography of the earth will greatly change.[1252] A stream will flow from beneath the temple[1253] and divide into two rivers,[1254] one flowing to the Great Sea, which we know as the Mediterranean Sea, and the other to the Dead Sea, causing the land to flourish. The Dead Sea itself will become fresh water filled with fish, though its swamps and marshes will remain salty.[1255] The desert and wastelands will thrive with vegetation.[1256] There will be plenty of rain when needed,[1257] an abundance of food,[1258] and the land will be luxurious, like the Garden of Eden.[1259] Wild beasts will be removed from the land.[1260] At the present, nature is subject to futility and is groaning together in agony, waiting for the deliverance from its bondage to decay by the saints.[1261] However, this is not its original or natural state. Nature will be restored to conditions like the Garden of Eden, with the animals at

---

[1251]   Isaiah 61:9b; Jeremiah 32:40–42
[1252]   Zechariah 14:4, 8, 10
[1253]   Ezekiel 47:1–2; Joel 3:18
[1254]   Zechariah 14:8
[1255]   Ezekiel 47:1–12
[1256]   Isaiah 35:1–2, 6–7
[1257]   Isaiah 30:23; Ezekiel 34:26; Joel 2:23
[1258]   Isaiah 27:6; 30:23
[1259]   Ezekiel 36:34–35
[1260]   Ezekiel 34:25, 28
[1261]   Romans 8:19–22

peace with each other and people.[1262] Israel's population will greatly multiply.[1263] People will have improved health[1264] and live much longer.[1265]

Spiritual

These are the spiritual blessings. During the Church Age, Christians share some of the spiritual blessings that Israel will experience during the Millennium. The writer of Hebrews says these include the forgiveness of sins,[1266] eternal redemption,[1267] being perfected for all time those who are being sanctified,[1268] and direct access to God without a priest as a go-between.[1269] They have an advocate to God, as Jesus is our lawyer who defends us before God the Father,[1270] and a clean conscience.[1271] Paul writes that Christians have the spiritual blessing of being indwelt by the Holy Spirit,[1272] as well as Israel, during the Millennium.[1273] Aside from forgiving and cleansing Israel's sin at Jesus' 2nd

---

[1262] Isaiah 11:6–9; 65:25

[1263] Ezekiel 36:37–38 (see Genesis 22:17 from the Abrahamic covenant)

[1264] Isaiah 29:18; 35:5–6

[1265] Isaiah 65:20–22

[1266] Hebrews 9:15, 26; 10:17–18

[1267] Hebrews 9:12

[1268] Hebrews 10:10, 14

[1269] Hebrews 10:19–20

[1270] Hebrews 9:24

[1271] Hebrews 9:8–9 with 9:14; 10:22

[1272] Romans 8:9; 1 Corinthians 6:19

[1273] Ezekiel 36:26–27; 39:29

Coming,[1274] God will internalize His laws in their hearts,[1275] enabling them to obey His laws.[1276] The whole world will know the Lord as the water covers the seas.[1277] It will be an era of ongoing joy.[1278]

End Rebellion

What does the end of the Millennium teach us? Even though mankind will be living under a perfect government with Edenic conditions in the absence of Satan or his demonic host, he will still be a sinner and naturally stray from God. After 1,000 years, Satan will be released from the bottomless pit[1279] and allowed to deceive the nations. He will rapidly deceive a vast, innumerable multitude of people from the nations,[1280] signifying that there will be a very large number of people during Jesus' reign who secretly rebel against Him. This is because open rebellion will be met with death during Jesus' earthly reign.[1281] Satan will gather them to make war, marching them onward to Jerusalem. His vast army will surround the city.[1282] Then, God will bring down fire

---

[1274] Zechariah 13:1; Romans 11:26–27
[1275] Jeremiah 31:33; Ezekiel 11:19
[1276] Ezekiel 36:26–27
[1277] Isaiah 11:9; Jeremiah 31:34
[1278] Isaiah 61:7
[1279] Revelation 20:7
[1280] Revelation 20:8
[1281] Isaiah 66:24
[1282] Revelation 20:9a

and immediately incinerate them.[1283] In this way, the wicked will be purged at the end of the Millennium. After the Millennium comes the 2nd general resurrection.

How does becoming familiar with the Millennium help Christians in their daily living and decision-making?

Application

1. First, God keeps His promises, no matter how long it takes. We need to hang on and trust Him.

2. Second, God is in control. He is in control of the little things in our lives, our life

3. journey, and our society. He is in control of human history.

4. Third, God restores what is broken. He will restore the nation of Israel and He will restore broken and damaged or twisted areas of our lives if we allow Him. But He operates on His own timetable, not ours.

In this lesson on the Millennium, we learned that Jesus' return is premillennial. He will literally return to reign on earth for 1,000 years. The study of the New Covenant supports the Millennium, for this is when its complete fulfillment takes place. In the next lesson, we will study the New

---

[1283] Revelation 20:9b

Covenant. To view the chart for this section, go to https://rbeteach71.wixsite.com/justified-sinners/charts.

STUDY E: THE NEW COVENANT

I t is important to understand the New Covenant, as it is a key piece in comprehending how the Triune God is working to restore lost fellowship with sinful mankind. Getting to know the New Covenant helps us see how God is working throughout history in this process.

First, we are going to examine the New Covenant using the framework of the Abrahamic covenant and the inter-related covenants. Second, we will discover what role the Trinity plays in the New Covenant. And third, we will take a look at seven unconditional and everlasting features of these covenants.

Abrahamic Covenant

First, to comprehend the New Covenant, one must understand how it fits into the Abrahamic Covenant. The Abrahamic Covenant promised a land, a seed, and a blessing. Three separate covenants fulfill this promise. The Land Covenant promised a land with specific land boundaries. The Davidic Covenant promised a seed: an eternal king and an everlasting kingdom. The New Covenant promised blessings: national, physical, and spiritual.

The Abrahamic covenant is God's agenda throughout the Ages. God gave it as an unconditional[1284] and everlasting[1285] covenant to Abraham,[1286] Isaac,[1287] and Jacob[1288] over 4,000 years ago. It is referenced throughout the Old[1289] and New Testament[1290] of God's promise[1291] and oath[1292] to Israel. A great nation[1293] will come from Abraham[1294] through Isaac,[1295] then Jacob,[1296] whose descendants will be innumerable.[1297] They will be promised a land with its specified boundaries[1298] as an everlasting possession,[1299] and God will be their God.[1300] Through Abraham, Isaac, and Jacob's offspring, who

---

[1284]   Genesis 15:7–11, 17 (It is unconditional because the only one who has to keep the terms of the covenant is God [15:17–18]).

[1285]   **Genesis 17:7–8**

[1286]   Genesis 12:1–3, 6–7; 15:1–21

[1287]   Genesis 26:1–5

[1288]   Genesis 28:3–4, 12–14

[1289]   Exodus 2:23–25 *with Genesis 15:13–14, 16, 18*; Leviticus 26:40–45; Joshua 1:2–4 (conquest in Joshua based on the Abrahamic covenant); 2 Kings 13:22–23; Nehemiah 9:7–8; Ezekiel 20:41–42.

[1290]   Luke 1:67 with 72–75; Galatians 3:13–18

[1291]   Genesis 12:1–3, 6–7

[1292]   Genesis 15:1–20 **(17–18)**

[1293]   Genesis 15:5, 13–14

[1294]   Genesis 12:2

[1295]   Genesis 17:19, 21

[1296]   Genesis 28:3–4, 12–14

[1297]   Genesis 22:17

[1298]   Exodus 23:31; Number 34:2–12

[1299]   **Genesis 17:8**

[1300]   Genesis 17:7–8

is also a descendant of King David,[1301] all the families[1302] and nations[1303] of the earth will be blessed. The apostle Paul says the offspring is Jesus.[1304] The Abrahamic covenant is still awaiting fulfillment, which will happen when Jesus comes a second time to rule the earth during the Millennium.

Land Covenant

The Land Covenant[1305] addresses the Abrahamic covenant's promise of a land. The Land Covenant was conditional.[1306] According to Leviticus 26 and Deuteronomy 28, obedience brought blessings,[1307] and disobedience brought judgment. It was prophesied that if the people of Israel continued to ignore God's judgment, they would be thrown out of the land.[1308] Disobedience would cause them to lose their land and their kingdom. They would not recover it until they nationally repented of their sins.[1309] The land promised to Abraham, Isaac, and Jacob, and later in the Land Covenant through Moses, still hasn't been fulfilled. Due to their lack

---

[1301] Jeremiah 33:25–26

[1302] Promise to Abraham (Genesis 12:3); Jacob (28:14)

[1303] Promise to Abraham (22:18); Isaac (26:4)

[1304] Galatians 3:16

[1305] Deuteronomy 29:1

[1306] Deuteronomy 29:1, 10–15, 22–28

[1307] Leviticus 26:3–13; Deuteronomy 28:1–14

[1308] Leviticus 26:14–33; Deuteronomy 28:15–68; Daniel 9:4–15 (**verses 11, 13**)

[1309] Jeremiah 3:12–18

of faith and disobedience,[1310] the land boundaries were not met when Israel entered the Promised Land and conquered it, during the kingdom under Saul, David, or Solomon, or any time since then. Because Israel rebelled against God and broke His covenant with them, He cast them out of the land and put foreign rulers over them.[1311] Israel's land and kingdom are still waiting to be restored in the future without foreign rule[1312] when the nation of Israel repents by humbling itself, acknowledges and forsakes its sin, and decides wholeheartedly to obey God's commands.[1313]

Davidic Covenant

The Davidic Covenant[1314] addresses the Abrahamic Covenant's promise of a seed. It clarified Abraham's seed. David was promised a descendant to rule forever and an everlasting kingdom.[1315] This promise was unconditional.[1316] It will be fulfilled through Jesus, the promised Messiah and King, at His 1st Coming through His family line,[1317] and at His 2nd

---

[1310] Numbers 33:51–53, 55 (tells what happens if they don't drive out the people living in the land); Joshua 1:2–4; 13:1–13; Judges 2:1–3

[1311] Leviticus 26:14–15, 17, 31–33, 38–39; Daniel 9:4–15 [**verses 11 and 13**]

[1312] Deuteronomy 28:36. See Gentile rule over Israel, even while the nation is in the land with Luke 21:24; Romans 11:25; Daniel chapter 2, 7

[1313] Deuteronomy 30:1–10; 2 Chronicles 7:14

[1314] 2 Samuel 7:10–16; Psalm 89:30–37 (**36–37**)

[1315] 2 Samuel 7:12–13, 16

[1316] Jeremiah 33:17, 20–21, 25–26

[1317] 2 Samuel 7:12–13 with Matthew 1:1; Luke 1:32

Coming *with His earthly reign and everlasting kingdom.*[1318] At its fulfillment, Jesus will be on the throne of David,[1319] where He reigns over Israel[1320] and the whole earth,[1321] judging them[1322] from Jerusalem.[1323] King David,[1324] also referred to as the prince in Ezekiel,[1325] will physically rule over the nation of Israel,[1326] and Jesus' twelve disciples will rule over its twelve tribes.[1327]

New Covenant

The New Covenant addresses the Abrahamic Covenant's promise of a blessing. The New Covenant[1328] is unconditional,[1329] everlasting,[1330] and future.[1331] It is provided on the basis

---

[1318] 2 Samuel 7:12–13, 16 with Luke 1:31–33

[1319] 2 Samuel 7:11–16; Luke 1:31–33

[1320] Isaiah 9:6–7; Micah 5:2

[1321] Zechariah 9:9–10; 14:9, 16–17

[1322] Isaiah 11:3–5; 16:5

[1323] Zechariah 14:16–17

[1324] Jeremiah 30:9

[1325] Ezekiel 37:25

[1326] Ezekiel 37:22, 24–25; Hosea 3:5

[1327] Matthew 19:28

[1328] Jeremiah 31:31–37; Ezekiel 37:15–28

[1329] Jeremiah 31:35–37

[1330] Jeremiah 32:40

[1331] The houses of Israel and Judah, will become one nation [Ezekiel 37:15–22], will return to the land [Ezekiel 37:21], and live there forever in peace and safety with David as their king, God dwelling in their midst as their God, a rebuilt temple, *and distinct from the other nations of the earth* [Ezekiel 37:25–28]); Zechariah 9:9–**11** (The New Covenant will occur when Israel's awaited king is ruler over the earth); Romans 11:25–**27** (This passage clarifies that the New

of a blood covenant,[1332] which is Jesus' death on the cross[1333] and mediated by Him.[1334] Jesus is the go-between God the Father and the recipients of the covenant.

The New Covenant, prophesied by the prophet Jeremiah, clarified the blessings. The blessings are national, physical, and spiritual. The Church participates in many of the spiritual blessings through its partial fulfillment, inaugurated by Jesus' death on the cross. But the national and physical[1335] blessings were promised specifically to the nation of Israel when their kingdom would be restored to them. The complete fulfillment of the New Covenant takes place in the Millennial kingdom when Jesus bodily rules.

The New Covenant is partially completed by the Church during the Church Age, which is made up of Gentiles and a remnant of Jews. The Church shares in many of its blessings now[1336`] through its union with Jesus[1337] as His body, the

---

Covenant will occur after the "Time of the Gentiles." This does not happen until after Daniel's 70th week [Daniel 9:27 – Tribulation] when God's earthly kingdom is set up [Daniel 2:35, 44 with 7:13–14, 27]).

[1332] Zechariah 9:9–11 (In this covenant provided on the basis of blood, the king will bring peace to Jerusalem and the nations, and he will rule the whole world.)

[1333] Hebrews 9:14–15; **13:20**

[1334] Hebrews 8:6–13

[1335] None

[1336] Romans 11:11–24; Ephesians 2:11–22; 2 Corinthians 3:6 with New Covenant in Hebrews (The New Covenant is a superior ministry [Hebrews 8:1–6] and has a superior mediator [Jesus] than the Land Covenant [Hebrews 8:6–13], providing spiritual blessings).

[1337] Galatians 3:16 (Christ fulfills the promise that the families and nations of the earth will be blessed through Abraham's offspring); Galatians 3:27–29 (in being united to Christ, there is no distinction between Jews and Gentiles).

Church.[1338] These spiritual blessings are the forgiveness of sins,[1339] eternal redemption,[1340] being perfected for all time those who are being sanctified,[1341] and direct access to God without a priest as a go-between.[1342] They include having an advocate to God, as Jesus is our lawyer who defends us before God the Father,[1343] a clean conscience,[1344] and the indwelling of the Holy Spirit.[1345]

The complete fulfillment of the New Covenant takes place in the future. It will come to pass when Israel's kingdom is restored at Jesus' 2nd Coming. Jesus vowed not to return until Israel as a nation embraced Him as their king and Savior.[1346] At this time, the entire nation will repent of their sin[1347] and embrace their Messiah (king[1348] and Savior[1349])

[1338]   Ephesians 1:22–23

[1339]   Hebrews 9:15, 26; 10:17–18

[1340]   Hebrews 9:12

[1341]   Hebrews 10:10, 14

[1342]   Hebrews 10:19–20

[1343]   Hebrews 9:24

[1344]   Hebrews 9:8–9 with 9:14; 10:22

[1345]   Romans 8:9; 1 Corinthians 6:19

[1346]   Jesus won't return until the nation of Israel embraces Him as their king and Savior, whom they rejected and killed (Matthew 23:37–39). He is proclaimed as king at His first coming, riding into Jerusalem on a donkey (Matthew 21:1–11), then both as king riding on a donkey into Jerusalem, and presented as king over the earth during the New Covenant (Zechariah 9:9–11). All the families and individuals in Israel will bitterly weep over their Savior and king whom they killed (Zechariah 12:10–14).

[1347]   Isaiah 59:20; Ezekiel 36:31–33a

[1348]   John 18:33–37; 19:19–22

[1349]   Acts 13:23; 1 John 4:14

whom they previously rejected and killed.[1350] While the New Covenant is different than the Land Covenant, both focus on national repentance. When God foretold that Israel would be uprooted from the land and serve foreigners due to their disobedience, He also declared that He would remove His punishment, forgive and cleanse their national sins,[1351] and fully restore them as a nation[1352] without being under foreign rule.[1353] This would happen after the nation of Israel repented[1354] by humbling itself, acknowledging and forsaking its sin, and deciding to wholeheartedly obey His commands.[1355] The New Covenant's national and physical blessings are specifically for the nation of Israel in the Millennium.

National

These are the national blessings. The separate houses of Israel and Judah have been separated for almost 3,000 years. They will be gathered from the surrounding countries

---

[1350] Acts 3:14–15

[1351] Zechariah 13:1; Romans 11:26–27

[1352] Ezekiel 37:15–28

[1353] Jeremiah 30:8–9 says that Israel will no longer be ruled by foreigners and David will be their king. This is in the context of Israel (30:3–4, 10) being restored to the land (30:3, 10), without the rule of foreign leaders over them (30:8) after the Tribulation (30:7).

[1354] The theme of the nation of Israel repenting after disobedience to God's laws runs throughout the Old and New Testaments. It was a prerequisite to returning to the land after exile and restoring Israel's kingdom (Deuteronomy 30:2, 10 [context is 30:1–10]; Jeremiah 3:12–18; Daniel 9:13–14; Matthew 4:17; Acts 3:12–21 [**vs. 19**]).

[1355] Deuteronomy 30:1–10; 2 Chronicles 7:14

and given the land of Israel,[1356] where they will be joined as one nation.[1357] In peace and safety,[1358] David will rule as their king[1359] in Jerusalem[1360] with the Millennial temple in their midst.[1361] God will dwell among them[1362] and promise never to turn away from them again.[1363] They will be distinct from the surrounding nations.[1364] They will have a great reputation,[1365] receive no more threats or insults from other nations,[1366] and their cities will be rebuilt and inhabited.[1367]

Physical

These are the physical blessings. God will bless the nation of Israel.[1368] The desert and wastelands will thrive with vegetation.[1369] There will be plenty of rain when needed,[1370] an

---

[1356] Ezekiel 37:21, **25–26**

[1357] Ezekiel 37:22 with 37:15–19

[1358] Jeremiah 32:37; Ezekiel 37:26

[1359] Ezekiel 37:22, 24–25; Hosea 3:4–5

[1360] Jeremiah 30:4, 8–9, 17–18, 21; Jerusalem will be rebuilt and never destroyed again (Jeremiah 31:38–40)

[1361] Ezekiel 37:26, 28

[1362] Ezekiel 37:23, 27; Zechariah 2:10

[1363] He will never turn away from them again, and they will never turn away from Him as a nation (Jeremiah 32:40)

[1364] Isaiah 61:9

[1365] Zechariah 8:22–23

[1366] Ezekiel 34:28–29

[1367] Ezekiel 36:33, 36, 38

[1368] Isaiah 61:9b; Jeremiah 32:40–42

[1369] Isaiah 35:1–2, 6–7

[1370] Isaiah 30:23; Ezekiel 34:26; Joel 2:23

abundance of food,[1371] and the land will be luxurious like the Garden of Eden.[1372] Wild beasts will be removed from the land.[1373] At the present, nature is subject to futility and is groaning together in agony, waiting for the deliverance from its bondage to decay by the saints.[1374] However, this is not its original or natural state. Nature will be restored to conditions like the Garden of Eden, with the animals at peace with each other and people.[1375] Israel's population will greatly multiply.[1376] People will have improved health[1377] and live much longer.[1378]

Spiritual

These are the spiritual blessings. Along with the blessings mentioned that the Church shares, which we have already mentioned, God will internalize His laws in their hearts,[1379] enabling them to obey His laws.[1380] The whole

---

[1371]   Isaiah 27:6; 30:23
[1372]   Ezekiel 36:34–35
[1373]   Ezekiel 34:25, 28
[1374]   Romans 8:19–22
[1375]   Isaiah 11:6–9; 65:25
[1376]   Ezekiel 36:37–38 (see Genesis 22:17 from the Abrahamic covenant)
[1377]   Isaiah 29:18; 35:5–6
[1378]   Isaiah 65:20–22
[1379]   Jeremiah 31:33; Ezekiel 11:19
[1380]   Ezekiel 36:26–27

world will know the Lord as the water covers the seas.[1381] It will be an era of ongoing joy.[1382]

First, we examined the New Covenant using the framework of the Abrahamic Covenant and the interrelated covenants. Second, let's see what role the Trinity plays in the New Covenant. Its plan is instituted by God the Father. Jesus' death on the cross started the New Covenant, but it won't be fulfilled until the Millennium when He bodily rules. In the Church Age and the Millennium, the Holy Spirit will indwell the people of God.

Third, having understood the New Covenant within the larger framework of the Abrahamic Covenant, we will go on to one other area they have in common. The unconditional and everlasting covenants have seven features that are foundational.

Seven Features of the Unconditional Covenants

- First, Israel will be a nation forever.[1383]

- Second, Israel will possess her land forever.[1384]

- Third, Israel will have a king forever.[1385]

[1381]   Isaiah 11:9; Jeremiah 31:34
[1382]   Isaiah 61:7
[1383]   Jeremiah 31:35–36; Ezekiel 37:15–22, **26,** 28
[1384]   Ezekiel 37:25
[1385]   Jeremiah 33:17, 20–21, 25–26

- Fourth, Israel will have a throne forever.[1386]

- Fifth, there will be a kingdom forever.[1387]

- Sixth, there will be an everlasting new covenant.[1388]

- *And seventh, there will be many abiding blessings.* These are the forgiveness of sins,[1389] eternal redemption,[1390] being perfected for all time those who are being sanctified,[1391] and direct access to God without a priest as a go-between.[1392] They include having an advocate to God as Jesus is our lawyer who defends us before God the Father,[1393] a clean conscience,[1394] God dwelling among His people,[1395] and the indwelling of the Holy Spirit.[1396] In the abiding blessings, an era of justice and righteousness will prevail[1397] because

---

[1386] 2 Samuel 7:13, 16; Psalm 89:3–4, 29, 36–37

[1387] Daniel 2:35, 44 with 7:14, 18, 27

[1388] Isaiah 61:8–9; Jeremiah 33:23–26

[1389] Jeremiah 31:34; [See also Micah 7:18–20]); Hebrews 9:15, 26; 10:17–18

[1390] Hebrews 9:12

[1391] Hebrews 10:10, 14

[1392] Hebrews 10:19–20

[1393] Hebrews 9:24

[1394] Hebrews 9:8–9 with 9:14; 10:22

[1395] Ezekiel 37:23, 27

[1396] Ezekiel 36:26–27; 39:29; Romans 8:9; 1 Corinthians 6:19

[1397] Isaiah 9:7; 42:1–4

Jesus will enact swift judgment[1398] and rule with a rod of iron over the nations.[1399] There will be worldwide peace[1400] and worldwide knowledge of the Lord.[1401]

We have reviewed three areas of the New Covenant. First, what it is in relation to the Abrahamic Covenant and interrelated covenants. Second, what role the Trinity plays in the New Covenant. And third, we looked at seven unconditional and everlasting features of these covenants, which are foundational. A key theme of the New Covenant is repentance. This is what the Triune God is using to restore lost fellowship with sinful mankind. To view the chart for this section, go to https://rbeteach71.wixsite.com/justified-sinners/charts.

[1398]   Malachi 3:5

[1399]   Psalm 2:8–9 with Revelation 19:15–16

[1400]   Isaiah 2:2–4; Zechariah 9:10

[1401]   Isaiah 11:9; Jeremiah 31:34

25. TRIBULATION

We are looking at the end times biblical concepts through the lens of five key questions that define one's position on future biblical events. We already looked at the first two questions: is Jesus' return literal, and is He physically returning to the earth or not? This led us to the biblical concepts of the 2nd Coming and the Two General Resurrections. If one believes Jesus' return is literal and in the future, it leads to the third question: is Jesus' return pre-Millennial? In our last lesson, we learned that the study of the New Covenant supports the Millennial view that when Jesus returns, He will bodily reign on earth for 1,000 years. This is when the complete fulfillment of the New Covenant takes place. If one believes that Jesus' return is pre-Millennial, this takes one to the fourth question. Is the Tribulation going to happen in the future? Are the Old and New Testament prophecies about the Tribulation still awaiting future fulfillment, or have they mainly happened?

Concept: The Tribulation is the worst period of time in all of human history. The second half could well be called hell on earth, as it is the Great Tribulation.[1402] It will last seven years[1403] and is Daniel's 70th week.

There are three main reasons why the Tribulation will occur. We will look at the final time of judgment for the nation of Israel, the time of judgment for those who do not follow Jesus and rebel against God, and a world revival. First, it is the final time of judgment for the nation of Israel. It is to complete the seventy weeks of judgment under foreign rule for Israel's disobedience against God's covenant.[1404] This judgment prepares them, as spiritually hardened people,[1405] to nationally repent of their sin[1406] and accept their King and Messiah, whom they rejected at His 1st Coming when they see His return.[1407]

Second, it is a time of judgment for those who dwell on the earth. It is for those people who do not follow Jesus and rebel against God.[1408] And third, the Tribulation is used to bring about a world revival among every nation, people group, and language. More people will decide to follow

---

[1402] Matthew 24:21

[1403] Daniel 9:27

[1404] Daniel 9:24, 27 (See also Daniel chapter 9 as context in which Daniel confessed the sins of Israel because they did not keep God's covenant and how God responded)

[1405] Romans 11:7–10, 25

[1406] Isaiah 59:20; Ezekiel 36:31–33a

[1407] The day of Jesus' triumphal entry when he came riding into Jerusalem on a donkey (Matthew 21:1–11), He prophesied over Jerusalem saying that because the nation of Israel rejected Him as king and Messiah, He would not return until they embraced Him as their king and Messiah (Matthew 23:37–**39**).

[1408] Revelation 3:10; 8:13

Jesus at this time than in all of human history.[1409] *During the Tribulation period, these three purposes will be fulfilled through a series of judgments on earth carried out under Jesus' authority given by God the Father*[1410]: *seven seals,*[1411] *seven trumpets,*[1412] *and seven bowls of wrath.*[1413]

Revelation covers the majority of Tribulation events. The book is structured[1414] around three divisions:[1415] the past, the present, and the future. It also has seven groups of seven, with various inserts between these groups,[1416] helping the reader understand its progression of events. Before the series of judgments, God is on the throne, with Jesus present.[1417] Chapters four and five demonstrate that God is sovereign and in control of the events that will be happening on earth during this time period.

"Daniel's 70th week"[1418] is the Tribulation after the Church and the Holy Spirit are removed, who both hold back sin. We will take a look at the events of the Tribulation. We will see the first half of the Tribulation with the rise of the

---

[1409] Matthew 24:14; Revelation 7:9, 14
[1410] Revelation 5:1–5, 7–10; 6:1
[1411] Revelation 5:1
[1412] Revelation 8:6
[1413] Revelation 16:1
[1414] Revelation 1:19
[1415] Things that were (Revelation 1), things that are (Revelation 2–3), and things that are to come (Revelation 4–22).
[1416] Larkin, Clarence. *The Book of Revelation.* (New York: Cosimos, 1919), 13–15.
[1417] Revelation 5:6
[1418] Daniel 9:27

Anti-Christ and the key events. We will look at the middle of the Tribulation, where there are significant changes, and we will look at the second half of the Tribulation, where the Anti-Christ is the world ruler for three and a half years. We will see his agenda and consequences. First, let's look at the first half of the Tribulation, the rise of the Anti-Christ. It will begin with the Anti-Christ making a peace treaty with Israel for seven years,[1419] who will later be revealed as "the lawless one."[1420] The Jewish temple will be rebuilt, and the sacrificial system will be practiced again.[1421] Israel will live peacefully and be prosperous in the land. In his rise to power, there will be a ten nation confederacy, ruled by ten kings[1422] who are ruling the whole world under the authority of the world religious system. The unified world religious system[1423] will rule the nations of the earth,[1424] brutally persecuting and killing followers of Jesus.[1425] By deception,[1426] the Anti-Christ will rise among these ten rulers and remove

---

[1419]   Daniel 9:27a

[1420]   2 Thessalonians 2:3, 8–9

[1421]   Daniel 9:27a with 8:11–14 & 12:11

[1422]   Daniel 7:7, 20, 24

[1423]   In the Old Testament the words harlot (or harlotry) and prostitute (or prostitution) were commonly used terms to describe following after false gods, or false religion (Numbers 25:1–2; 1 Chronicles 5:25; Isaiah 57:3–9). The great harlot (Revelation 17:1, 5) represents the false religious system, also the great city which controls the kings of the earth (17:18). The waters on which she sits are the peoples, multitudes, nations, and tongues (17:1 with 15).

[1424]   Revelation 17:18

[1425]   Revelation 17:6

[1426]   Daniel 8:23, 25

three of them, bringing three of the ten nations under his authority in his initial rise to power.[1427]

Halfway through the Tribulation,[1428] *many things will happen in rapid succession.* Satan will be permanently cast out of heaven.[1429] He will give the Anti-Christ his authority.[1430] The ten kings who rule the world under the authority of the world religious system will give their authority to the control of the Anti-Christ.[1431] They will destroy the world religious system,[1432] which had ruled over the nations,[1433] and the Anti-Christ will take control over the whole earth.[1434] He will replace world religion, as his image alone must be worshipped.[1435] The Anti-Christ will break the peace treaty with Israel.[1436] He will take away the temple sacrifices[1437] and carry out the abomination of desolation in the temple.[1438] He will declare himself there as God, greater than anyone on earth or anyone or anything else to be worshipped.[1439] Jesus

---

[1427] Daniel 7:8, 20, 24

[1428] Time, times, & half a time (Daniel 7:25; 12:7) = 42 months (Revelation 11:2; 13:5) = 1,260 days (Revelation 11:3)

[1429] Revelation 12:7–12

[1430] Revelation 13:2, 4

[1431] Revelation 17:12–13, 17

[1432] Revelation 17:16

[1433] Revelation 17:18

[1434] Daniel 7:23–25; Revelation 13:5, 7

[1435] Revelation 13:8, 15–17

[1436] Daniel 9:27

[1437] Daniel 9:27 with 8:11–14

[1438] Daniel 9:27; Matthew 24:15

[1439] 2 Thessalonians 2:3–4

warned about the abomination of desolation. He stated that when it happened to flee to the mountains, not going back for anything, for then there would be a great tribulation, the most horrific time in human history.[1440] The Anti-Christ will attempt to annihilate the people of Israel, but God will enable some to miraculously flee to a place of safety for the rest of the Tribulation.[1441] During the second half, two-thirds of the Jews will be killed, and one-third will escape.[1442] Then, he will relentlessly persecute those who follow Jesus. At the middle of the Tribulation, the two witnesses of God will begin to prophesy in Jerusalem and continue for forty-two months,[1443] before the Anti-Christ overcomes and kills them. They will be resurrected, and God's judgment will fall as a testimony to His power.[1444]

For forty-two months, the Anti-Christ will rule over the whole earth.[1445] This will be the second half of the Tribulation. He will change the "times and the law."[1446] He will make great boasts, uttering blasphemy against God's name and

---

[1440] Matthew 24:15–21; Mark 13:14–19

[1441] Revelation 12:13–16

[1442] Two thirds will die (Zechariah 13:7–9)

[1443] It is not the beginning of the Tribulation, as the temple will already be desecrated and the Gentiles will have control of the city, not Israel (Revelation 11:2–3). Jesus affirms this in Luke 21:24.

[1444] Revelation 11:7–13

[1445] Daniel 7:23–25; Revelation 13:5, 7

[1446] Daniel 7:25

heaven.[1447] The false prophet will promote the Anti-Christ,[1448] who is worshipped by the nations and unbelieving Israel.[1449] The Anti-Christ and false prophet will deceive many people.[1450] The mark of the beast will be used to promote the worship of the Anti-Christ.[1451] He will force everyone to wear his mark on the right hand or forehead, or they will not be able to buy or sell without it.[1452] All who take it will be eternally damned.[1453] He will openly persecute those who follow Jesus. At the end of this appointed time, Jesus will return to save His people, judge those who oppose Him, then rule as king.

In this study, we have seen three reasons why the Tribulation will happen, how the book of Revelation is structured, and key events during the beginning, middle, and end of the Tribulation. Why do we, as believers, need to understand this time period? How does it affect the way we approach life?

[1447] Revelation 13:5–6
[1448] Revelation 13:11–17
[1449] Revelation 13:3–4, 8, 12, 14–15
[1450] Revelation 13:13–14; Daniel 8:23, 25
[1451] Revelation 13:16–18
[1452] Revelation 13:16–17
[1453] Revelation 14:9–11

Application

1. First, we need to realize Satan is not in control. God is, even when we can't see it. We have to trust Him, knowing we don't see the whole picture, like Job in the Bible.

2. Second, God will not let sin go unpunished. Sooner or later, He will judge it.

3. And third, evil can't overcome God or His people who trust in Him to the end.

The Tribulation will happen in the future. This leads us to the final question that defines one's position on future biblical events. Is the Rapture pre-Tribulation? In the following lesson, we will examine the Rapture. To view the chart for this section, go to https://rbeteach71.wixsite.com/justified-sinners/charts.

26. RAPTURE

We are looking at the end times biblical concepts through the lens of five key questions that define one's position on future biblical events. We looked at the first two questions: is Jesus' return literal, and is He physically returning to the earth or not? If one answers yes to both questions, this leads one to the third question: is Jesus' return pre-Millennial? When Jesus returns, if He will bodily reign on earth for 1,000 years, this takes one to the fourth question. Is the Tribulation going to happen in the future? If the Tribulation is future, this leads us to the fifth and final question. Is the Rapture pre-Tribulation?

Concept: In last session, we looked at the Tribulation. In this lesson, we will study two major aspects of the Rapture. One, does the Rapture happen before the Tribulation? Two, is there a difference between the Rapture and the 2nd Coming of Jesus?

The Bible does not explicitly state when the Rapture occurs, but two main arguments strongly support a pre-Tribulation Rapture. First, the Tribulation is a time of judgment for Israel, not the Church. Secondly, the restrainer must be removed before the Anti-Christ is revealed.

Before we examine how the Tribulation is a time of judgment for Israel, but not the Church, let's see how the Tribulation fits into Daniel's seventy weeks. It is the final time period of judgment appointed for the people of Israel because they did not keep God's covenant in the Old Testament.[1454] Jeremiah called the Tribulation Jacob's trouble,[1455] and Jesus said it would be a time of wrath upon the people of Israel.[1456] During the second half, two-thirds of the Jews would be killed.[1457] The Tribulation judgments and persecution of the Jews will cause the nation of Israel to nationally repent of their sins.[1458] They will accept their king and Messiah they had previously rejected and killed when they see Him return at His 2nd Coming.[1459] This national repentance ushers in the restoration of the kingdom of Israel[1460] without being under foreign rule.[1461]

[1454] Daniel 9:24, 27. See also Daniel chapter 9 as context in which Daniel confessed the sins of Israel because they did not keep God's covenant and how God responded.

[1455] Jeremiah 30:7

[1456] Luke 21:23

[1457] Zechariah 13:7–9

[1458] Isaiah 59:20; Ezekiel 36:31–33a

[1459] The day of Jesus' triumphal entry when he came riding into Jerusalem on a donkey (Matthew 21:1–11), He prophesied over Jerusalem saying that because the nation of Israel rejected Him as king and Messiah, He would not return until they embraced Him as their king and Messiah (Matthew 23:37–**39**).

[1460] Ezekiel 37:15–28

[1461] Jeremiah 30:8–9 says that Israel will no longer be ruled by foreigners and David will be their king. This is in the context of Israel (30:3–4, 10) being restored to the land (30:3, 10), without the rule of foreign leaders over them (30:8) after the Tribulation (30:7).

There are three supporting reasons why this judgment period is not for the Church. First, there will be a time of terrible persecution for those who follow Jesus. During the first half, the unified world religious system,[1462] who will rule over the nations of the world at this time,[1463] will brutally and mercilessly persecute the followers of Jesus.[1464] After that, the Anti-Christ will destroy the world's religious system[1465] and rule over the whole earth.[1466] He will mercilessly persecute the followers of Jesus.[1467]

Second, the Church is never mentioned in this time of wrath. In Revelation, the Church is mentioned before the Tribulation in chapters 1–3 and at the end of the Tribulation in chapters 19 and following, but not during the Tribulation events itself. The entire Tribulation judgment is for the people of Israel and those who dwell upon the earth, those who don't follow Jesus and rebel against God.[1468] But it is not for the Church.

[1462]   In the Old Testament the words harlot (or harlotry) and prostitute (or prostitution) were commonly used terms to describe following after false gods, or false religion (Numbers 25:1–2; 1 Chronicles 5:25; Isaiah 57:3–9). The great harlot (Revelation 17:1, 5) represents the false religious system, also the great city which controls the kings of the earth (17:18). The waters on which she sits are the peoples, multitudes, nations, and tongues (17:1 with 15).

[1463]   Revelation 17:18

[1464]   Revelation 17:6

[1465]   Revelation 17:16

[1466]   Daniel 7:23–25; Revelation 13:5, 7

[1467]   Revelation 17:6

[1468]   Daniel 9: 24, 27; Revelation 3:10; 8:13

Third, in the context of the Rapture passage, Paul says the Church is not destined to wrath but will be removed beforehand.[1469]

The second main argument why the Church will not go through the Tribulation but will be raptured before it begins is because the restrainer who holds back sin must be removed before the Anti-Christ is revealed.[1470] This is either the Holy Spirit who "convicts the world concerning sin and righteousness and judgment,"[1471] or the New Testament believers who are indwelt by Him.[1472] Either hold back sin. However, if the Holy Spirit is removed, the Christians won't be there either since the Church Age is characterized by the Holy Spirit indwelling the believers. The Church must be removed before the Anti-Christ is revealed.

When will the Anti-Christ be revealed? It either refers to the middle of the Tribulation or when it begins. First, he reveals his true nature when he enters the Holy of Holies in the temple, committing the abomination of desolation and declaring himself as God.[1473] Secondly, he reveals his identity when he makes a strong covenant of peace with Israel to start the Tribulation and the Jewish temple is rebuilt,[1474]

[1469]   1 Thessalonians 5:**9** with 5:2–4; same context as 4:13–18

[1470]   2 Thessalonians 2:7–8

[1471]   John 16:8

[1472]   1 Corinthians 6:19; Ephesians 1:13–14

[1473]   2 Thessalonians 2:3–4

[1474]   In this future date the temple sacrifices are being stopped. For it to be stopped, the Jewish temple first has to be rebuilt, something that has never happened

which is currently on the third holiest Muslim religious site. The second is much more likely as believers will know who the Anti-Christ is at the beginning of the Tribulation. He won't be free to openly and actively deceive until the restrainer is removed. If the restrainer is removed before the Tribulation, it will give him time to actively deceive.[1475] The people who understood the truth of the gospel and rejected it will be deceived and will embrace the Anti-Christ. They will be condemned.[1476]

The two main arguments are that the time of judgment is for the nation of Israel, not the Church, and that the Church is removed before the Anti-Christ is revealed. The evidence strongly supports a pre-Tribulation Rapture.

Second, is there a difference between the Rapture and the 2nd Coming of Jesus? Several biblical verses and passages draw a clear distinction between the Rapture and the 2nd Coming. The following chart shows seven differences between the two.

First, the 2nd Coming gives clear signs that the end is near, but no Rapture passage talks about Jesus' return preceded by signs. Second, every passage about the 2nd Coming is in the context of tribulation and judgment, but in the Rapture, they don't talk about any judgments. The Rapture passages don't mention any Tribulation before the event. Just Jesus

---

since its destruction in 70 A.D. (Daniel 9:27 with 8:11–14).
[1475]   2 Thessalonians 2:9–10; Daniel 8:23–25
[1476]   2 Thessalonians 2:10–12

promising to return for His people. Third, in the 2nd Coming, Jesus literally descends to earth, landing on Mt. Olives, but in the Rapture, Jesus meets His people in the air, those who are alive and those who have already died in Christ, and nobody else sees them. Fourth, physical changes occur on the earth at the 2nd Coming, but the Rapture passages don't talk about physical changes on the earth. Fifth, the Resurrection is after Jesus' descent. In the Rapture, the resurrection happens at the same time as Jesus' partial descent. Sixth, in the 2nd Coming, the destination of the believers is back to earth, and in the Rapture, the destination of believers is going with Jesus to heaven. And seventh, the whole world will see the 2nd Coming of Jesus, but the Rapture is secret like a thief in the night. Finally, Matthew 24 covers the Rapture in verses 32–44, the Tribulation in verses 15–22, and the 2nd Coming in verses 29–31.

2nd Coming	Rapture
1. The 2nd Coming gives clear signs that the end is near.	**1.** No Rapture passage talks about Jesus' return preceded by signs.
2. Every passage about the 2nd Coming is in the context of tribulation and judgment.	**2.** They don't talk about any judgments. The Rapture passages don't mention any tribulation *before* the event, just Jesus promising to return for His people.
3. Jesus literally descends to earth, landing on Mt. Olives.	**3.** Jesus meets His people in the air (those who are alive and those who have already died), and no one else sees Him.
4. Physical changes occur on the earth at the 2nd Coming	**4.** The Rapture passages don't talk about physical changes on the earth.
5. The resurrection is after Jesus' descent	**5.** The resurrection happens at the same time as Jesus' partial descent.
6. The destination of believers is back to earth.	**6.** The destination of believers is going with Jesus to heaven.

7. The whole world will see the 2nd Coming of Jesus.	**7.** The Rapture is secret, like a thief in the night.

Finally, Matthew 24 covers the *Rapture* (32–44), the *Tribulation* (15–22), and the *2nd Coming* (29–31).

Why is it important for Christians to understand the Rapture? How does it affect how they live?

Application

1. First, Jesus' return will come at any time, unexpectedly. Paul wrote in 1 Thessalonians 5:2, "For you yourselves know full well that the day of the Lord will come just like a thief in the night." Are you ready?

2. Second, Christians are spared from the Tribulation.

3. And third, those who understand the gospel and reject it may not have another chance to follow Jesus when He returns. Paul prophesies in 2 Thessalonians 2:8–12, "Then the lawless one will be revealed whom the Lord will slay with the breath of His mouth and bring to an end by the appearing of His coming; that is, the one whose coming is in accord with the activity of Satan,

with all power and signs and false wonders, and with all the deception of wickedness for those who perish, because they did not receive the love of the truth so as to be saved. For this reason God will send upon them a deluding influence so they will believe what is false, in order that they all may be judged who did not believe the truth, but took pleasure in wickedness."

In this study, we have examined the Rapture. It will happen before the Tribulation. It is completely distinct from Jesus' 2nd Coming. The Rapture questions conclude the five key questions that define one's position on future biblical events. First, is Jesus' return literal? Second, is He physically returning to the earth or not? Third, is Jesus' return Pre-Millennial? Fourth, is the Tribulation going to happen in the future? And fifth, is the Rapture pre-Tribulation? The Rapture marks the end of the Church Age, which is between Daniel's 69th and 70th weeks. Our next lesson is the study of the Church Age. To view the chart for this section, go to https://rbeteach71.wixsite.com/justified-sinners/charts.

STUDY F: CHURCH AGE:

The Church Age is one of God's judgments for the nation of Israel, like Daniel's seventy weeks and the Times of the Gentiles. In this study, we will define it, see why it happened, what its time frame is, and how it relates to the following topics. What is the relationship of the Church Age and the nation of Israel to the New Covenant? What is the relationship between the Church Age and the Old Testament Sacrifices? What is the relationship between the Church Age and the Tabernacle? And what is the relationship between the Church Age and the Seven Biblical Feasts?

Define It

First, we will define it. The Church Age is the time period when God chooses to work with the Gentiles and a remnant of Jews as the people of God instead of the nation of Israel. It is placed on the prophetic calendar of Daniel's seventy weeks between the 69th and 70th week.[1477]

[1477]   Daniel 9:26

Reason for It

What is the reason for it? The Church Age happened because the people of Israel rejected and killed their king and Messiah. In the Old Testament, the coming of the promised king and Messiah was understood as a one-time event, where He would come to save people from their sin[1478] and restore the kingdom of Israel to them,[1479] reigning as their king[1480] and king over the earth.[1481]

When John the Baptist and Jesus were announcing the nearness of the awaited kingdom to the Jewish nation and people,[1482] entrance to its promised fulfillment was conditional upon Israel repenting[1483] and accepting their king and Messiah. However, since they rejected Him,[1484] Jesus said He would not return until the nation of Israel would embrace

---

[1478]   Isaiah 53:5–6; 10–12

[1479]   It was expected the kingdom would be restored to Israel (Ezekiel 37:15–28). The Old Testament predicted this coming kingdom (Zechariah 9:9–10; 14:9) and New Testament passages confirm they were waiting for it (Matthew 19:28; Luke 19:11; **Acts 1:6**).

[1480]   Isaiah 9:6–7; Micah 5:2

[1481]   Zechariah 9:9–10; 14:9, 16–17

[1482]   Matthew 3:2; 4:17; In Mark 1:14–15 Jesus said the time of the seventy weeks in Daniel 9:24–27 was to be fulfilled.

[1483]   The theme of the nation of Israel repenting after disobedience to God's laws runs throughout the Old and New Testaments. It was a prerequisite to returning to the land after exile and restoring Israel's kingdom (Deuteronomy 30:2, 10 [context is 30:1–10]; Jeremiah 3:12–18; Daniel 9:13–14; Matthew 4:17; Acts 3:12–21 [**vs. 19**]).

[1484]   Acts 3:14–15

Him.[1485] Jesus told the Jewish leaders they would reject and kill Him as their Messiah. As a result, God would transfer the kingdom from the people of Israel to the Gentiles for a time.[1486] Since the people of Israel rejected and killed their King and Messiah, their entrance to the kingdom was denied until a further date when they later embrace Him nationally. Because of their rejection, God removed the kingdom from their hands and gave it to the Gentiles until the fullness of the Gentile would come in.[1487]

Paul also explains this. He wrote that the nation of Israel as a whole (except for a Jewish remnant[1488]) is excluded from the people of God for a time,[1489] and Gentile believers are grafted into it in their place.[1490] The majority of God's saving work would be with the Gentiles, not the Jews, until the full-

---

[1485] The day of Jesus' triumphal entry when he came riding into Jerusalem on a donkey (Matthew 21:1–11), He prophesied over Jerusalem saying that because the nation of Israel rejected Him as king and Messiah, He would not return until they embraced Him as their king and Messiah (Matthew 23:37–**39**). When they see Him at His return (Revelation 1:7), they will nationally repent (Isaiah 59:20; Ezekiel 36:31–33a) and individually mourn over their king and Messiah whom they had previously rejected and killed (Zechariah 12:10–14).

[1486] Parable of the vineyard/tenants is where the kingdom of Israel is removed and given to the Gentiles (Matthew 21:33–46). Parable of the wedding feast has the same meaning (Matthew 22:1–14).

[1487] Romans 11:25

[1488] God has not rejected the people of Israel, but has kept a remnant of believing Jews during this time period (Romans 11:1–6).

[1489] Romans 11:15, 17, 19–20, 24–27

[1490] Romans 11:11–24

ness of the Gentile believers have come in.[1491] During the Church Age, the people of Israel are spiritually hardened.[1492]

Time Frame

What is this time frame? The Church Age began on the day of Pentecost[1493] and will end at the Rapture, before the Tribulation period. As the beginning happens as an outpouring of the Holy Spirit on the Church on the Day of Pentecost, the end is marked by a falling away from the faith of people professing to be Christians.[1494] This unknown period of time, the Church Age, is mentioned in Daniel 9:26–27 between the 69th [1495] and 70th [1496] weeks of Daniel. During this era, Daniel prophesied three things. First, the nation of Israel's Messiah and King would be rejected and killed. Second, Jerusalem and the temple would be destroyed, causing the nation of Israel to no longer exist. Third, Israel would become a nation again, living in their land and offering sacrifices in their temple. Jesus prophesied this time of judgment for the nation of Israel when He declared to His disciples that the temple would be destroyed.[1497] This gap of time is

---

[1491] Romans 11:25
[1492] Romans 11:7–10, 25
[1493] The Day of Pentecost is the birth of the Church (Acts 2:1 with Acts 2).
[1494] 2 Thessalonians 2:3; 1 Timothy 4:1–3; 2 Timothy 4:3–4
[1495] The end of the 69th week is Jesus' Triumphal entry.
[1496] Daniel 9:27
[1497] Daniel 9:26; Matthew 24:1–2

also clearly seen in various Old Testament prophecies that refer to Jesus' 1st and 2nd Coming as a one-time event, even though there is a considerable time period between the two occurrences.[1498] The apostle Paul calls this undefined time, which we know as the Church Age, a mystery not revealed in the Old Testament.[1499] After the Tribulation, the completion of Daniel's seventy weeks, the kingdom of Israel will be later reestablished.[1500] This is the ultimate fulfillment of the New Covenant,[1501] the Millennial[1502] Kingdom.

The Relationship of the Church Age and Nation of Israel to the New Covenant

What is the relationship of the Church Age and the nation of Israel to the New Covenant? To comprehend the New Covenant, one must first understand how it fits into the Abrahamic Covenant. The Abrahamic Covenant is made up of a land, seed, and blessing. The land is further explained in the Land Covenant, the seed is further explained in the

---

[1498]   The following are some passages that include both Jesus' first and second coming together with a large gap of time in between their fulfillment (Isaiah 61:1–2 [See Jesus' commentary on Isaiah 61:1–2 in Luke 4:16–21]; Zechariah 9:9–10)

[1499]   Colossians 1:24–27 (**25–26**)

[1500]   Jeremiah 30:8–9 says that Israel will no longer be ruled by foreigners and David will be their king. This is in the context of Israel (30:3–4, 10) being restored to the land (30:3, 10), without the rule of foreign leaders over them (30:8) after the Tribulation (30:7).

[1501]   Ezekiel 37:15–28

[1502]   Revelation 20:6

Davidic Covenant, and the blessing is further explained in the New Covenant. The New Covenant's partial completion is experienced during the Church Age, promised in Jeremiah 31:31–34 and repeated in Hebrews 8:8–12. It is provided on the basis of a blood covenant,[1503] which is Jesus' death on the cross[1504] and mediated by Him.[1505] Jesus is the go-between God the Father and the recipients of the covenant. Its complete fulfillment is carried out during the Millennium, at the end of Daniel's seventy weeks. Its physical and national blessings are specifically for the nation of Israel in the future,[1506] even though the Gentiles and a remnant of Jews share in some of its spiritual blessings now[1507] through their union with Jesus[1508] as His body, the Church,[1509] during the Church Age. These spiritual blessings are the forgive-

---

[1503] Zechariah 9:9–**11** (In this covenant provided on the basis of blood, the king will bring peace to Jerusalem and the nations, and he will rule the whole world.)

[1504] Hebrews 9:14–15; **13:20**

[1505] Hebrews 8:6–13

[1506] The houses of Israel and Judah, which will become one nation (Ezekiel 37:15–22), will return to the land (Ezekiel 37:21), live there forever in peace and safety with David as their king, God dwelling in their midst as their God, a rebuilt temple, *and distinct from the other nations of the earth* (Ezekiel 37:25–28).

[1507] Romans 11:11–24; Ephesians 2:11–22; 2 Corinthians 3:6 with New Covenant in Hebrews (The New Covenant is a superior ministry [Hebrews 8:1–6] and has a superior mediator [Jesus] than the Palestinian Covenant [Hebrews 8:6–13], providing spiritual blessings).

[1508] Galatians 3:16 (Jesus fulfills the promise that the families and nations of the earth will be blessed through Abraham's offspring); Galatians 3:27–29 (in being united to Christ, there is no distinction between Jews and Gentiles).

[1509] Ephesians 1:22–23

ness of sins,[1510] eternal redemption,[1511] being perfected for all time those who are being sanctified,[1512] and direct access to God without a priest as a go-between.[1513] <u>They include having an advocate to God, as Jesus is our lawyer who defends us before God the Father,[1514] a clean conscience,[1515] and the indwelling of the Holy Spirit.[1516]</u>

The Relationship between the Church Age and the Old Testament Sacrifices

What is the relationship between the Church Age and the Old Testament Sacrifices? During the Church Age, the Old Testament sacrifices are gone, fulfilled in Jesus. Animal sacrifices were not offered to save one's soul but for God's people to live in relationship with their Creator, who is holy. "The sin offerings could never take away sin.[1517] All they could do was to point to one who could. But they illustrated a very important point: the death of an innocent life is required to satisfy a Holy God's wrath against sinners. In the Old Testament sins were passed over when people offered acceptable

---

1510   Hebrews 9:15, 26; 10:17–18
1511   Hebrews 9:12
1512   Hebrews 10:10, 14
1513   Hebrews 10:19–20
1514   Hebrews 9:24
1515   Hebrews 9:8–9 with 9:14; 10:22
1516   Romans 8:9, 1 Corinthians 6:19
1517   Hebrews 10:4, 11

sacrifices to God by faith. It is, in fact only in the cross where God the Father fully satisfies His own righteousness against sin, and thus demonstrates His righteousness."[1518] Jesus offered Himself as the perfect sin offering to God. His one-time payment is sufficient forever for all who take hold of it through faith in Jesus.[1519]

The Relationship between the Church Age and the Tabernacle

What is the relationship between the Church Age and the Tabernacle? In the Church Age, there is no Tabernacle or temple. However, the tabernacle and its elements are directly fulfilled in Jesus at His 1st Coming. The Tabernacle itself speaks to us of the Incarnation. Jesus, as God, dwells among His people. John 1:14 declares, "And the Word became flesh and dwelt or tabernacled among us..."

The Tabernacle has seven pieces of furniture[1520] which are positioned in the place of a cross.[1521] We have the Brazen Altar, the Laver, the Altar of Incense, the Ark of the Cove-

---

[1518] Romans 3:21–26

[1519] Hebrews 9:26; 10:10, 12, 14

[1520] Exodus 31:6–9

[1521] The Ark of the Covenant with the Mercy Seat resting on top of it, and the Altar of Incense were facing each other, separated by the veil (Exodus 30:1, 6). The Brazen Altar was before the door (Exodus 40:6). the Laver was between the tent of meeting (Holy Place) and the Brazen Altar (Exodus 40:7). The Table of Shewbread was on the north side (Exodus 40:22) and the Candlestick was on the south side (Exodus 40:24). They were opposite each other (Exodus 26:35).

nant, and the Mercy Seat, which draw a straight line. To the left of the Altar of Incense, we have the Candlestick, and to the right, we have the Table of Shewbread. So we have a straight line, and then we have a line that crosses it.

The Brazen Altar represents the cross of Jesus, the place of sacrifice.[1522] Jesus was also the sin offering,[1523] which, through the sacrifice of Himself, paid for all the sins of the world.[1524] He is the only way to God.[1525]

In the New Testament, the Laver stands for cleansing or sanctifying believers through the washing of water by the Word. Ephesians 5:27–29 declares, "Christ loved the church and gave Himself up for her, that He might sanctify her, having cleansed her by the washing of water with the word, so that He might present the church to Himself in splendor, without spot or wrinkle or any such thing, that she might be holy and without blemish." Jesus is the Word of God[1526] who cleanses us through the Word and work of the Holy Spirit to be presented holy and blameless as a Church before God the Father.

The Candlestick represents Jesus, the Light of God[1527] and the only way to God the Father. This comes through

---

[1522] John 1:29 with I Peter 2:24

[1523] John 1:29 with I John 2:1; 4:10. See also Isaiah 53:10

[1524] Propitiation is sacrifice (1 John 2:2; 4:10). His sacrifice of Himself takes away the sins of the world (Hebrews 9:26; 1 John 2:2).

[1525] John 14:6

[1526] John 1:1–2, 14

[1527] John 8:12

conviction of sin by the Holy Spirit. Jesus fulfills Old Testament promises of the coming of the "light" of salvation and the "light" of God.[1528]

The Altar of Incense represents Jesus, our Intercessor, who advocates for us to God the Father when we sin.[1529] Psalm 141:2 says incense are the prayers of the saints.[1530] When believers pray, they are to pray to God the Father[1531] through the Holy Spirit,[1532] in the name of Jesus.[1533]

The Table of Shewbread represents Jesus, the Bread of God.[1534] Jesus is our daily bread, and we are dependent on Him for our daily needs. We are dependent on Him in place of ourselves to live the Christian life.

The Veil is not one of the seven pieces of furniture. It separates the Inner Court from the Holy of Holies. At Jesus' death, it was torn in two,[1535] indicating that believers now have direct access to God the Father[1536] through His sacri-

---

[1528] Jesus fulfills Old Testament promises of the coming of the "light" of salvation and the "light" of God (Isaiah 49:6; Acts 13:47; 26:23)

[1529] Jesus is our intercessor (advocate) before the Father (Romans 8:34; 1 John 2:1)

[1530] See also Revelation 8:3–4 with 5:8

[1531] Matthew 6:9–13

[1532] Romans 8:26

[1533] John 14:13–14

[1534] John 6:30–33, **35, 48–51**

[1535] Matthew 27:51

[1536] Hebrews 10:19–20

ficial death.[1537] The writer of Hebrews says that the Veil is Jesus' flesh.[1538]

The Ark of the Covenant represents the presence of God. God's presence dwelt there,[1539] and anyone who approached it would immediately die.[1540] Jesus is God, so when He became human and dwelt among man, He was fulfilling God's presence among His people.[1541]

Jesus is the Mercy Seat.[1542] [1543] He is the place for the sin offering of the people in the Holy of Holies. He is also the high priest[1544] who offered the sacrifice for the sins of the people and sprinkled its blood on the Mercy Seat,[1545] just as the high priest did once a year on the Day of Atonement.[1546] The difference is that Jesus, as high priest, completed the Day of Atonement when He not only offered the sacrifice,

---

[1537]   Hebrews 9:11–14, 24–28

[1538]   Hebrews 10:19–20

[1539]   Exodus 25:21–22

[1540]   2 Samuel 6:6–7

[1541]   John 1:14

[1542]   Wallace, Dan. "Class Notes," NT 105 Exegesis of Romans, Dallas: Dallas Theological Seminary, Fall 2009. (His notes on Romans 3:21–26 says that the correct translation for propitiation means Mercy Seat)

[1543]   As the Mercy Seat (Romans 3:25), He is the place for the sin offering of the people in the Holy of Holies (Leviticus 16:2, 14–15).

[1544]   Hebrews 2:17; 8:1. Because he was fully man He was a merciful and high priest who could understand people's struggle with sin's temptations (Hebrews 4:14–15)

[1545]   Hebrews 9:25–26 ("blood of another" was the blood of the bull and goat sprinkled on the Mercy Seat [Leviticus 16:14–15])

[1546]   Leviticus 16:2, 14–15 (Hebrews 9:7, 25), 30, 34

but the sacrifice He presented to God was Himself.[1547] It was a sacrifice one time, forever paying for the sins of the world.[1548] Because God the Father sees Jesus' blood covering sinners,[1549] believers have direct access to the Mercy Seat in God's presence.[1550] The Mercy Seat[1551] represents Jesus as the only way for sinful man to meet Holy God and, as a sinner at the same time, be declared righteous before God[1552] and enter His presence.[1553]

The Relationship between the Church Age and the Seven Biblical Feasts

What is the relationship between the Church Age and the Seven Biblical Feasts? In the first five books of the Old Testament, the people of Israel were instructed to celebrate seven yearly feasts.[1554] **These Seven Biblical Feasts point toward the 1st and the 2nd Coming of Jesus. The first three feasts look towards His 1st Coming.** These are the *Pass-*

[1547] Hebrews 7:26–27; 9:11–12

[1548] Propitiation is sacrifice (1 John 4:10). His sacrifice of Himself takes away the sins of the world (Hebrews 9:26; 1 John 2:2).

[1549] Hebrews 9:12, 25–26

[1550] Hebrews 10:19–20

[1551] Also called the throne of grace in Hebrews 4:16 (God's throne is associated with the Mercy Seat [see Ezekiel 43:4–8 {vs 7} with Ezekiel 10:1])

[1552] Romans 3:23–24; 5:18–19; 2 Corinthians 5:21

[1553] Hebrews 10:19–20

[1554] Leviticus chapter 23

over, the *Feast of Unleavened Bread*, and the *Feast of First Fruits*. They carry out the work of the Church.

The *Passover*[1555] and the *Feast of First Fruits*[1556] are fulfilled in Jesus' death and resurrection, and the Passover is replaced by the Lord's Supper.[1557] Jesus is the Passover lamb,[1558] who was crucified during the Passover.[1559] Like the lamb, Jesus was without defect[1560] and when sacrificed,[1561] none of His bones were broken.[1562] His act of sacrificing Himself[1563] paid for the sins of the world.[1564] It is the acceptance of His death for us that causes God the Father to pass over people's sins[1565] because He sees the blood of Jesus covering them instead of their sins.[1566]

The Feast of First Fruits foreshadows Jesus' resurrection. In the same way that God accepted the first fruits for the entire harvest, Jesus is the first fruit of all believers, whom God also accepted. Jesus' resurrection is the first

---

[1555] Lord's Passover (Leviticus 23:5); Feast of the Passover (Exodus 34:25)

[1556] Leviticus 23:9–14

[1557] Matthew 26:17–29 (26–29) with 1 Corinthians 11:23–26

[1558] 1 Corinthians 5:7 with John 1:29

[1559] Matthew 26:2; John 19:14–16

[1560] Exodus 12:5 with 2 Corinthians 5:21; 1 Peter 1:18–19

[1561] John 11:49–53

[1562] Exodus 12:46 with John 19:31–33, 36

[1563] Hebrews 7:26–27; 9:11–12

[1564] Hebrews 9:26; 1 John 2:2

[1565] Romans 3:21–26 (**25**)

[1566] Hebrews 9:12, 25–26

fruits of believers,[1567] who will be resurrected and will be transformed to be like Him.[1568]

The Feast of Unleavened Bread is about the removal of sin. Leaven is associated with sin.[1569] As the people of Israel were to remove leaven from their houses during this feast, believers are to continuously remove sin from their lives as cleansing to be in fellowship with the Triune God. Eating unleavened bread gives a picture of believers breaking from their previously sinful life and walking holy before God.[1570] Jesus is the unleavened bread, who lived a sinless life,[1571] and believers take part in His life.[1572]

The Feast of Weeks is also known as the Day of Pentecost.[1573] It is not part of the Spring Feasts or the Fall Feasts. It is in between, just as the Church Age is between the 1st and 2nd Coming of Jesus. The Feast of Weeks anticipates the

---

[1567] 1 Corinthians **15:20**, 23

[1568] Philippians 3:20–21; 1 John 3:2

[1569] Leaven is like sin, which spreads throughout a person and organization (1 Corinthians 5:6–8). Leaven is likened to malice and wickedness (1 Corinthians 5:8), hypocrisy (Luke 12:1), false doctrine (Galatians 5:7–9), and compared to the wrong teaching of the Pharisees and Saducees (Matthew 16:6, 12).

[1570] 1 Corinthians 5:7–8

[1571] knew no sin (I2 Corinthians 5:21), did no sin (1 Peter 2:22), and in Him is no sin (1 John 3:5).

[1572] John 6:30–33, 35, 48–51

[1573] The Feast of Weeks (Exodus 34:22) was called the Day of Pentecost in the New Testament (Acts 2:1). The Feast of Weeks was also called Feast of Harvest (Exodus 34:22 with 23:16) and the Day of First Fruits (Numbers 28:26 – also called the Feast of Weeks). *It is not to be confused with the Feast of First Fruits.*

inauguration of the Church. It is when the Holy Spirit indwelt the believers.[1574]

The last three feasts point towards His 2nd Coming. These are the *Feast of Trumpets*, the *Day of Atonement*, and the *Feast of Tabernacles*. The Feast of Trumpets looks forward to Israel's future regathering at the end of the Tribulation period.[1575] The Feast of Tabernacles is also called the Feast of Booths.[1576] It pictures the restoration of Israel's kingdom God has prepared for them when their Messiah returns and they receive Him.[1577]

At His 1st Coming, Jesus partially completed the Day of Atonement as an acceptable sacrifice to God the Father when He, as high priest, entered the Holy of Holies in the heavenly Tabernacle with His blood.[1578] He offered Himself there as a sacrifice one time, forever paying for the sins of the world.[1579] However, the future fulfillment of the Day of Atonement is Israel's national conversion and following

---

[1574] Acts 2, Joel 2:28

[1575] Matthew 24:29–31

[1576] The Feast of Tabernacles (Leviticus 23:34; Zechariah 14:16) is also called Feast of Booths in some translations. Feast of ingathering (Exodus 23:16).

[1577] Zechariah 12:10–13:1 (Israel's response to Jesus' return); see Isaiah 35 (millennial blessings). The feast will be celebrated with Jews and Gentile nations (Zechariah 14:16–19).

[1578] Hebrews 9:11–12. The blood is the life of a creature (Leviticus 17:11), so Jesus shedding His blood was the innocent Son of God offering the sacrifice of Himself for the sins of the guilty world.

[1579] Hebrews 9:26; 1 John 2:2

cleansing at Jesus' 2nd Coming, based on His death at His 1st Coming.[1580]

In this study, we have learned that the Church Age is one of God's judgments for the nation of Israel, just like "Daniel's Seventy Weeks" and "The Times of the Gentiles." We have defined it, seen why it happened, what its time frame is, and how it relates to the following topics. What is the relationship of the Church Age and the nation of Israel to the New Covenant? What is the relationship between the Church Age and the Old Testament Sacrifices? What is the relationship between the Church Age and the Tabernacle? And finally, what is the relationship between the Church Age and the Seven Biblical Feasts?

The Church Age ends at the Rapture. This leads us to the final biblical doctrine in this study on redeeming God's image-bearers, which is the Eternal State, when mankind is in full fellowship with the Triune God again. To view the chart for this section, go to https://rbeteach71.wixsite.com/justified-sinners/charts.

[1580]   Hebrews 9:23–**28** with Matthew 23:37–39 (Jesus won't return until the nation of Israel as a whole acknowledges and turns to Him as their king and Savior they previously rejected and killed); Zechariah 12:10–13:1

27. ETERNAL STATE

We have been studying the end times biblical concepts through the lens of five key questions, ending with the Rapture and its relation to the Church Age. In this final lesson, we will examine the Eternal State. In redeeming God's image-bearers, the Eternal State is after the fourth stage, the Resurrection, when the Triune God is in fellowship with redeemed mankind.

The Eternal State begins after the 2nd Resurrection, the Great White Throne Judgment.[1581] All the righteous will be in heaven and the wicked in hell, humanity and the demonic host. The Triune God will have restored lost fellowship between Himself and mankind due to sin. Sinless humanity will be in fellowship with God, having been conformed to His image.[1582] When God created mankind in the beginning, He was in full fellowship with Adam and Eve. Sin entered the world, breaking fellowship between God and the human race. Since then, the Triune God has been actively working throughout history to restore sinful mankind to Himself. In this restored fellowship, Revelation 21:3 says that God will live in the midst of His people.

[1581] Revelation 20:11–15
[1582] Philippians 3:20– 21; 1 John 3:2

In the Eternal State, five things that we know as permanent will be missing. There will be no more sorrow or pain.[1583] Death will be eliminated.[1584] There will no longer be night[1585] or sun,[1586] for the light comes from God the Father and Jesus.[1587] According to Revelation 21:1, the present heaven and earth are destroyed, and a new heaven and earth are created.[1588] Everything is made anew.

There will be seven new things in heaven: a new heaven, a new earth, a new city, new nations, a new river, a new tree of life, and a new throne. First, there will be a new heaven.[1589] Second, there will be a new earth without any sea.[1590] Third, the new city, Jerusalem, will descend from heaven.[1591] It will be 1,500 miles cubed,[1592] with 216-foot wide walls[1593] made of the stone of jasper.[1594] The city is of pure gold, like clear glass.[1595] The wall has twelve foundation stones. Each stone

---

[1583]   Revelation 21:4

[1584]   Revelation 21:4 and Isaiah 25:8

[1585]   Revelation 21:25; 22:5

[1586]   Revelation 21:23

[1587]   Revelation 21:23; 22:5

[1588]   This is not the new heavens and new earth that the prophet Isaiah refers to (Isaiah 65:17–25) during the Millennium when Jesus is ruling the earth, Satan is bound, and man still has his sin nature.

[1589]   Revelation 21:1

[1590]   Revelation 21:1

[1591]   Revelation 21:2, 10

[1592]   Revelation 21:16

[1593]   Revelation 21:17

[1594]   Revelation 21:18, 11

[1595]   Revelation 21:18

is made of a different precious jewel,[1596] with one of the twelve disciples' names on each one.[1597] It has twelve gates, three on each side,[1598] each one made of a single pearl.[1599] On each gate, one of the names of Israel's twelve tribes is written.[1600] An angel is stationed at each gate.[1601] And the street of the city is pure gold, like transparent glass.[1602] There is no temple in the city or sun. For the temple is God the Father and Jesus,[1603] and the light comes from them.[1604] Fourth, there will be new nations.[1605] Fifth, there will be a new river flowing from the throne of God in Jerusalem through the middle of the city's street.[1606] Six, there will be a new tree of life on either side of the river, with twelve different fruits, one for each month.[1607] And seven, there will be a new throne, with God the Father and Jesus on it.[1608] Jesus will rule forever in the eternal kingdom.[1609] The Holy Spirit will be there, too. [1610]

[1596]   Revelation 21:14, 19–20
[1597]   Revelation 21:14
[1598]   Revelation 21:12–13
[1599]   Revelation 21:21
[1600]   Revelation 21:12
[1601]   Revelation 21:12
[1602]   Revelation 21:21
[1603]   Revelation 21:22
[1604]   Revelation 21:23; 22:5
[1605]   Revelation 21:24–26
[1606]   Revelation 22:1–2
[1607]   Revelation 22:2
[1608]   Revelation 22:3
[1609]   Daniel 7:13–14; Revelation 11:15
[1610]   Revelation 22:17

The Eternal State is significant to Christians because it reveals that this is not the only life they have. And the future is far better than the present. How should it affect the way they live?

Application

1. The Eternal State brings hope for the future. Paul says in 1 Corinthians 15 that if there is no resurrection, our faith is worthless. The Christian life is a waste of time, and those who believe in and practice it are to be more pitied than anyone on earth. But since Jesus rose from the dead, we, as Christians, have hope. Our future in heaven is guaranteed. And in that future, we will have no more pain or sorrow. Our struggles and suffering will be gone.

2. Death is a doorway to heaven. We should not fear it.

3. We should have no shame when we share Jesus with others. We offer them hope. Without Jesus, people don't have real hope.

In this lesson, we have studied the Eternal State. It is the end game of Redeeming God's image bearers. It is after the fourth stage of the redemptive cycle, the resurrection, when God has restored fellowship with mankind. In the Eternal State, sinless humanity is in fellowship with the Triune God, having been conformed to His image. In the next lesson, we will explain how the Triune God is working throughout history to redeem sinful mankind. To view the chart for this section, go to https://rbeteach71.wixsite.com/justified-sinners/charts.

Redeeming God's Image-Bearers Throughout History

I. Abrahamic Covenant

A. Abrahamic Covenant—Fulfilled in Three Separate Covenants

  1. Land Covenant

  2. Davidic Covenant

  3. New Covenant

  4. Abrahamic Covenant: Still Awaiting Fulfillment

B. National Rebellion Leads to *Judgment*

  1. Judgment: Times of the Gentiles

  2. Judgment: Daniel's Seventy Weeks

  3. Judgment: Transfer of the Kingdom

  4. Judgment: How It Will Be *Removed*

   a. Process

   b. 1st and 2nd Coming

   c. Seven Biblical Feasts (God's Calendar)

  3. Judgment: Tribulation Leads to National Repentance

C. Abrahamic Covenant = Millennium

II. God's Sovereign Plan of Redemption

A. Supersedes Mankind's Hardened Heart

B. Historical Overview

C. 1st and 2nd General Resurrections: Redemption or Condemnation

D. Millennium Reveals Mankind Is by Nature Sinful and Rebellious Towards God

E. Accept Redemption or Receive Condemnation

F. Conclusion

Redeeming God's Image-Bearers Throughout History

The Triune God is working throughout history to bring sinful mankind back into fellowship with Him. He knew mankind would sin and rebel against His Creator and planned to restore mankind to Himself from before the world began.[1611]

This outline will help us understand the study of Redeeming God's image bearers throughout history. We will look at two major sections: the Abrahamic Covenant and God's sovereign plan of redemption. When God made a promise to Abraham, He promised a land, seed, and blessing. These are fulfilled in three separate covenants: the Land Covenant, the Davidic Covenant, and the New Covenant. The Abrahamic Covenant is still awaiting fulfillment. Israel's national rebellion against God's covenant leads to judgment.[1612] The judgments are the Times of the Gentiles, Daniel's Seventy Weeks, and the transfer of the kingdom. We will look at how the judgment will be removed. We will look at the process, how God is working in the 1st and 2nd Coming to redeem His people back to Himself, and God's calendar of Seven Biblical

---

[1611]   1 Peter 1:18–20

[1612]   Daniel 9:24, 27. See also Daniel chapter 9 as context in which Daniel confessed the sins of Israel because they did not keep God's covenant and how God responded.

Feasts. And finally, we will see how, during Daniel's seventy weeks, the Tribulation leads to national repentance. The Abrahamic Covenant promised over 4,000 years ago will be fulfilled in the Millennium.

Secondly, we will look at God's sovereign plan of redemption. How it supersedes mankind's hardened heart, we will look at the historical overview, how it leads to the 1st and 2nd general resurrections redemption or condemnation, how the Millennium reveals mankind is by nature sinful and rebellious towards God, how God's sovereign plan of redemption leads man to choose to accept redemption or receive condemnation, and then a conclusion.

Abrahamic Covenant—Fulfilled in Three Separate Covenants

The Abrahamic Covenant. When God promised Abraham a land, seed, and blessing,[1613] Abraham could not have known that the promise would take over 4,000 years to complete. The Land Covenant promised a land with specific land boundaries.[1614] The Davidic Covenant promised a seed: an eternal king and an everlasting kingdom.[1615] The New Covenant promised blessings: national, physical, and spiritual.[1616]

[1613] Genesis 12:1–3; 15:1–21
[1614] Exodus 23:31; Number 34:2–12
[1615] 2 Samuel 7:12–13, 16
[1616] Jeremiah 31:31–37; Ezekiel 37:15–28

Land Covenant

First, we will look at the Land Covenant.[1617] The Land Covenant was conditional.[1618] According to Leviticus 26 and Deuteronomy 28, obedience brought blessings,[1619] and disobedience brought judgment. If the people of Israel continued to ignore God's judgment, they would be thrown out of the land.[1620] Disobedience would cause them to lose their land and their kingdom. They would not recover it until they nationally repented of their sins.[1621]

Davidic Covenant

Second, we will look at the Davidic Covenant.[1622] The Davidic Covenant clarified Abraham's seed. David was promised a descendant to rule forever and an everlasting kingdom.[1623] This promise was unconditional.[1624] It could not be derailed.

New Covenant

Third, we will look at the New Covenant.[1625] The New Covenant was prophesied by the prophet Jeremiah and

---

[1617] Deuteronomy 29:1
[1618] Deuteronomy 29:1, 10–15, 22–28
[1619] Leviticus 26:3–13; Deuteronomy 28:1–14
[1620] Leviticus 26:14–33; Deuteronomy 28:15–68; Daniel 9:4–15 (**verses 11, 13**)
[1621] Jeremiah 3:12–18
[1622] 2 Samuel 7:10–16
[1623] 2 Samuel 7:12–13, 16
[1624] Jeremiah 33:17, 20–21, 25–26
[1625] Jeremiah 31:31–37; Ezekiel 37:15–28

clarified the blessings. The blessings are national, physical, and spiritual. The Church participates in many of the spiritual blessings through its partial fulfillment,[1626] inaugurated by Jesus' death on the cross.[1627] But the national and physical blessings were promised specifically to the nation of Israel when their kingdom would be restored to them.[1628] The complete fulfillment of the New Covenant takes place in the Millennial kingdom when Jesus bodily rules.

Abrahamic Covenant: Still Awaiting Fulfillment

The land, seed, and blessing first promised to Abraham is still awaiting fulfillment, which will happen when Jesus comes a second time. The promise of over 4,000 years ago will not be fulfilled until there is national repentance.[1629] When the Law was given during Moses' time, God prophesied in Leviticus 26 and Deuteronomy 28 that if the people of Israel were to obey Him, they would be blessed. If they

---

[1626]   Romans 11:11–24; Ephesians 2:11–22; 2 Corinthians 3:6 with New Covenant in Hebrews (The New Covenant is a superior ministry [Hebrews 8:1–6] and has a superior mediator [Jesus] than the Land Covenant [Hebrews 8:6–13], providing spiritual blessings).

[1627]   Hebrews 9:14–15; **13:20**

[1628]   The houses of Israel and Judah, which will become one nation (Ezekiel 37:15–22), will return to the land (Ezekiel 37:21), live there forever in peace and safety with David as their king, God dwelling in their midst as their God, a rebuilt temple, *and distinct from the other nations of the earth* (Ezekiel 37:25–28).

[1629]   The theme of the nation of Israel repenting after disobedience to God's laws runs throughout the Old and New Testaments. It was a prerequisite to returning to the land after exile and restoring Israel's kingdom (Deuteronomy 30:2, 10 [context is 30:1–10]; Jeremiah 3:12–18; Daniel 9:13–14; Matthew 4:17; Acts 3:12–21 [**vs. 19**]).

disobeyed Him and worshipped other gods, they would be cursed. If they continually ignored God's judgment, He would escalate His punishments and eventually remove them from the land, causing foreigners to rule over them. God promised to restore their kingdom when they nationally repent.

National Rebellion Leads to *Judgment*

We will see how Israel's national rebellion leads to judgment. Because the nation of Israel rebelled against God and broke His covenant with them, He cast them out of the land and put foreign rulers over them. Near the end of the Babylonian exile, Daniel prayed, confessing the sins of his nation, Israel, and asking God to return his people to their land at the end of seventy years according to God's promise through Jeremiah the prophet.[1630] Daniel prayed to God for three things: to forgive the sins of the nation of Israel, rebuild the city of Jerusalem, and restore the temple.[1631] God sent His messenger, Gabriel, to tell Daniel that seventy weeks of judgment would be decreed for his people, Israel, and their city, Jerusalem.[1632] During that time, the nation of Israel and the city of Jerusalem would be under the control of foreign rulers, called the Times of the Gentiles.

[1630]   Daniel 9:2; Jeremiah 25:11–12
[1631]   Daniel 9:16–19
[1632]   Daniel 9:20–24

Judgment: Times of the Gentiles

The Times of the Gentiles[1633] is that period of time in which the Promised Land, given by God to Abraham and his descendants, is controlled by foreign rulers, and the Davidic throne is empty of any rightful heir in the Davidic line.[1634] The Times of the Gentiles begins with Nebuchadnezzar's invasion of Jerusalem in 605 B.C. and continues until the Messiah returns to the earth at the end of the Tribulation Period. During this time, four world empires rule over the nation of Israel: the Babylonian Empire, the Medo-Persian Empire, the Greek Empire, and the Roman Empire, including the Revived Roman Rmpire.[1635]

Judgment: Daniel's Seventy Weeks

The seventy weeks prophesied in Daniel are God the Father's appointed time of judgment for the nation of Israel. Its purpose is to bring them to national repentance and restore their kingdom.[1636] The everlasting righteousness that comes after this time of judgment is when Jesus will bodily rule the earth[1637] and the Holy Spirit will indwell the people of God.[1638] In Daniel's Seventy Weeks, each week is a

---

[1633]   Luke 21:24

[1634]   Hosea 3:4–5

[1635]   Daniel chapters 2, 7

[1636]   Daniel 9:24

[1637]   Zechariah 9:9–10; 14:9, 16–17

[1638]   Ezekiel 36:26–27; 39:29

week of years, not days. Each week stands for seven years. Jesus' Triumphal Entry completed the 69th week.[1639]

Judgment: Transfer of the Kingdom

Next, we will look at the judgment, the transfer of the kingdom, which we know as the Church Age. The coming of the promised king and Messiah in the Old Testament was understood as a one-time event, where He would come to save people from their sin[1640] and restore the kingdom of Israel to them,[1641] reigning as their king[1642] and king over the earth.[1643]

[1639] "When one investigates the calendars of ancient India, Persia, Babylonia and Assyria, Egypt, Central and South America, and China it is interesting to note that they uniformly had twelve thirty day months, making a total of 360 days for the year, and they had various methods of intercalculating days so the year would come out correctly. Although it may be strange to present day thinking it was common in those days to think of a 360 day year" (Hoehner, Harold. *Chronological Aspects of the Life of Christ* [Dallas: Dallas Theological Seminary, 1973], 135–136). The prophet Daniel and apostle John did this in calculating the second half of the Tribulation, the second half of the "70th week" (Time, times, & half a time [Daniel 7:25; 12:7] = 42 months [Revelation 11:2; 13:5] = 1,260 days [Revelation 11:3]). "From the time Artaxerxes decree authorized Nehemiah to rebuild Jerusalem's walls in 444 B.C. (Nehemiah 2:1–8) until the day of Jesus' triumphal entry into Jerusalem (Zechariah 9:9 with Matthew 21:1–11) was exactly '69 weeks,' or 483 years according to the 360 day year calendar" (Ibid, 138).

[1640] Isaiah 53:5–6; 10–12

[1641] It was expected the kingdom would be restored to Israel (Ezekiel 37:15–28). The Old Testament predicted this coming kingdom (Zechariah 9:9–10; 14:9) and New Testament passages confirm they were waiting for it (Matthew 19:28; Luke 19:11; **Acts 1:6**).

[1642] Isaiah 9:6–7; Micah 5:2

[1643] Zechariah 9:9–10; 14:9, 16–17

When John the Baptist and Jesus were announcing the nearness of the awaited kingdom to the Jewish nation and people,[1644] entrance to its promised fulfillment was conditional upon Israel repenting[1645] and accepting their king and Messiah. Late in His ministry, Jesus told the Jewish leaders they would reject and kill Him as their Messiah. As a result, God the Father would transfer the kingdom from the people of Israel to the Gentiles for a time.[1646] As predicted, the people of Israel rejected and killed their king and Messiah, and their entrance to the kingdom was denied until a further date when they would later embrace Him nationally. Because of their rejection, God removed the kingdom from their hands and gave it to the Gentiles until the fullness of the Gentiles would come in.[1647] The Church Age happened because the people of Israel rejected and killed their king and Messiah.

The Church Age is the time period when God chooses to work with the Gentiles and a remnant of the Jews as the people of God instead of the nation of Israel and is placed in the prophetic calendar of Daniel's seventy weeks between

---

[1644]   Matthew 3:2; 4:17; In Mark 1:14–15 Jesus said the time of the seventy weeks in Daniel 9:24–27 was to be fulfilled.

[1645]   The theme of the nation of Israel repenting after disobedience to God's laws runs throughout the Old and New Testaments. It was a prerequisite to returning to the land after exile and restoring Israel's kingdom (Deuteronomy 30:2, 10 [context is 30:1–10]; Jeremiah 3: 12–18; Daniel 9:13–14; Matthew 4:17; Acts 3:12–21 [**vs. 19**]).

[1646]   Parable of the vineyard/tenants is where the kingdom of Israel is removed and given to the Gentiles (Matthew 21:33–46). Parable of the wedding feast has the same meaning (Matthew 22:1–14).

[1647]   Romans 11:25

the 69[1648] and 70[1648] week.[1648] Paul also explains this. He wrote that the nation of Israel as a whole (except for a Jewish remnant[1649]) is excluded from the people of God for a time,[1650] and Gentile believers are grafted into it in their place.[1651] The majority of God's saving work would be with the Gentiles, not the Jews, until the fullness of the Gentile believers has come in.[1652] During the Church Age, the people of Israel are spiritually hardened.

The Church Age began on the day of Pentecost[1653] and ended at the Rapture before the Tribulation starts. This unknown time period is mentioned in Daniel 9:26–27 between the 69th and 70th weeks of Daniel. During this era, Daniel prophesied three things. First, the nation of Israel's Messiah and king would be rejected and killed. Second, Jerusalem and the temple would be destroyed, causing the nation of Israel to no longer exist. Third, Israel would become a nation again, living in their land and offering sacrifices in their temple. Jesus prophesied this time of judgment for the nation of Israel when He declared to His disciples that the temple would be destroyed.[1654] This gap of time is

---

[1648] Daniel 9:26

[1649] God has not rejected the people of Israel, but has kept a remnant of believing Jews during this time period (Romans 11:1–6).

[1650] Romans 11:15, 17, 19–20, 24–27

[1651] Romans 11:11–24

[1652] Romans 11:25

[1653] The Day of Pentecost is the birth of the Church (Acts 2:1 with Acts 2).

[1654] Daniel 9:26; Matthew 24:1–2

also clearly seen in various Old Testament prophecies that refer to Jesus' 1st and 2nd Coming as a one-time event, even though there is a considerable time period between the two occurrences.[1655] The apostle Paul calls this undefined time, which we know as the Church Age, a mystery not revealed in the Old Testament.[1656]

Judgment: How It Will Be Removed

Overview

Now, we will see how the judgment is removed. First, let's take a look at the process. The 1st and 2nd Comings of Jesus are intertwined, and both work toward the nation of Israel's repentance. At His 1st Coming, God the Father sent the Son to be the Savior of the world.[1657] The Holy Spirit impregnated Mary,[1658] giving Jesus the Father's nature.[1659] Jesus grew up being fully human because of His mother, yet fully God at the same time.[1660] He had a human nature like everyone else,[1661] except without sin[1662] and the natural tendency to sin.

[1655]   The following are some passages that include both Jesus' first and second coming together with a large gap of time in between their fulfillment (Isaiah 9:6–7; 61:1–2 [See Jesus' commentary on Isaiah 61:1–2 in Luke 4:16–21]; Micah 5:2; Zechariah 9:9–10)

[1656]   Colossians 1:24–27 (**25–26**)

[1657]   1 John 4:14

[1658]   Matthew 1:18–23

[1659]   Hebrews 1:3 with John 10:30

[1660]   Philippians 2:6–7

[1661]   Hebrews 2:14, 17

[1662]   Hebrews 4:15

Because He was a sinless man, He could die in mankind's place.[1663] The death of Jesus on the cross pays for the sins of the world,[1664] including the national rebellion and sins of the nation of Israel. But the nation of Israel must repent of their sins nationally to be cleansed,[1665] remove God's judgment, and restore their kingdom.[1666] Jesus vowed not to return until national repentance first occurred. [1667] Jesus stated that the Father appointed the time of His return. Not even Jesus knew when it would happen while He was on earth.[1668] At His return, the Holy Spirit would bring conviction and repentance to His people.[1669]

1st and 2nd Coming

Next, we will look at how God is working to redeem mankind and remove judgment through the 1st and 2nd Coming. Let's compare the Triune God's judgment and restoration of His people during the 1st and 2nd Coming when He is redeeming them. First: At the 1st Coming, Jesus is Savior,

---

[1663]   Philippians 2:7–8; Hebrews 2:17

[1664]   Hebrews 9:26; 1 John 2:2

[1665]   Zechariah 13:1; Romans 11:26–27

[1666]   Ezekiel 37:15–28

[1667]   The day of Jesus' triumphal entry when he came riding into Jerusalem on a donkey (Matthew 21:1–11), He prophesied over Jerusalem saying that because the nation of Israel rejected Him as king and Messiah, He would not return until they embraced Him as their king and Messiah (Matthew 23:37–39). When they see Him at His return (Revelation 1:7), they will nationally repent (Isaiah 59:20; Ezekiel 36:31–33a) and individually mourn over their king and Messiah whom they had previously rejected and killed (Zechariah 12:10–14).

[1668]   Matthew 24:36

[1669]   Zechariah 12:10–13:1

and at the 2nd Coming, Jesus is Judge and Ruler. Second: At the 1st Coming, the people of Israel nationally reject their Messiah, and at the 2nd Coming, the people of Israel nationally repent and embrace their Messiah. Third: At the 1st Coming, the people of Israel are still under God's appointed judgment, and at the 2nd Coming, God's judgment is removed. Next is the section of Daniel's seventy weeks. Fourth: At the 1st Coming, the people of Israel are put under foreign rulers during Daniel's seventy weeks, and at His 2nd Coming, the people of Israel are a sovereign nation with a king when Daniel's seventy weeks have been completed. Lastly is the section of kingdom lost, kingdom restored. Fifth: At the 1st Coming, the Day of Atonement is partially fulfilled when Jesus offered Himself as the once-for-all sacrifice to pay for the sins of the world. At this time, the kingdom is still lost. At the 2nd Coming, the Day of Atonement is completely fulfilled at Israel's national repentance and cleansing. This is when the kingdom is restored.

Seven Biblical Feasts (God's Calendar)

And finally, we will look at God's calendar, Seven Biblical Feasts. The Seven Biblical Feasts are also tied to Jesus' 1st and 2nd Coming. They are also working to deal with sin and bring God's people back into a relationship with Him through repentance, then fellowship.

The Spring calendar feasts point to Jesus' 1st Coming. Jesus was crucified on the feast of Passover.[1670] He is the perfect lamb offered to God to pay for the sins of the world[1671] from the beginning to the end of history. The *Feast of Unleavened Bread* points toward Jesus, who lived a sinless life,[1672] giving Him the right to die as man in mankind's place for sin.[1673] Jesus fulfills the Feast of First Fruits at His resurrection.[1674]

The Fall calendar feasts allude to Jesus' 2nd Coming. At the *Feast of Trumpets*, the people of Israel are regathered when Jesus comes to set up His Father's earthly kingdom.[1675] When the surviving people of the nation of Israel see Jesus coming in the clouds at His return, they will bitterly mourn over their rejection of Him,[1676] nationally repent,[1677] and be cleansed from their sin.[1678] This is the *complete fulfillment* of the *Day of Atonement*. During Jesus' 1,000-year earthly reign as king over all the earth, He will call the nations to celebrate and worship Him once yearly at the *Feast of Tab-*

[1670]   Matthew 26:2; John 19:14–16

[1671]   John 1:29

[1672]   Knew no sin (2 Corinthians 5:21), did no sin (1 Peter 2:22), and in Him is no sin (1 John 3:5).

[1673]   Philippians 2:7–8; Hebrews 2:17

[1674]   1 Corinthians **15:20**, 23

[1675]   Matthew 24:29–31

[1676]   Zechariah 12:10–14 with Revelation 1:7

[1677]   Isaiah 59:20; Ezekiel 36:31–33a

[1678]   Zechariah 13:1; Romans 11:26–27

ernacles in Jerusalem.[1679] It is a celebration of God dwelling among His people.

The Feast of Weeks is also called the Day of Pentecost. It is not part of the Spring feasts pointing to His 1ˢᵗ Coming or the Fall feasts foreshadowing His 2ⁿᵈ Coming. It takes place between them. It marks the beginning of the Church Age with the initial indwelling of the Holy Spirit in Acts 2. Fifty days elapse between the Feast of First Fruits, which is Jesus' resurrection, and the Feast of Weeks, which is the coming of the Holy Spirit upon the Church.[1680] Take a minute to look at the chart to review what we have covered with the 1st and 2nd Coming and the Seven Biblical Feasts.

Judgment: Tribulation Leads to National Repentance

The end of Daniel's 70ᵗʰ week is the Tribulation, which leads to national repentance. As mentioned before, the people of Israel are spiritually hardened.[1681] The apostle Paul said a veil covers their hearts.[1682] They are spiritually blind. Israel won't be restored to their land and city Jerusalem as a sovereign nation, without living under foreign rule, until they

---

1679   Zechariah 14:16–19

1680   Pentecost is the Feast of Weeks, or seven sevens. From when the Passover lamb was offered, the day after the following Sabbath when the Feast of the First Fruits was celebrated (Exodus 23:18–19; 34:25–26 with Leviticus 23:11), count seven full weeks to the Day of Pentecost (Leviticus 23:15). It is called Pentecost because "you shall count 50 days to the day after the seventh Sabbath…" (Leviticus 23:16).

1681   Romans 11:7–10, 25

1682   2 Corinthians 3:14

nationally repent of their sin[1683] and embrace their Messiah and King they have previously rejected.[1684] God will use the Tribulation to bring this about, ending Daniel's seventy weeks and ushering in the restoration of Israel's kingdom. This is the 70th week of Daniel, seven years of judgment on earth.[1685] Jesus declares this the worst time in human history.[1686] The Church will not pass through any of this period of judgment but will be raptured beforehand, and the Holy Spirit will be removed.[1687] Only the Father knows when this time would happen. Not even Jesus knew while on earth.

The beginning of the Tribulation will start with the Anti-Christ making a treaty with the nation of Israel for seven years.[1688] He will break it halfway throughout[1689] and attempt to annihilate all of its people.[1690] God will grant him the right to rule the earth, and the Anti-Christ's rule will be backed by the full authority of Satan.[1691] His global reign of terror and destruction will force people to choose between God and the Anti-Christ. At this time, Jesus carries out judgments

---

[1683] Isaiah 59:20; Ezekiel 36:31–33a

[1684] Acts 3:14–15

[1685] Daniel 9:24, 27

[1686] Matthew 24:15–21; Mark 13:14–19

[1687] 2 Thessalonians 2:7–8

[1688] Daniel 9:27

[1689] Daniel 9:27; 2 Thessalonians 2:3–4

[1690] Revelation 12:13–16

[1691] Revelation 13:2, 4

upon the earth,[1692] *seven seals,*[1693] *seven trumpets,*[1694] *and seven bowls of wrath,*[1695] planned out beforehand by God the Father.[1696] The Holy Spirit allows sin to play out unrestrained.[1697] A worldwide explosion of the gospel will ensue, and people from every nation, language group, dialect, and tribe will come to Jesus.[1698] At the end of the Tribulation, God the Father will send Jesus back to earth. He will come with His armies,[1699] and the surviving third left of the people of Israel[1700] will nationally repent. Each family and individual will bitterly mourn that the one who is coming is He whom they rejected and killed as a nation over 2,000 years ago.[1701] They will repent as an entire nation and be cleansed of their sin.[1702]

1692   Revelation 5:1–5, 7–10; 6:1

1693   Revelation 5:1

1694   Revelation 8:6

1695   Revelation 16:1

1696   Revelation 5:1–7 (**1, 7**)

1697   2 Thessalonians 2:7–8

1698   Matthew 24:14; Revelation 7:9, 14

1699   Jude 14–15; Revelation 19:11–16, 19

1700   Zechariah 13:7–9

1701   Zechariah 12:10–14; Revelation 1:7

1702   Zechariah 13:1; Romans 11:26–27

Abrahamic Covenant = Millennium

The Abrahamic Covenant is fulfilled in the Millennium. At His return, Jesus will judge the wicked[1703] and set up His kingdom under the authority of God the Father.[1704] The Holy Spirit will indwell those who follow Jesus.[1705] The nation of Israel will be restored and be given the highest place among the nations of the world.[1706] King David will be resurrected as king and will rule over the nation of Israel.[1707] The Abrahamic Covenant's promise of a land, seed, and blessing will be fulfilled during the restoration of Israel's kingdom, the Millennium. The nation of Israel will receive full possession of the land as spelled out by Moses.[1708] Through Jesus, an eternal king will rule over an everlasting kingdom, which was promised to David.[1709] It will inaugurate a new world society known for its everlasting righteousness, as foretold in Daniel.[1710] It will bring in national, physical, and spiritual blessings. Concerning national blessings, the prophet Ezekiel foretold reuniting the separate houses of Israel and

---

[1703]   Joel 3:1–2, 11–14; Matthew 25:31–46

[1704]   Daniel 7:13–14

[1705]   Ezekiel 36:26–27; 39:29

[1706]   Zechariah 8:22–23

[1707]   Ezekiel 37:22, 24–25; Hosea 3:4–5

[1708]   Ezekiel 37:21, **25–26** (Exodus 23:31 and Numbers 34:2–12 with Ezekiel 47:13–23; 48:1–29)

[1709]   2 Samuel 7:12–13, 16 with Luke 1:31–33

[1710]   This era of righteousness and justice (Isaiah 9:7; 42:1–4) is because Jesus will enact swift judgment (Malachi 3:5) and rule with a rod of iron over the nations (Psalm 2:8–9 with Revelation 19:15–16).

Judah into one nation, which has been separated for about 3,000 years.[1711] Daniel wrote that the Millennial temple would be built.[1712] Haggai the prophet said it would be more magnificent than Solomon's temple.[1713]

God's Sovereign Plan of Redemption

In "Redeeming God's Image-Bearers Throughout History," we looked at the section on the Abrahamic Covenant. Now, we are going to transition to God's sovereign plan of redemption. We will start with how it supersedes mankind's hardened heart.

Supercedes Mankind's Hardened Heart

When God made a promise to Abraham, He knew there would be significant obstacles. Even so, He continued to reiterate the same message throughout the Old[1714] and New Testaments.[1715] It could not be activated apart from His disobedient, obstinate people confessing their sins and repenting nationally. But His promise also could not

---

[1711]   Ezekiel 37:22 with 37:15–19

[1712]   Daniel prayed for the restoration of the temple in Daniel 9:17. It was promised in Daniel 9:24 with the "anointing of the most holy." It was also promised by other Old Testament prophets (Ezekiel 37:26, 28; Zechariah 6:12–13, 15)

[1713]   Haggai 2:6–9

[1714]   Exodus 2:23–25 *with Genesis 15:13–14, 16, 18*; Leviticus 26:40–45; Joshua 1:2–4 (conquest in Joshua based on the Abrahamic covenant); 2 Kings 13:22–23; Nehemiah 9:7–8; Ezekiel 20:41–42.

[1715]   Luke 1:67 with 72–75; Galatians 3:13–18

be ruined by His people's disobedience. It could not be defeated by His people's rejection of Him. It could not be nullified by His people's indifference to His ways. It could not be set aside by His people's spiritually hardened hearts. When God sets out to accomplish His purposes, nothing sinful mankind can do to thwart them. It is true that mankind has a choice to accept or reject Him as their Creator, but even so, God will bring to pass what He has promised and override their rebellion. God used His promises to Abraham to work throughout history to bring sinful mankind back to Himself, to redeem His image bearers.

Historical Overview of God **Redeeming** Mankind

We will look at the historical overview of God redeeming mankind. As a quick overview, God's promise to Abraham over 4,000 years ago was a land, seed, and blessing. This was further explained in the Land Covenant with specific land boundaries, in the Davidic Covenant with an eternal king and everlasting kingdom, and in the New Covenant with national, physical, and spiritual blessings. This promise won't be fulfilled until the Millennium. The nation of Israel never fully possessed the land due to their disobedience.[1716] Disobedience to God's covenant caused them to lose their

---

[1716]   Joshua 13:8–19:51 with Joshua 13:1–7; 16:10; 17:7–18; Judges 1

land and their kingdom.[1717] God appointed judgment through the Times of the Gentiles and Daniel's seventy weeks, which would not be removed apart from national repentance.[1718] At the end of the 69th week, Jesus entered Jerusalem on a donkey and allowed the people of Israel to proclaim Him as king.[1719] But the nation of Israel chose to reject and crucify Him instead of embracing Him as Savior.[1720] As a result, God the Father removed the kingdom from the nation of Israel and gave it to the Gentiles for a time,[1721] which we know as the Church Age. Soon after the Jews crucified their king and Messiah, God sent the Romans to destroy their nation. Jerusalem and its temple were destroyed in 70 A.D. The nation of Israel is together again before Daniel's 70th week, as prophesied in Daniel 9:26–27. The final week of judgment allotted for the nation of Israel is the Tribulation. The Church will be raptured beforehand, for they are not appointed for God's time of wrath.[1722] The Tribulation will open the eyes of the people of Israel to the truth about Jesus, causing the sur-

---

[1717] Leviticus 26:14–15, 17, 31–33, 38–39; Daniel 9:4–15 (**verses 11 and 13**)

[1718] The theme of the nation of Israel repenting after disobedience to God's laws runs throughout the Old and New Testaments. It was a prerequisite to returning to the land after exile and restoring Israel's kingdom (Deuteronomy 30:2, 10 [context is 30:1–10]; Jeremiah 3:12–18; Daniel 9:13–14; Matthew 4:17; Acts 3:12–21 [**vs. 19**]).

[1719] Matthew 21:1–11

[1720] Acts 3:14–15

[1721] Parable of the vineyard/tenants is where the kingdom of Israel is removed and given to the Gentiles (Matthew 21:33–46). Parable of the wedding feast has the same meaning (Matthew 22:1–14).

[1722] 1 Thessalonians 5:**9** with 5:2–4; same context as 4:13–18

viving remnant[1723] to nationally repent[1724] and bitterly mourn over their rejection of Him when they see Him return.[1725] They will be cleansed,[1726] delivered from their oppressors,[1727] and formed as a nation. Their kingdom will be restored,[1728] David will rule as king over Israel,[1729] Jesus will reign over the earth,[1730] and there will be a worldwide knowledge of God as the waters cover the seas.[1731]

[1723]   Zechariah 13:7–9

[1724]   Isaiah 59:20; Ezekiel 36:31–32

[1725]   Zechariah 12:10–14

[1726]   Zechariah 13:1; Romans 11:26–27

[1727]   Jeremiah 30:8–9 says that Israel will no longer be ruled by foreigners and David will be their king. This is in the context of Israel (30:3–4, 10) being restored the land (30:3, 10), without the rule of foreign leaders over them (30:8) aff the Tribulation (30:7 – see also Daniel 12:1).

[1728]   Ezekiel 37:15–28

[1729]   Ezekiel 37:22, 24–25; Hosea 3:5

[1730]   Zechariah 9:9–10; 14:9, 16–17

[1731]   Isaiah 11:9; Habakkuk 2:14

Redemption or Condemnation:
1st and 2nd General Resurrections

In God's sovereign plan of redemption, there is a 1st and 2nd general resurrection, which leads to redemption or condemnation. There are two general resurrections: the Resurrection of the Righteous and the Resurrection of the Wicked. They are separated by Jesus' 1,000 earthly reign.[1732] The Resurrection of the Righteous happens between the Rapture of the Church and the end of the Tribulation period, Daniel's 70th week. In both resurrections, Jesus is the Judge. The Father gave Him authority to judge the righteous and the wicked.[1733] The Resurrection of the Wicked occurs after the Millennium. At the Great White Throne judgment, Jesus will judge all of the unsaved from the beginning of the world until its end according to their works and because their name is not found in the Book of Life. They will be thrown into the lake of fire.[1734] Satan and all the disobedient angels o rebelled against God Almighty by following him will be vn into the Lake of Fire, which was prepared specifi- r them.[1735]

.NERS

Millennium Reveals Mankind Is by Nature Sinful and Rebellious Towards God

In God's sovereign plan of redemption, Millennium reveals mankind is by nature sinful and rebellious towards God. The Resurrection of the Righteous and the Wicked is separated by the Millennial kingdom. At this time, there are perfect world conditions. Nature is restored to its Edenic state,[1736] and mankind is under a perfect world government. Yet, at the end of Jesus' 1,000 global reign, there will be a mass rebellion against Him when Satan is released from his 1,000-year bondage.[1737] This reveals mankind's sinful nature and natural rebellious state towards God–man is not good. He is wicked by nature. Then comes the judgment.

Accept Redemption or Receive Condemnation

In God's sovereign plan of redemption, we see that man must choose to accept redemption or receive condemnation. At the judgment of the wicked, Jesus will not be the only one to condemn the wicked. He will use other people throughout history to condemn them. The people of Nineveh will rise up at the judgment and condemn the gen-

---

[1736]   Isaiah 11:6–9; 65:25
[1737]   Revelation 20:7–8

eration who heard Jesus' message and saw His miracles, for they repented at the preaching of Jonah. Jesus is superior to Jonah.[1738] The queen of Sheba will rise up at the judgment and condemn the same generation because she came from the ends of the earth to hear Solomon's wisdom. Jesus is greater than Solomon.[1739] Moses will rise up and accuse this generation.[1740] Due to their rejection of Jesus' message and signs, condemnation will be greater for those cities that heard Jesus' message and saw His miracles than Sodom and Gomorrah.[1741] This seems to suggest that those who hear the truth and reject Jesus' message throughout history will certainly be condemned by other people throughout history at the Great White Throne judgment, not just Jesus Himself. You see, man has a sin nature and has a natural rebellious state towards God. God is working throughout history to redeem sinful, rebellious mankind and will accomplish His purposes set before the foundation of the earth, regardless of man's disobedience, indifference, and spiritually hardened hearts. Either people respond to the gospel or reject His message and are condemned.

[1738]   Matthew 12:41; Luke 11:32
[1739]   Matthew 12:42; Luke 11:31
[1740]   John 5:45
[1741]   Matthew 10:15

Conclusion

In the beginning, man sinned and was thrown out of the Garden of Eden. Since then, the Triune God has been working throughout history to bring sinful mankind to repentance and into relationship with Him. In the Eternal State, sinless, redeemed mankind will be without a sin nature,[1742] and death will be abolished.[1743] Holy God and perfected mankind will be in full fellowship with one another forever.[1744] To view the chart for this section, go to https://rbeteach71.wixsite.com/justified-sinners/charts.

[1742] Philippians 3:20– 21; 1 John 3:2

[1743] 1 Corinthians 15:26; Revelation 20:4

[1744] Revelation 21:3

About the Author

Timothy Musgrave graduated from Dallas Theological Seminary in 2015 with a ThM and accreditation in Greek, Hebrew, Bible, Theology, and Christian Education. He has served as a hospice and trauma chaplain. His professional work and ministry have been in encouraging, giving hope, and developing people in crisis all over the spectrum. The author has been married for twenty years and has three children.

www.ingramcontent.com/pod-product-compliance
Lightning Source LLC
LaVergne TN
LVHW010439070225
802954LV00005B/5